Gilbert Simondon's
Psychic and Collective Individuation
A Critical Introduction and Guide

DAVID SCOTT

EDINBURGH
University Press

For Lisa, your idea

Edinburgh University Press Ltd
The Tun - Holyrood Road
12(2f) Jackson's Entry
Edinburgh EH8 8PJ
www.euppublishing.com

Typeset in 11/13pt Monotype Ehrhardt by
Servis Filmsetting Ltd, Stockport, Cheshire
and printed and bound in Great Britain by
CPI Group (UK) Ltd, Croydon CR0 4YY

A CIP record for this book is available from the British Library

ISBN 978 0 7486 5450 5 (hardback)
ISBN 978 0 7486 5451 2 (webready PDF)
ISBN 978 0 7486 5449 9 (paperback)
ISBN 978 0 7486 9574 4 (epub)

Contents

Acknowledgements

First I would like to acknowledge Carol MacDonald at Edinburgh University Press for all her assistance along the way, especially for how easy she made this process. I would like to thank Len Lawlor, my friend and role model, Robert Bernasconi, who made my philosophical path possible, and Tom Nenon for his inspired teaching. A special thanks is owed to Steve DeCaroli and Valerie Saint-Amand for their encouragement. I also would like to acknowledge Patricia and Ken Scott who prepared the way for my writing this book. And lastly and most importantly, I am especially grateful to my amazing wife for her tireless editing and proofreading skills (with jokes in the margins). Her editorial and philosophical skills are incomparable.

Abbreviations

CI   *Communication et information: cours et conférences (Communication and Information: courses and conferences)*

FIP   "Forme, Information, Potentiels" ("Form, Information, Potentials")

IGPB   *L'individu et sa genèse physico-biologique (Individuation and its Physico-Biological Genesis)*

II   *Imagination et invention (1965–1966) (Imagination and Invention: 1965–1966)*

IL   *L'individuation à la lumière des notions de forme et d'information (Individuation in Light of the Notions of Form and Information)*

IPC   *L'individuation psychique et collective (Psychic and Collective Individuation)*

MEOT   *Du mode d'existence des objets techniques (Of the Mode of Existence of Technical Objects)*

Introduction

THE TEXT

Gilbert Simondon's *L'individuation psychique et collective* (*Psychic and Collective Individuation*, hereafter IPC) is an exceptional work that emerges out of the fog of chatter and philosophical loquacity with an impact that extends far beyond the number of readers who actually turn its pages. For too long Simondon has been the treasured secret of a significant, restricted, and admiring coterie – most significantly among them Gilles Deleuze, Simondon's steadfast advocate. But we can also count among the admirers of Simondon's work Georges Canguilhem, Maurice Merleau-Ponty, Isabelle Stengers, and Bernard Stiegler.

If Simondon was known at all, it was largely on the merits of *Du mode d'existence des objets techniques* (*Of the Mode of Existence of Technical Objects*, hereafter MEOT), published in 1958. The stated goal of MEOT is a better knowledge of technical objects. Simondon argues that by better understanding our relationship with the technical objects fashioned to regulate our existence in the world, we create for ourselves the possibility of a new idea of what it means to be human, on the basis of a knowledge that correlates technology with human processes of existence. Human reality *lives* through technology. A machine's structures function by fixing and crystallizing the human gesture. In fact, today MEOT continues to draw the most attention, particularly in Media Studies and Communication Studies researching the role technology plays in the development of culture across the disciplines. Still, we must remain cognizant that, while MEOT is undoubtedly important, having obvious far-reaching implications, Simondon himself saw it as only an adjunct to his shockingly brilliant primary doctoral thesis, *L'individuation à la lumière des notions*

1

de forme et d'information (*Individuation in Light of the Notions of Form and Information*, hereafter IL). Let us say, MEOT concretely dramatizes the descriptive metaphysics and epistemology presented in his primary thesis. It would not be until 2005 that the full thesis would be published. Beside MEOT, only the first part of the main thesis, *L'individu et sa genèse physico-biologique* (*Individuation and its Physico-Biological Genesis*, hereafter IGPB) was published during Simondon's lifetime in 1964. IPC is the second part of his main thesis; however, it was not published until 1989. Because IPC was intended by Simondon to be the final part of his main thesis, IL – the convergence of the reflections of the two prior works, MEOT and IGPB – I take it as bringing to full maturity his philosophical thought.

TWO SUPPOSITIONS: "IT IS DIFFICULT" AND "IT IS PHILOSOPHY"

Two suppositions organize my study of Simondon's IPC: Simondon's work is extremely difficult and it is a work of philosophy. One should not be under any illusions that Simondon's work is easy to read. He makes the reader work. It must be said that Simondon is not a graceful writer. His sentences are clogged with subordinate clauses, chained not always comfortably with semi-colons. His syntax often turns back upon itself. He also has a tendency not to qualify his pronoun references. When reading him in French, one often has the feeling of being swept downstream by a violent current, with only momentary rests where the river pools between rocks. This pause is only momentary and then we readers are swooshed downstream, sometimes pushed beneath the surface, sometimes catching an overhanging branch and pulling ourselves above the surface as we are carried along. We have to ask ourselves, what is the nature of this difficulty? And is whatever we encounter in his work worth the struggle?

I would posit that Simondon's writing is actually the logical extension of the stress he places on the *operational* nature of thinking. That is to say, Simondon's own prose and his way of structuring IPC illustrates through its mode of expression the very operation of individuation that is this work's object at the level of thought. Its repetitions and paradoxes stem from the fact that IPC takes itself to be the dramatization of thought in action. The difficulty of Simondon's writing style takes itself to be both a reflection on the practice of "doing" philosophy and a reflection of the individuation of thought. "Reflective intuition" is how Simondon describes the nature of thought's operationality when thinking is engendered in thought. And more specifically, philosophical intuition is not just a forming of *a priori* or *a posteriori* knowledge, philosophy situating itself somehow before or after what it has knowledge of; instead, the act of doing philosophy is, for

Simondon, an operation that makes itself contemporaneous with the existence of the being it intuitively *grasps*.

This brings me to the second supposition orienting my study of IPC. I
would like to affirm unequivocally that IPC, and my own critical study of
it, are works of philosophy. How could we not take this to betray anything
other than a kind of willful naivety, especially if we place it within the
context of current market trends and the state of the publishing industry?
For alas, who reads philosophy today? This is probably a question for
another day. For now I must insist that my exposition and analysis, critical
and speculative, insists on finding its point of orientation within the meth-
odologies, questions, problems, and traditions of philosophy. More pro-
grammatically this means that the many references in IPC to theories and
concepts borrowed from physics, biochemistry, physiology, embryology,
sociology, and psychology will not be fully addressed. Part of the reason for
this is practical: I do not want to risk writing a work too much longer than
the text it hopes to explain. However, more theoretically, it is clear that
in the resources Simondon draws upon to formulate the problem of individuation (the pre-Socratics, Plato, Aristotle, Kant, Nietzsche, Spinoza),
his particular identification of this problem is fundamentally ontological
(ontogenesis), as is the manner he adopts for its explication. Lastly, I
believe it would be dangerous for me to insinuate that Simondon implicitly
accepts a hierarchical relationship between philosophy and the sciences,
with the latter more important. I am compelled to favor philosophy over
science for at least one reason: because of the stress Simondon places on the
role of reflexivity, both as the very operational mode of philosophy and as
the impetus for the constitution of the sciences as knowledge. "All philosophical activity, by reason of the reflexivity of thought, is also a reform of
the mode of knowledge, and has repercussions for a theory of knowledge"
(MEOT 233).

And yet I remain fully aware that by restricting my analysis of IPC to
philosophy, its methods and traditions, I risk placing this study at cross-
purposes with itself. For I believe that what makes Simondon's work challenging and important is the very thing I would seem to be denying: it is
radically interdisciplinary. Or rather, Simondon is radically transdisciplinary.[1] My study finds Simondon's work to exemplify a primary principle:
thinking is an event that erupts at the intersection of different knowledges,
at the point of their diffractions. For me this does not deny the philosophical significance of IPC, but affirms it even more. Philosophy happens in
the margins of knowledge, where knowledge professes innocence but
is incapable of reflecting on its own culpability, its own will to power.
Thinking is not, therefore, intellectuality; it is the experience of thought's
limits. Moreover, true thought can only ever happen by transcending its

own limits (often self-imposed). As such, to engender thinking within thought can only ever be transdisciplinary. Or as Simondon dramatizes it, it must be transductive and trans-individuating of itself. This study sees Simondon and this particular work as the announcing of a "new category of philosopher" whose taste and inclinations are the reverse of his predecessors. Simondon is in every sense, as Nietzsche claims, a philosopher of the "dangerous Perhaps."[2] Which is to say, Simondon is a philosopher whose very thought takes itself to be necessarily incomplete, inchoate, and, therefore, experimental.

Certainly, the challenge facing my study of IPC is to explore the implications of Simondon's achievement. In so doing, I clarify the terms, concepts, and categories operational in his work, and I identify those philosophers with whom a dialogue is crucial. These requirements are united in support of my *critical* engagement with Simondon's text. For I believe that we have only just begun to appreciate the way *Psychic and Collective Individuation* verifies Simondon as our contemporary.

Still, I must admit that there will be moments when I will appear to violate the academic rules of discourse and decorum, which all us "scholars" supposedly consent to – knowingly or not – when we read and, most importantly, write about a philosophical text. Without pretending to be solicitous, I would, nonetheless, ask readers for their indulgence at these moments. I am trying to exploit certain paths into IPC, which at first might seem non-existent, save for the few traces left after Simondon's thinking passes through the thickets of the philosophical tradition. Every passing shadow and brief encounter, however oblique, set and met, is useful I believe not so much for reconstructing his thought, or filling in gaps, but for amplifying it and affirming, as a result, the virtuosity of Simondon's inventive strangeness.

GENERAL PROBLEMATIC, PRINCIPLES, AND DESCRIPTION

The history of philosophy has accorded great metaphysical and epistemological weight to the notion of the individual. The most explicit illustration of the theoretical and speculative privilege conferred on the individual or individuality by the history of philosophy is substantialist metaphysics, that is, that metaphysics which considers being as either one or many unified and presumed essences or "substances." Hylemorphism is the prevalent schema of thought adopted to explain and bring into actuality the substantialist metaphysics presupposed by a whole series of theoretical and speculative theories. Thus, the individual is born, it is said, from a form encountering matter. The hylemorphic schema places the principle of individuation *anterior* to individuation; if individuation, that is to say the becoming of the individual, is synonymous with form encountering matter, then this puts the principle of individuation outside of the act of their being related to one another. In the instance of hylemorphism, the relationship of form and matter, the principle of individuation is presumed to be outside of the hylemorphic operation. Thus, it is a matter of metaphysically re-describing what Simondon calls the "obscure zone" lying between the articulation of form and matter, where the operation of individuation occurs, which brings about their encounter, yet is neglected by hylemorphism. It is a matter also of contesting the underlying metaphysics that justifies this relationship on the grounds that it is an encounter between two already unified and formed "substances." Atomism is one theory that organizes itself on the assumption that there is a pre-existing principle of individuation, which determines how they are supposed to compose themselves to create a world without changing their own immutable natures. The principle of individuation is given as a fact pre-existing the operation of individuation, which it supposedly determines. First supposed is the existence of the principle of individuation, and then this principle brings about an operation of individuation that, finally, causes the constituted individual to appear.

Simondon contests the method, and the presumed temporality imposed on individuation by the metaphysics of substantialism and the hylemorphic schema. The individual is only one element produced by individuation; the individual is neither the sole goal nor motivating impetus for individuation happening. One does not pass rapidly through stages of individuation to finally realize in the end the individual, perfect and self-contained and exhausting being. What if one began the search for individuation not with the individual but with individuation itself? What if the individual were not privileged as the final outcome and, thus, the only beginning from which we worked backward to find the conditions for its being confirmed? What if, instead, we attempted to grasp individuation in the fullness of the unfolding of its reality? What if we sought to comprehend the individual without necessarily having recourse to the presumptions of knowledge responsible for granting its ontological and epistemological privilege? What if, to use Simondon's own words, we sought "to know the individual *through* individuation rather than to know individuation starting from the individual" (IPC 12)? "To know" individuation starting from the individual reduces individuation to no more than a re-presentation of the posited individual, whose principle of becoming pre-exists what it supposedly determines, while "to know" the individual through individuation forces a fundamental reformulation of categories of knowledge raising their ontological status to that of a problem, thereby shifting the ontological presumption from being to becoming, from substance to individuation. It means the principle of genesis becomes internally generated from within the process of individuation itself. In other words, individuation generates for itself and out of itself its own principle of ontogenesis, only ever relative to those conditions or potentialities maintained with itself which nurture its occasion.

> Individuated being is not substance but rather the putting into question of being, being through a problematic, divided, reunited, carried in this problematic, which sets itself up through it and causes it to become. *Becoming is not the becoming of individuated being but the becoming of the individuation of being:* what happens occurs in the form of a putting into question of being, in other words, in the form of the element of an open problematic, which is the individuation of resolved being: the individual is contemporary of its becoming for this becoming is its individuation; time itself is essence, not as development starting from an origin or tendency towards some end but, rather as resolute constitution of being. (IPC 224)

So, at one level, it would not be inaccurate to say that the entirety of Simondon's thought hinges on a simple strategy of reversal or, as he calls it, a "return": to attain the full knowledge of the individual we begin not with the individual (presumed to be fully constituted or individuate) but with a return to individuation, considering it the "primordial" operation by which the individual becomes, and of which individuals are "modalities." It is not being that conditions becoming, it is becoming that conditions being. Being is becoming; becoming has being. It is a strategy so simple, yet its implications are surprising. The individual is grasped then as only a relative reality, a certain phase of being in the midst of bringing into reality the potentialities of pre-individual reality that precede it and condition its becoming actual. As Gilles Chatelet lyrically writes, "The state of the preindividual is the promise of becoming."[3] This promise is made actual by Simondon's formulation of what he calls "transduction." Traversing physics, biology, the psychic, and the social, transduction describes an operation by which an activity of thought or being is born from the propagation of the pre-individual reality little by little, from one problematic region to another, each subsequent region amplifying the one prior to it, producing a transformation, a new phase of reality. "Becoming is in effect perpetuated and renewed resolution, incorporating resolution, proceeding via crises, and as such its sense is in its center, not at its origin or end" (IPC 223).

Transduction is explicitly theorized by Simondon to counter the kind of dialectical thought that would characterize becoming as a "third term" born from the reduction of individuation to the movement of the "negation of negation," until all contradictions and oppositions are negated once they are subsumed into a higher formal unity of being. Simondon describes transduction, instead, as a state of dephasing of being, whereby being is forced to disclose to itself the pre-individual tensions, in the form of information, which provide the condition for its individuation. Once the condition for its own individuation is set, the condition exists for transductively passing along the pre-individual catalyst for other individuations, and on and on from one individual being to another individual being. Transduction is a potentially inexhaustible process.

What is more, according to Simondon, the individual never exists alone; it is only ever relative to the milieu associated with its existing, for every individual is only the secondary manifestation of a more primary operation of individuation. According to Simondon, individuation is not a matter of representation or the emanation; it is through individuation that a partial and relative resolution of a pre-individual reality is attained in the "form" an individual assumes, where certain incompatibilities and tensions constitute the problem internal to being and the potential for new individuations to be brought into conjunction and become compatible – if only for a time. On the basis of this reversal Simondon's thought justifies to itself, and dramatizes the need for, an entirely unique and groundbreaking rethinking of the method for doing philosophy, and the utter and complete rewriting of the history of philosophy. Old problems are remade – especially the ancient problem of how to describe the relation constituting both the individual and the collective; and new problems appear – for example, how to account for a new relationship between the human and the technical object.

The importance of Simondon's work stems from its directly engaging the metaphysics that inform social and psychological theories customarily used to justify setting the individual over and against the collective. Implicitly, these theories ground themselves in a metaphysics that assumes the individual and the collective to exist only ever as already individuated beings or "substances." Simondon contests the conception of the individual and the collective made possible by this kind of metaphysics because it lends itself to the lie that the individual and the collective can exist independently of one another. Such a conception further promotes the idea that both have an existence outside the "relational activity" or "operation of individuation" that requires their reciprocal codependency. Simondon asserts, "the psychosocial is transindividual" (IPC 193).[4] The "transindividual" is the attainment of the unity of the individuation of the collective and the individual. It is, in brief, the "relation of relations." As an ethical and political concept – epistemologically and ontologically fabricated – the transindividual leads quite naturally to "*Humanism without Man*" erected, as Muriel Combes writes, "on the ruins of philosophical anthropology."[5]

7

INTELLECTUAL HISTORICAL CONTEXT I:
PHENOMENOLOGY AND STRUCTURALISM

In this section I would like to provide historical context for IPC by focusing on the way Simondon's own formulation of individuation is situated at the point of diffraction separating phenomenology and structuralism. Each takes itself to demarcate a specific path, from a specific point, which each uses to distinguish one from the other. The point of diffraction I would suggest is the problem of genesis, more specifically, the genesis of subjectivity.

Phenomenology is motivated by the need to problematize our so-called mundane or naive experience of the world. Its stated desire to "return to things themselves" is meant to redirect our thinking to reflect on how the world is given to us as phenomena we experience through touch, sight, taste, sound. It is because it allows us to reflect on how we come to believe in the existence of the reality of this world, solely on the basis of perceptual faith, that the phenomenological reduction is the most basic method of Husserl's philosophy. It is a methodological pathway by which to contest the mundane empirical and psychical reality. It assumes as its philosophical goal the task of opening up epistemological breathing space, so that we might gain access to "transcendental subjectivity." The phenomenological reduction accomplishes this goal by putting the mundane world, or rather individual things, "in parenthesis" in order to force the theoretical gaze to reverse itself, to reflect upon its own cognitive activity, specifically, the operation by which the world is brought into a phenomenal reality. The problem of genesis becomes the central issue: how a "thing" attains its presence as existing in the world for the experiencing consciousness. For Husserl, this will be the basis for his developing a dynamic or genetic phenomenology to describe the "all-pervasive genesis that governs the whole life and development of the personal 'I'."[6]

But this genetic philosophy is just a preliminary step toward a transcendental phenomenology, according to Husserl. Here the phenomenological reduction acquires a new immediacy and focus. By disconnecting ourselves from the "natural attitude," which has us believe unconditionally and naively in the existence of this world, the phenomenological reduction as a method of knowing at once permits our attaining a systematic totality of knowledge through which we "transcend" the world and, at the same time, leads us back to the world, though now the world transformed into a *problem*, whose disclosure reveals that its significance, its meaning for us, emerges only in unison with the "absolute and concrete stream of the experience" of transcendental subjectivity.[7] The problem of phenomenological genesis is only truly thinkable at the level of the transcendental.

And yet, with the attaining of phenomenological transcendentalism, the problem of genesis acquires another transformation: "The true theme of phenomenology is neither the world on the one hand, nor a transcendental subjectivity which is to be set over and against the world on the other, but the *world's becoming in the constitution of transcendental subjectivity*."[8] Still, even through the entire series of reversals of theoretical gaze carried out by the phenomenological reduction, reflection remains both phenomenology's motive and means.

The emergence of the structuralist movement in the late 1940s and early 1950s was largely a reaction to existentialism as a philosophy of subjectivity and the subject: the French psychosocial broadening of German phenomenology. The first, more positive negotiation with structuralism is substantiated by Jacques Lacan's well-known paper "The Mirror State as Formative of the *I* Function."[9] Almost immediately Lacan's intentions are made clear when he asserts that the "I" function he is describing, in the manner he describes it, breaks with any philosophy that would ground itself in the *cogito*. Here he is speaking about phenomenology. The process of individuation, of a being's becoming a subject, occurs through an infant's "jubilant assumption" of an image, which structures the objectivity and unity sought by the infant's identification with it. The infant is individuated as individual subject by a fictional determination that structures the psychic reality prior to these encounters, although language restores to the subject the awareness of his or her functionality. He or she sees oneself in this image, identifies with it and becomes or is individuated as an "I," a "subject." The mirror stage has the purpose, according to Lacan, of establishing a relationship between an organism and its reality. The image gives to the infant a "symbolic matrix," a way to symbolically (that is, through language) represent to itself its subjective function in structuring its relation to the Other: to other beings and to the group or society more generally. And with this synthesis derived from the image, not only is the "permanence of I" symbolized but its alienation is also prefigured, for the subject does not give itself this fictional image, the Good Form. It is an imaginary ideal structured by a culture to make the internal inconsistencies and fractured being of the human infant coherent. The mirror image is a product of structures, of those modes of cultural and symbolic normalization (Oedipus complex) existing anterior to the subject's genesis.[10]

Unlike many of Simondon's generation who either adopted a structuralist orientation, if not its actual methods and concepts (Lacan), or who sought an active engagement on their own terms by radically reimagining it until it became virtually unrecognizable (Deleuze), Simondon seems barely to register that structuralism was in the ascendant at the time he was writing IPC. (This is especially surprising since Simondon at one point was an assistant to Lacan.) And yet this seeming lack of interest on his part should not make us too hasty. We might discern Simondon's negotiation with structuralism obliquely, in one positive sense and one negative sense. More positively, he exploits structuralism's stated imperative to "decenter" the subject, that is to say, to displace the role of the subject both theoretically and in terms of the importance given to subjectivity in the world. Negatively, the development of Simondon's ontogenetic perspective is clearly a reaction to what he finds to be insufficient in structuralism for accounting for the convertibility of structures or, in other words, the problem of genesis.

Structuralism clears theoretical space for Simondon to address the problem of genesis, to rethink the concept of the subject in terms of ontogenesis, and to raise the status of the symbolic (although for Simondon this dimension is not primary). We might read Lacan's paper as presenting a theory of individuation/individualization that frees Simondon to seek an ontological basis for rethinking the relationship of the psychic and the collective in addressing the problem of individuation. But Simondon is not a structuralist in any real or imaginary sense.

And it is here that we are able to appreciate how Simondon's theorizing of the ontological complementary relationship between operations and structures distance his thought from structuralism. Indeed, I would suggest that Simondon's formulation of the "Allagmatic" point of view is meant to counter the structuralist notion that all sciences are fundamentally structural and that the only true science is structuralist. Rather than epistemologically and ontologically privileging structures, which is to presuppose their invariant or at least pre-individuated being, which leads us back dangerously close to epistemologies of the individual and a metaphysics of "essences," Simondon favors operations or, rather, the relationship between structures and operations. An Allagmatic point of view is one that is attentive to the grasping of the event of operations as they bring structures into appearance or modify structures that transform operations into different operations. What is missing from structuralism is the *operationality of structures* themselves: the impetus and procedure for their becoming. What this means is that negatively, though never explicitly, Simondon's philosophy of individuation stands as a direct critique of structuralism because of the latter's inability to account for the convertibility of structures, the invention of new structures, or in other words, to directly grasp in its own assumptions the problem of genesis. Deleuze dramatizes this particular critique in his brilliantly ironic essay "How Do We Recognize Structuralism?" This essay is less about defining structuralism than reimagining structuralism as other than what it is: a philosophy of genesis, of the virtual. It is a kind of hilarious send-up: we recognize structuralism for what it is not.

> Structuralism is not at all a form of thought that suppresses the subject, but one that breaks it up and distributes it systematically, that contests the identity of the subject, that dissipates it and makes it shift from place to place, an always nomad subject, *made of individuations, but impersonal ones, or of singularities, but preindividual ones.*[11]

It is the decentering of the subject and subjectivity that permits Simondon to see how, in fact, the subject has an existence because "it is placed into question" by the transindividual reality that structures it. It is this transindividual reality that is made available for us to grasp once the subject is put into question. We will turn to this relationship between Simondon and Deleuze later on.

It is quite evident that Simondon's Allagmatic theory, as well as his method of transduction, is modeled on the phenomenological reduction, particularly its transcendental variant. But it is also clear that Simondon is not in any sense a phenomenologist. The problem of individuation ceases to have any relevance for the phenomenological project; instead, it is the self-forming act of transcendental consciousness that gains prominence. Again, phenomenology violates his first principle: it grants an epistemological privilege to the individual subject by taking it as the starting point for its presumed genetic analysis.

More specifically, the "younger" generation of those philosophers arriving immediately after Sartre and Merleau-Ponty – Foucault, Deleuze, and Simondon's generation – reacted against the Hegelian-Marxist conception of the laboring subject, supposedly the purest symbol of historical subjectivity. Sartre perfectly exemplified this Hegelian-Marxist tendency when he argued, in *Critique of Dialectical Reason*, that "every human relation is historical" that all "relations between men are the dialectical consequence of practice to precisely the extent that they arise as a transcendence of dominating and institutionalized human relations."[12] Labor power is made concrete through the machine. In this way the laborer is transformed into a product, that is to say, social wealth. A new humanism is called for.[13] Foucault's intervention, perhaps, would settle this debate once and for all. Simondon's IPC is, at least from this perspective, a diversion from the path between the former squabble between phenomenologists and structuralist declarations that "man" is only a empirical-transcendental figment of language, labor, knowledge: phenomenology or structuralism, in either case, reflecting the too, too human desire to rebuff finitude.

INTELLECTUAL HISTORICAL CONTEXT II: FREUDO-MARXISM

Another intellectual movement dominant at the time IPC was being composed was the attempt to find a point of correspondence between the thought of Sigmund Freud and Karl Marx. On the one hand, Simondon's work directly engages with Freudian notions in order to formulate the relationship of sexuality to personality, and to discover linkages between the psychological and the social. On the other hand, IPC explicitly and directly takes up Marx's overriding preoccupation with labor – the formations of collectivity – not to mention his oblique references to colonialism and the "pre-revolutionary" state of being. For these reason, IPC would seem to share the same preoccupations as explicitly Freudo–Marxists works like Marcuse's *Eros and Civilization*, Lyotard's *Libidinal Economy*, and Deleuze and Guattari's *Anti-Oedipus*.

I would like to reserve a more thorough engagement with Freud and Marx until later in order to take up the specific texts Simondon references in IPC. For now, however, I will simply sketch in very broad outlines the aspects of Freudianism and Marxism which are brought to a point of convergence in Freudo-Marxism.

Marx argues in the *Grundrisse* that production constitutes a social body or "social subject." That is to say, it is a process of subjectivaton relative to the need for a particular subjectivity to take part in its respective form of production. Labor or work is brought about by the social conditions of production, within which the individual acts. In *Group Psychology and the Analysis of the Ego*, Freud begins from the "fundamental fact" that an individual in a group is subjected to society via an alteration in its mental activity. This becomes possible with the removal of inhibitions on instincts specific to each individual by ceding of control of those inclinations to the "higher organization" of the group. Freud is interested in providing a psychological explanation for this mental change, which becomes necessary upon the assumption of membership by an individual of a group. In a group the individual is brought under conditions that permit the individual's being liberated from the repression of the unconscious instinctual impulses. Freud identifies the role played by the *libido* – the energy regarded as a quantitative magnitude (though not actually measurable) of those instincts which relate to sexual love, as well self-love, love for parents and children, friendship, love for humanity, for abstract ideas and concrete objects, etc. All are traceable to this same instinctual impulse.[14] Further, the libido attaches itself to the satisfaction of vital needs. Love instincts are diverted from the original sexual aims, though without a diminution of energy. Thus, in mankind as a whole, as in the individual, love alone acts as the civilizing factor by transforming egoism into altruism. It is precisely the inhibiting of sexual impulsions that insures lasting ties between people. Each individual is bound by libidinal ties to the leader and to other members of the group.

Felix Guattari writes, "Any theoretical development bearing upon class struggle at this time should be concerned primarily with its connection with libidinal production and its impact on the creativity of the masses."[15] Freudo-Marxism takes seriously Freud's suggestion that the libido is the socialization of the energy produced by sexual drives, such that this drive is transformed through production into a sublimated object of love or desire. Freudo-Marxism fosters "a parallelism between social production and desiring production."[16] Capitalism is nurtured by the libido via the force of labor in the nineteenth century and by consumerism in the twentieth century. Hence, "every political economy is libidinal,"[17] according to Lyotard, because every political economy is solely determined and preoccupied with the organizing of desires.

Bernard Stiegler, the philosopher who most admits taking his cues from Simondon's thought, is in fact a more contemporary updating of Freudo-Marxism. Stiegler argues that there is a need for rescuing and updating the discredited notion of the critique of political economy, taking into account the movement from exchange to commerce spurred by a new libidinal energy, which causes a mutation of production on the basis of new digital ("grammaticological") technologies and, therefore, a mutation in the social desires leading to the "functionalization of social relations." Here we have the birth of "a new consumerism" ("proletarianized consumer"), reflected in the parallel re-envisioning of labor. For Stiegler, Marxism has arrived at the limit of its own usefulness in trying to analyze the fictitious capital generated within this new technological age and must be bolstered with Simondonian concepts filtered through a Freudian perspective.[18]

Still there is a definite sense that Simondon intends his conception of the psychosocial to be read in a way opposed to the Freudo-Marxist notion of the libidinal economy. According to Freud, the libido is quantitative. What is more, it is fundamentally tied to the act of identification (with the object in place of the ego-ideal). Once again, we discover another means by which to ontologically privilege the individual over individuation. Both Freudanism and Marxism ultimately find their motivating problem in how to procure for the group precisely those features that are characteristic of the individual but extinguished in him by the formation of the group. Thus, the aim (for psychoanalysis or Marxist analysis) is to equip the group with the attributes of the individual. The Simondonian concept of the psychosocial is created to directly contest this goal; it is the transindividual. The psychosocial is the bearer of those pre-individual and impersonal forces which act as the charge for potentially new individuations. Rather than instituting some basis for communication between individual consciousnesses, the psychosocial provides the opportunity for the "synergy and common structuration of beings" (IPC 193).

GILLES DELEUZE, SIMONDON'S ADVOCATE

Unquestionably, Gilles Deleuze is the philosopher most responsible for bringing Simondon's work to the public, even in France. Therefore, it is not merely coincidental that in nearly all of Deleuze's published works – from *Difference and Repetition* to *Logic of Sense* to *Thousand Plateaus* and *What is Philosophy?* – Simondon's theses or concepts can be implicitly detected or explicitly identified. And although it is certainly the case that more often than not IGPB is the work Deleuze references, I would argue this is more a matter of the circumstances of its earlier publication than proof of Deleuze's indifference toward IPC. Indeed, given their friendship it is more than probable that Deleuze well knew the full thesis and read it. In fact, as I will suggest, there is an oblique reference to IPC in his review of IGPB.

Although it would be ridiculous for us to reduce Deleuze's own philosophical brilliance to the status of a kind of philosophical talent scout or the rescuer of eccentrics from the "island of misfit philosophers," nonetheless there is truth in the fact that an inextricable element of how Deleuze conceives philosophical practice is what he calls a "minor" or minoritarian line of thought within the traditional (or "major") history of philosophy. Deleuze's works are rich with forgotten, marginalized, anomalous, and unconventional thinkers and writers (Bousquet, Ruyer, Lautman, Wolfson, Maimon, Tarde), who are relevant not because they add color or exoticism to his thought but because they open up new paths for exploration. Deleuze's works do not counter the established philosophical "canon" as much as they reveal the points of weakness, the pressure points of tension that might engender thinking by bringing philosophy to the threshold where it either collapses into itself or must risk putting into question its grounds for judging who or what belongs to its narrative. Minoritarian thought forces majoritarian thought into risking continuous variation or, to use Deleuze's language, the "deterritorialization" of the history of philosophy and those texts deemed worthy for inclusion. It introduces a "line of escape" from the majoritarian categories, purposes, and accepted ways of speaking. If it wants to be creative, it forces the history of philosophy to confront the necessity for its own "becoming-minor." This is why the history of philosophy has a vested interest in ensuring that some thinkers continue to be judged "non-philosophical" and, thus, unsuitable for belonging to its tradition. The "history of philosophy" does not want to be creative; it wants scholars not philosophers. Scholars seek tenure and conference invitations, philosophers do not. "Is there a hope for philosophy, which for a long time has been an official, referential genre? Let us profit from this moment in which antiphilosophy is trying to be a language of power."[19] And yet, as Deleuze carefully reminds us, the major and the minor are inextricably tied to one another. Simondon is a minor philosopher in the specific sense Deleuze means, not in the sense that his thought is secondary to the more famous. This is why Deleuze continuously returns to Simondon, and continuously promotes his thought, even if obliquely through his own indirect and transformative usage. Simondon is that minoritarian philosopher. He forces philosophy to stammer, to run on at the mouth, to trip over its own discourse. Simondon discomforts us philosophers.

The points at which comparisons might be made between Simondon and Deleuze are really too many for me to address in the brief space I have given myself in this introduction. I would not really do either philosopher justice if I merely enumerated where they agreed and where they disagreed. Such an exercise would be pedagogically useful; however, I will leave it for others to carry out. Instead, I would like to begin my comparison by detailing the ontological justification Deleuze discovers in Simondon. To this end I will focus on Deleuze's *Difference and Repetition* and his 1966 book review of Simondon's IGPB, in which Simondon makes his earliest appearance. And then, rather than tracing every time Simondon appears in Deleuze's works thereafter – like a game of "where's Waldo?" – I will focus on one text, "Immanence: A Life." This is Deleuze's final published text, appearing just before his death in 1995. What makes this final text interesting from my perspective is that Simondon's name never actually appears, yet I would argue that it is in many ways Deleuze's most Simondonian work.

Before turning more directly to the ontological imperative as Deleuze sees it, which establishes his attraction to Simondon's thought, I would like to suggest that there is a more general philosophical orientation that makes the affinity between both thinkers inevitable: both Simondon and Deleuze fundamentally orient their thought on the basis of the Spinoza–Nietzsche nexus.[20] It is this nexus and the metaphysical and epistemological imperatives prescribed by it that prepare the ground for Deleuze and Simondon's ontological like-mindedness. As the reader progresses through this study this will become ever more apparent, I hope.

For now let us take Deleuze's promoting Simondon's thought as a way to clarify what he calls "the contemporary renaissance of ontology."[21] What is the nature of this ontological renaissance? What is it that Deleuze determines links all the different ontologies of his day? Or, perhaps it should be said: what is it that determines any one philosophy to be worthy of joining the revitalization of ontology? According to Deleuze the renaissance is inaugurated by those ontologies that exploit the full ontological scope of the "question–problem complex." It is the discovery of the question and the problematic as transcendental elements "which belong essentially to being, things, and events," that far from being merely epistemological or heuristic devices, are themselves corresponding to Being. As such, Deleuze argues that internal and constitutive to Being itself is a fundamental problematic, a "disparity" or difference that, while signifying its "greatest powerlessness," nonetheless is the point where this powerlessness is transmuted into potentially its greatest power.[22] And it is precisely Simondon's return to the problem of individuation that qualifies his central place in this new ontological renaissance. As Deleuze writes, "Individuation emerges like the act of solving such a problem, or – what amounts to the same thing – like the actualization of a potential and the establishing of communication between disparates." Thus, the beingness of the problematic is internal to the act of individuation; it is the integrating of the "elements of disparateness into a state of coupling" that ensures they internally resonate within whatever actual individual results from it.[23] But even more, for Deleuze, Simondon's primary innovation is the role given to the pre-individual. This means "Being is never One," that is, Being never achieves a state in which it is fully stable and completely individual. It is only ever more-than-one, metastable. As Deleuze concludes in his review, "As individuated, [Being] is still multiple, because it is 'multiphase,' 'a phase of becoming that will lead to new processes.'"[24]

It is in "Immanence: A Life" that Deleuze brings us to what is the most important and difficult question that must be asked about how we establish the relationship between these two philosophers: do both these philosophers embrace a philosophy of immanence? For Deleuze, obviously, the question is a resounding "yes"; for Simondon, however, the answer is more nuanced and complex and certainly uncertain. For now I will outline how Deleuze characterizes the connection between immanence and individuation in this final published essay. My interpretation of Simondon's response will be more fully spelled out in Chapter 4 of this study.

In this final piece of writing it becomes immediately clear that what both connects and differentiates Deleuze and Simondon is their relationship to the transcendental. Simondon makes no claims to trying to refashion Kantianism, or to rescue the transcendental from any confusion with transcendence, whereas, for Deleuze, the resources for accomplishing both these tasks lie in Simondon's work. Most particularly, what distinguishes Deleuze from Kant is that Deleuze ascertains that the ontology of the problem operates as a transcendental field. It is the problem of individu-ation. In our being forced to confront this problem, we are able to access the transcendental. For Deleuze, individuation is the pure and absolute "unthought," operating beneath all forms, and yet it is inseparable from the grounds that make these forms available. It is precisely the intensive field of individuation or individuating difference, in other words the prob-lematic being, that functions as the transcendental, as the condition of the organization and determination of individuals, forms, species. According to Deleuze, "the transcendental field escapes all transcendence – as object or subject – and, so, for this reason, it can be defined 'as a pure plane of immanence.'"[25] Yet this absolute plane of immanence itself is only ever experienced, lived in "a life."

And it is a life's being conditioned by this plane of individuation, pre-individual and impersonal, which the individual continues to bear, that ensures a living individuality remains, to whatever degree, impersonal and at least relatively incomplete. "The life of such individuality is eclipsed by the singular immanent life of a man who no longer has a name, though he can be mistaken for no other."[26] A life is, on this account, however partially, anonymous and indefinite, even after individuation when it becomes a singularity. This is because not only is a life conditioned by pure immanence, but it never fully divorces itself from its share of the transcen-dental circumstance which makes individuation possible. Indeed, this is why Deleuze never says a being is "individuated." Instead, he says that individuation leads to the creation of a singular "event," a singularity. This is a life. And what is a singularity but a momentary pause in individuation, overdetermined by a singularity's relation to other singularities, other lives, and other milieus of individuation? It is the totality of these actions which Deleuze describes as "absolute immanence."

However, the main element that demonstrates Deleuze's altering of Simondon's process of individuation involves the notion of the virtual. The ontological status, which the indefinite plane of immanence initially possesses, is that of the virtual prior to its becoming individuated as subject or object. Deleuze describes the movement of the pre-individual and impersonal becoming singular and individual as that by which "the virtual becomes engaged in the process of actualization as it follows the plane which gives it its proper reality."[27] Simondon quite definitely rejects the notion of the virtual. The taking of form is the passage from real meta-stability to a stable state. But this operation, for Simondon, has nothing to do with the notion of virtuality, which he argues is composed by an imag-ined ideal state ("Good Form"). In other words, completely opposite to Deleuze, who worries that one might confuse the virtual and the possible,[28] Simondon finds them to be synonymous. Instead, "potential, conceived as potential energy, is of the *real*, for it expresses the reality of the metastable state, and its energetic situation" (IPC 68 n.14). Rather than a process of actualization, Simondon describes it as the operation of "transduction."

Here Simondon finds the justification for his method, reflecting its operationality, that is, the action by which it occurs: transduction or the transductive. "The thought that we name *transductive* does not consider as the unity of a being that which is conferred by the form *informing* matter, but by a defined regime of the operation of individuation, which founds being in an absolute manner" (209). The cohesion of being is achieved not by the relationship of form and matter; it is a regime of activity of "converting structure into function and function into structure." As such, individuation develops at the "very center of being" prior to dephasing; before the terms marking the extremes of its individuated status – as "object" or as "subject" – there is the "internal resonance," wherein being communicates with itself, and from which emerges the possibility of dephasing and every individuation. In other words, as was previously mentioned, this action of convertibility of structure and operation, otherwise called "Allagmatic," describes ontology as a "general theory of operations," of the exchanges and modifications of being, of relation, whose importance lies in the fact that this action unites the means and principle discovering self-justification through the transductive practice at its interior. "Being is relation, for the relation is the internal resonance of being in relationship to itself, the fashion by which it reciprocally conditions in the interior of itself, splitting and reconverting itself into a unity" (210). All thought that seeks to fully grasp individuation is, for Simondon, finally genetic, insofar as it is primarily characterized as a systematic effort to construct an Allagmatic point of view, that is, a point of view that originates from the convertibility of structure and operation, specifically their reciprocal relationship. But, more generally, philosophy is the authorizing of thinking all objective structural reality as a complex of relations; in short, the being of becoming. As a result, Simondon writes, "One can only comprehend the unity starting from individuation, absolute ontogenesis" (210). It is ontogenesis that is the creation of a new perspective, a new way to orient oneself in thought:

> Ontogenesis would become the point of departure for philosophical thought; it would truly be first philosophy, anterior to the theory of knowledge [episte-mology] and to an ontology that would accompany the theory of knowledge. Ontogenesis would be the theory of the phases of being, anterior to objective knowledge that is a relation of individuated being to the milieu, after indi-viduation. The existence of the individuated being as subject is anterior to knowledge; first, a study of individuated being must precede the theory of knowledge. Anteriorly, to every critique of knowledge (*connaissance*) arises

the knowledge (*savoir*) of ontogenesis. Ontogenesis precedes critique and ontology. (163)

A GNOSEOLOGICAL THESIS: THE LEAP INTO ONTOGENESIS

This Critical Introduction and Guide to Simondon's IPC has an implied thesis which it carries out through the choices it makes in identifying and structuring the problem of individuation. Orienting this study is the hypothesis that the directing goal of Simondon's philosophy of ontogenesis more generally is what I am calling the *ontologicalization* of knowledge. Which is to say, the "leap into ontology" is done in parallel with Simondon's reformulation of philosophical practice and his reconceiving it as a mode of "intuition" or "grasping" of a kind of ontological understanding – what I call a pure *understanding without knowledge*. One cannot fully appreciate Simondon's ontological imperative without taking into account the associated *gnoseological* imperative inextricably tied to it.[29]

Epistemologically, logic is said to deal only with propositional enunciations relative only to those individual beings that have been individuated as "object" or "subject." Simondon argues that a theory of being (or ontology) must be instituted that is anterior to all logic. Such a theory, according to Simondon, would be able to provide the grounds for a more adequate logic, for the simple reason that there is nothing that proves beforehand that being is individuated in only one possible manner. But what if, instead of a single individuation, there were multiple individuations, existing all together though not always at the same speed and in the same intensity? And what if these individuations reciprocally inflected one another, so that we had to think of each of these modes of individuation as expressive of the being of becoming, each equally real in their inequality? At the very least, Simondon argues, several logics would also have to exist, each corresponding to a defined type of individuation. The classification of ontogenesis permits our *"pluralizing logic."* In other words, in seeking to make logic "philosophical," Simondon makes it ontogenetic. The implications for the axiomatization of knowledge are made immediately apparent once we follow Simondon's lead and take into account pre-individual being insofar as it is the engendering source of potentialities nurturing the respective incidents of individuation. Pre-individual being "cannot be contained in a preliminary logic, no norm or system detached from its content can be defined: *only the individuation of thought in completing itself, can accompany the individuation of other beings*" (IPC 30, my italics). Therefore, ontogenetic logic (logic now transformed after the ontogenetic leap) is neither an immediate or mediate knowledge. We cannot have *epistemological* knowledge of individuation. We are left, instead, with a grasping of knowledge itself as already implicated in the individuation of being; it is an operation of knowing that occurs "parallel to the known operation." For "we cannot, in the usual sense of the term, *know individuation*; we can only *individuate, individuate ourselves,* and *individuate in ourselves (individuer, nous individuer, et individuer en nous)*" (30). As a result, Simondon stresses, "What is grasped, therefore, *lies in the margin of knowledge.*" One does not have knowledge "about" individuation (as if that were so easy). Rather individuation is grasped in grasping itself (reflecting upon itself) as it constructs itself; knowledge must implicate itself as an active participant in the operation of individuation itself. In doing so, "knowledge" structures itself as an analogy between two operations of individuation: thought and being. In this regard, knowledge is nothing more or less than the mode of communication between them. "The individuation of the real exterior to the subject is grasped by the subject thanks to the analogical individuation of knowledge in the subject; but it is *through the individuation of knowledge* and not by knowledge alone that the individuation" of all other beings, "non-subject" so-called beings, is grasped. "Beings can be known by means of the knowledge of the subject but the individuation of beings can only be grasped by the individuation of the knowledge of the subject" (30).[30]

Knowledge, on this account, is nothing more than the retrieval of these lines of development, with each reprising its preceding individuation. Unlike Kant, it is not a matter of disclosing in the subject *a priori* forms of space and time, coherent with the brute *a posteriori* givenness of the world. Knowledge cannot any longer be defined by taking something to be objectively and subjectively sufficient to be true. In making the theoretical shift of focus from the terms to be explained (subject, object) to the domains providing the grounds for their emergence, their signification, Simondon finds support for his claim that "the individual cannot any longer be identified with a isolated elementary being" (IL 488). At issue is not the individual but the system of thought or domain of being that makes it possible. For Simondon, "subject-being" and "object-being" emerge from the same "primitive reality," the pre-individual field of forces. Thought, which now appears to institute an inexplicable relation between object and subject, is the prolonging of the initial individuation. Knowledge is, for Simondon, only a subsequent individuation; and, thus, it *is* what it reflects: the individualization that makes the individuated being's real and actual existence. What this means is that "knowledge's *conditions of possibility* are identical with the individuated being's *causes of existence*" (IPC 127). Knowledge in the ordinary sense must be rethought. Ontology and epistemology must be put into sync with one another by the event of individualization, so that each reciprocally expresses the necessity for the other. As a result, we are directed to the shared conditions making them possible. Beyond its own self-justifying conditionality, there is no universality of knowledge *in itself*.

For us to think with Simondon and not merely to explicate his concepts is to invite ourselves into the heart of the ontologization of thought. For such a "transductive operation" in method correlates itself and is, at the same time, in correlation with the "leap" (as I am referring to it) that Simondon carries out, from the ontology of substances (object) to the ontology of ontogenesis (relation).

> The individual being, as the principle of the notion of substance that governs all logic, must be considered via individuation as the operation that founds and instigates being; ontogenesis is anterior to the logic and ontology. The theory of individuation must, therefore, be considered as a theory of the phases of being, of its becoming insofar as it is essential. (223)

Indeed, what I call "the leap" is precisely this requisite perspectival orientation inextricably tied to the gnoseological leap, insofar as each provides the other with justification.[31]

Axiomatization of the human sciences is, for Simondon, possible only on the basis of the leap that is one with an ontologization of thought (from an ontology of essence and substance to an ontology of relation). In place of a unity of explicative principles, Simondon structures his axiomatic of the human sciences on the unity of tendencies, to attain a new idea of "form" (50, 52–3, 58).[32] Thus, Simondon's primary ambition is to formulate a general theory of the human sciences. The hope is that this will incite reflexive thought and, in so doing, incite as well the search for those conditions which make axiomatization possible to begin with. This project's success or failure is thus predicated on discovering in the notion of "information" a way to generalize transductivity (as *the ontologico-epistemological* operation) at the levels of the psychic, vital, and social.

READING STRATEGIES

Simondon's discourse is *performative*,[33] that is to say, it *is* what it enacts or the action it carries out. This is primarily the source of IPC's difficulty. Though I will make this connection more obvious later, Simondon calls this the "operative" level of being and thought. The performative is the operative. The problem is that to try to capture this performative or operational discursive dimension of ontology of ontogenesis is like trying to hold rushing water in one's hands. This is what is behind Simondon's use of semi-colons, stringing together ideas and phrases in a headlong rush of sentences that do not end so much as kind of pitter out. We only get the trace of its reality; after all it leaves our hands moist. But if we are not careful, lost to us is the water's actual rushing movement, the very act that defines its existence.

I would suggest the best way to read Simondon's text, practically, is to choose one of the two parts of the Introduction – I would personally choose the first section ("Position of the Problem of Ontogenesis"). It is this section that most directly establishes Simondon's approach and method. It is also the section of the Introduction that Simondon wrote with IPC in mind. An added benefit of choosing the first section of the Introduction over the second is that it fills in the missing elements of the first part of the larger thesis (IGPB). I would also suggest that the reader pay close attention to how Simondon's repetition of his main thesis and concepts are applied within the different chapters. For example, "information" has a different role to play in the chapter dealing with perception and affectivity, than in the chapter specifically focused on the individuation of the group relative to the individual. Each chapter seems almost to refashion the same concepts and the same fundamental structure relative to how they operate in addressing each new problem. This is something to which the reader should remain sensitive.

CHAPTER OUTLINE OF THIS STUDY

Chapter 1 focuses on Simondon's Introduction to IPC. Here I schematically outline the general problematic that directs Simondon's work, while indirectly establishing the basis for its connection to a larger philosophical project. In fact, I actually begin this chapter by integrating the final part of *L'individu et sa genèse physico-biologique*, "The Individuation of Living Beings," as it provided a transition from the primary focus on developing a theory of information at the level of biology to a theory of information at the level of the psychosocial. Chapter 2 concerns Chapter 1, Part I of IPC. At issue in this chapter is the psychological problem: how does the subject *qua* subject grasp separately objects as perceptual unities rather than as a confused continuum of sensations. This requires that one define the problem of individuation in relation to perception. Merleau-Ponty is Simondon's foil in this regard. Chapter 3 corresponds to Chapter 2, Part I of IPC. The fundamental motive for this chapter is Simondon's development of a theory of affectivity. Like Spinoza's ontology of affect, Simondon formulates a kind of ontology of affectivity in order to shift the ground for defining the "psychic" or mental. Chapter 4 focuses on the longest and most complicated chapter in IPC, Chapter 3, Part I. This chapter's difficulty derives from the structure Simondon adopts for it. Incorporating philosophy, sociology, psychology, myth, religion, and ethics, this chapter moves with the speed of its self-generating transductive logic. Its unity precisely expresses the regime of the activity generated by the internal differences arising from the relations established between the diverse discourses. At the heart of this chapter is a discussion of the transcendental and the empirical – individuation and individualization in the formulation of "personality." Finally, special attention is paid to the striking moment when Simondon reinterprets the famous "tightrope walker" scene from Nietzsche's *Thus Spake Zarathustra*. Chapter 5 corresponds to Chapter 1, Part II of IPC. Simondon distances himself from both phenomenology and structuralism by proposing that *relation* constitutes the group and individual; and for this reason, the relation realizes the "value of being" (ontology of relation). But really the most central aspect of this chapter is Simondon's formulation of the two individuations: vital individuation and the individuation of the group, the relation between the individuated and the social. Chapter 6 corresponds to Chapter 2, Part II of IPC. In this chapter I explicate the characterization by Simondon of signification or meaning as the establishing of the relation between subjects. The collective is born with information becoming significance. Meaning is the transindividual. In Chapter 6 I also address (and, perhaps, seek a remedy for) the absence of a discussion of language in IPC. Chapter 7 explicates the two main ideas proposed in the Conclusion to IPC: an ontogenetic ethics and a non-human humanism. I conclude this Critical Introduction and Guide to Simondon's *Psychic and Collective Individuation* with only the briefest of suggestions to the reader of a possible line of convergence for research: the "biopolitical" or "biopower."

NOTES

1. A good place to start for those looking for a discussion of the non-philosophical resources present in Simondon's texts – particularly cybernetics and depth psychology – is Pascal Chabot's book *The Philosophy of Simondon: Between Technology and Individuation*, recently translated into English (London: Bloomsbury, 2013).
2. Friedrich Wilhelm Nietzsche, *Beyond Good and Evil: Prelude to a Philosophy of the Future*, trans. Marion Faber (Oxford: Oxford University Press, new edn, 2008), 6.
3. Gilles Châtelet, *L'Enchantement du virtuel mathématique, physique, philosophie* (Paris: Rue d'Ulm, 2010), 212.
4. All translations are mine. Italicized text in quotations from Simondon's works follows the original, unless otherwise stated. In subsequent chapters, all page references in the main text are to IPC, unless otherwise stated.
5. Muriel Combes, *Gilbert Simondon and the Philosophy of the Transindividual*, trans. Thomas LaMarre (Cambridge, MA: MIT Press, 2013), 50.
6. Edmund Husserl, *Psychological and Transcendental Phenomenology and the*

Confrontation with Heidegger (1927–1931): The Encyclopaedia Britannica Article, the Amsterdam Lectures "Phenomenology and Anthropology," and Husserl's Marginal Notes in Being and Time, and Kant and the Problem of Metaphysics, trans. Thomas Sheehan and Richard E. Palmer (Dordrecht and Boston: Kluwer Academic Publishers, 1997), 167.

7. Eugen Fink, "The Phenomenological Philosophy of Edmund Husserl and Contemporary Criticism," trans. R.O. Elveton, in *The Phenomenology of Husserl: Selected Critical Readings*, ed. R.O. Elveton (Chicago: Quadrangle Books, 1970), 112.

8. Fink, "The Phenomenological Philosophy of Edmund Husserl," 130, Fink's italics.

9. Jacques Lacan, *Ecrits: The First Complete Edition in English*, trans. Bruce Fink (New York: Norton, 2006).

10. Lacan, *Ecrits*, 80.

11. Gilles Deleuze, "How Do We Recognize Structuralism?," trans. Michael Taormina, in *Desert Islands and Other Texts*, ed. David Lapoujade (New York: Semiotexte, 2004), 190, my italics.

12. Jean-Paul Sartre, *Critique of Dialectical Reason. Theory of Practical Ensembles*, trans. Alan Sheridan-Smith (London: NLB, 1976), 97, 98.

13. Sartre, *Critique of Dialectical Reason*, 241.

14. "Love relationships . . . constitute the essence of the group mind"; Sigmund Freud, *Group Psychology and the Analysis of the Ego*, trans. James Strachey (New York: Norton, 1989), 31.

15. Félix Guattari, *Chaosophy: Soft Subversions*, trans. David Sweet and Chet Wiener (New York: Semiotext(e), 1996), 190. Interestingly this comment comes within the context of a discussion in which Guattari contests the entire project of a Freud and Marx synthesis. For him it is a theoretical dead-end. This quite surprising initially, given his writing *Anti-Oedipus* with Deleuze. But then Guattari adds a caveat: he rejects the idea that either Freudianism or Marxism can ever totally overcome their fundamental incompatibilities. There is no way to join them together as whole-cloth, that is, in the entirety of their doctrines. However, "some bits of a 'dismembered' Marxism can and should converge with a theory and practice of desire; bits of a 'dismembered' Freudianism can and should converge with a theory and practice pertaining to class struggle" (ibid.). Thus, it is not that the very idea of joining Freud and Marx is impossible. It is that one should be under no illusion that to do so will not require a fundamental redefinition of the terms and conditions each appeals to, as well as those hidden suppositions each depends upon for their practice.

16. Gilles Deleuze and Félix Guattari, *Anti-Oedipus: Capitalism and Schizophrenia*, trans. Mark Seem, Robert Hurley, and Helen R. Lane (New York: Viking Press, 1977), 31.

17. Jean-François Lyotard, *Libidinal Economy*, trans. Iain Hamilton Grant (Bloomington: Indiana University Press, 1993).

18. Bernard Stiegler, *For a New Critique of Political Economy*, trans. Daniel Ross

(Malden, MA: Polity, 2010), 93. In an endnote Stiegler writes, "It is because the libidinal economy is *protentional* [a key term taken from Husserl's discussion of temporality referring to the "anticipation of the next moment"] and because capital is an organization of the production of protentions that capitalism is an epoch of libidinal economy" (140 n.16).

19. Gilles Deleuze and Félix Guattari, *Kafka: Toward a Minor Literature*, trans. Dana Polan (Minneapolis: University of Minnesota Press, 1986) 27. "Minor languages are characterized not by overload and poverty in relation to a standard or major language but a sobriety and variation that are like a minor treatment of the standard language, a becoming-minor of the major language. The problem is not the distinction between major and minor language; it is one of a becoming. It is a question not of reterritorializing oneself on a dialect or patois but of deterritorializing the major language." Gilles Deleuze and Félix Guattari, *A Thousand Plateaus: Capitalism and Schizophrenia*, trans. Brian Massumi (Minneapolis: University of Minnesota Press, 1987), 104.

20. "Yes, I did begin with books on the history of philosophy, but all the authors I dealt with had for me something in common. And it all tended toward the great Spinoza-Nietzsche equation." Gilles Deleuze, *Negotiations, 1972–1990*, trans. Martin Joughin (New York: Columbia University Press, 1995), 135.

21. Gilles Deleuze, *Difference and Repetition*, trans. Paul Patton (New York: Columbia University Press, 1994), 196.

22. Deleuze, *Difference and Repetition*, 199.

23. Deleuze, *Difference and Repetition*, 246.

24. Gilles Deleuze, *Desert Islands and Other Texts, 1953–1974*, trans. Michael Taormina, ed. David Lapoujade (Cambridge, MA: Semiotext(e), 2004), 89.

25. Gilles Deleuze, *Two Regimes of Madness: Texts and Interviews, 1975–1995*, trans. Ames Hodges and Mike Taormina, ed. David Lapoujade (New York: Semiotext(e), 2007), 389.

26. Deleuze, *Two Regimes of Madness*, 391.

27. Deleuze, *Two Regimes of Madness*, 392.

28. Deleuze, *Difference and Repetition*, 211–15.

29. I would like to rescue this ancient term *"gnoseology"* – as I translate it here – which seems to have long fallen out of favor, so as to define a "theory of knowledge" *now* ontologized, that is adequately and necessarily expressive and *in sync* with the very nature, the event and action of being *qua* becoming. In this way philosophy grasps things from the perspective of their true genesis. The more we grasp things in this way the more we understand the condition of individuation, which make them possible, Nature. Thus, *gnoseology* stands in contrast to "epistemology," more strictly speaking, as the theory of systematically organized and instituted knowledge, in other words, "science."

30. "The theory of individuation must be first in relation to other critical and ontological deductive studies. It is, in effect, what indicates how it is legitimate to cut up being in order to make it enter into the propositional relation. Prior to every particular category, there is that of Being, which is a response to the problem of individuation; for, in order to know how Being can be thought,

it is necessary to know how it individuates itself, for it is this individuation which is the support for the validity of every logical operation with which to be conformed. Thought is a certain mode of secondary individuation intervening after the fundamental individuation that constitutes the subject; thought is not necessarily capable of thinking being in its totality; it is second in relation to the condition of the subject's existence; but this condition of existence of the subject is not unique or isolated, for the subject isn't an isolated term having constituted itself; the substantialization of the subject as term is a facility that thought allows to be able to assist the genesis and justification of itself; thought searches to identify with the subject, in other words, to identify with its condition of existence in order not to be late on its own condition of existence" (IPC 222).

31. This is a concept I am developing in other works both published and soon to be published.

32. "If it is possible to generalize this scheme and to specify it by the notion of information, by the study of the metastability of conditions, we can require founding the axiomatic of a human science on a new theory of form" (IPC 65).

33. Bernard Stiegler, *Acting Out*, trans. David Barison, Daniel Ross, and Patrick Crogan (Stanford: Stanford University Press, 2009), 6.

1

Ontogenesis and the Concepts of Individuation

INTRODUCTION TO THE "INTRODUCTION"

The "Introduction" to IPC is fabricated from two disparate texts. This contributes to its somewhat lapidary nature, reflecting the strange heritage of the work's publishing history. The first text making up the Introduction was originally written to introduce the full and complete dissertation *L'individuation à la lumière des notions de forme et d'information.* The text, entitled "Form, Information, Potential, and Metastability," was originally delivered in 1960 at the meeting of the *Société française de philosophie.* And so this second text predates by four years the publication of the first text. As constituted, the Introduction presents several difficulties. Problems are introduced that are only vaguely or indirectly dealt with in IPC, or worse, abandoned. Undoubtedly, they had already been addressed in the dissertation section just prior to IPC (published separately as *L'individu et sa genèse physico-biologique*). Consequently, we have the feeling that we have walked into the middle of a discussion, begun long before we entered. Both texts making up the Introduction were written originally to be self-contained. Another unintended and unavoidable impression left by the editor's contriving of this Introduction is that it transforms the main text of IPC into an extended supplement to it.

In order to avoid repetition and redundancy, allowing for IPC's later chapters to fully develop its arguments and ideas, rather than offering a close exposition of this chapter, I will instead try to link this Introduction at the point where the larger dissertation leaves off: "The Individuation of Living Beings," the final part of IGPB, just prior to the beginning of IPC.

The relation to the prior work (or part) is made clear in this Introduction when Simondon establishes that his ambition is "to study the *forms, modes, and degrees of individuation* in order to replace the individual in being, according to the three physical levels: the vital, the psychic, and the psychosocial" (23). But, at least in IPC, we eventually come to realize that the levels of the physical and vital are assumed more than they are actually analyzed. Only IGPB takes the physical and vital relationship to be its primary focus. Whatever conclusions are arrived at in IGPB are taken for granted more often than not by IPC. Nonetheless, they establish the conditions for individuation at the level of the psychic and psychosocial. Given that IPC is intended to be the *psychosocial* realization of the physio-biological process of individuation, the Introduction usefully fills in the missing elements dealt with in IGPB: its more focused critical analysis of the foundations of the hylemorphic scheme, the search for a more dynamic scheme in energetics, and (what I call) the *re-formation* of form or the "Good Form." Simondon's main purpose, however, in the Introduction, whose groundwork was laid in IGPB at the level of biology, is to search for a principle of individuation *anterior* to the resultant individual.

We must not forget that Simondon's attempt to generalize the ontogenetic scheme is motivated by the requirement he discerns in psychology and sociology, which forces his adopting (and adapting) the notion of information. To what end? Ultimately, he hopes to realize an "axiomatic of the human sciences" (31) on the basis of a reformed theory of Form. The notion of information makes this possible.

FOUR ONTOGENETIC PARALOGISMS

Simondon organizes his research in opposition to what I will call four basic ontogenetic paralogisms. A logical paralogism is a fallacy that results from the syllogistic form itself, regardless of its content. The falseness of transcendental paralogism, on the other hand, relates to the improper appeal made to transcendental grounds justifying the adopting of the particular syllogistic form. The latter is a fallacy of human reason, according to Kant. Simondon is concerned that, because of these paralogisms, we have been led away from a true appreciation of the problem of individuation, the potential and productive unsettling of prescribed categories of knowledge, in rushing toward the dogmatic illusion of complete and stable being, promised by a substantialist metaphysic and delivered by a supporting schema. Ultimately, the paralogisms Simondon identifies reflect the requirements of a metaphysic conditioned by the self-same form of knowledge which would seek to make intelligible the principle of individuation independent of its operation, thereby ensuring that individuation is knowable, if only as either "object" or "subject." For this reason, I would call them *transcendental ontogenetic* paralogisms.

First Paralogism: The individual is granted ontological privilege as the "given" starting point, necessary if one hopes to disclose how genesis of the individual being progresses.

Second Paralogism: Individuation requires a principle anterior to itself.

Third Paralogism: In order for us to grasp the genesis of the individual, a *reversal* of perspective becomes necessary, which would disclose to us the principle most responsible for engendering it.

Fourth Paralogism: In searching for the principle of individuation *in a reality* that precedes individuation itself, it is to consider individuation as being only ontogenesis. (10)

The outcome of these paralogisms is that the principle of individuation is assumed to *pre*-figure the constituted individuality, predetermining the properties that the individual will have once it is constituted. In this sense, Simondon defines the "principle" in a manner similar to how it functions in medieval scholasticism. For medieval philosophers, a "principle" had an important significance. Not merely was it taken to be an obvious truth serving as a starting point from which to derive other truths, a general or foundational epistemological guide, but the answer to individuation must be sought in those "principles," which were said to explain *and* to constitute the processes of individuation. For scholastic thinkers, principles were as much metaphysical constituents as logical predicates. As much as they were rules or laws for making being intelligible, they were likewise assumed to provide beings with the grounds for existence. Simondon shares scholasticism's search for the principle of individuation of the individual, while demonstrating that it is an epistemological as well as a direct and active ontological invention.

Simondon worries that any perspective for research that confers ontological privilege to the constituted individual risks "not carrying out (*opérer*) a true ontogenesis, of not replacing the individual in the system of reality in which individuation occurs" (10). If there is an inclination to make the starting point for all thought the achieved individuated being, then Simondon's thesis is quite simple: we must investigate why the starting point of the individual is privileged above all others. For what reasons – metaphysical and epistemological – does it serve, and how might we account for it by passing through the stages of individuation leading to the individual? What this means ontologically, for Simondon, is that he seeks a *principle of individuation, not a principle of the individual*. Epistemologically, the challenge is how we grasp (*saisir*) ontogenesis in the full reality of unfolding, that is, "*to know the individuation via individuation, rather than individuation beginning with the individual*" (12).

In the end, these paralogisms concern the transcendental form of knowledge, which knowledge posits as necessary if one is to have any hope of "grasping" individuation. And so the conflict between an ontogenetic principle and these transcendental paralogisms arises from prohibiting Simondon's aspiration to reach a comprehension of individuation indistinguishable from its operation, a paralleling of what knows (thought) and what is known (being). He writes, "We are unable to, in the usual sense of the term, *know individuation*; we can only individuate, individuate ourselves, and individuate in ourselves; this *grasping* is, therefore, in the margins of knowledge properly speaking, an analogy between two operations, which is a certain mode of communication" (30).

IN THE OBSCURE ZONE OF THE NOTION OF FORM: CRITIQUE OF HYLEMORPHISM

According to Simondon, the notion of Form assumes a theoretical and methodological privilege not only for philosophers but also for scientists and social theorists because it seemingly encapsulates the very idea of being's unity and self-cohesion. Form, as notion or concept or idea, whether we desire it or not, draws its power from presupposing an underlying metaphysic and structure: the substantialist metaphysic and the hylemorphic schema of thought.

In a fascinating text called "L'histoire de la notion d'individu" (History of the Notion of the Individual)[1] Simondon proposes an alternative "history" of philosophy in which these two schemas operate, sometimes intersecting and sometimes diverging, while structuring the various speculative and scientific theories. A substantialist metaphysic takes being to be internally self-consistent, retaining a unity that is given in itself and founded on itself, unaltered by what lies outside it. The encounter between form and matter engenders the individual according to the hylemorphic scheme. Any substantialist thought is necessarily monist, seemingly opposed to the bipolarity endorsed by a hylemorphic scheme. And yet it is these two ways, hylemorphism and monistic substantialism, each distinct yet supportive of the other, Simondon argues, that science and social theory appropriate for the purpose of offering an explanation for the reality of the individual. But to do so requires posing, together, the problem of individuation by constituting for themselves a starting point in the existence of the individual. The individual is *given* to exist, which for this reason is taken to be the ideal starting point for re-ascending to those conditions giving birth to the individual. The human sciences and psychology, most particularly, seem trapped in a vicious logical circularity, where the individual is taken as engendering itself on the grounds that it is already given to itself as individual.

The ontological and epistemological privilege which has been granted to the individual by psychology, sociology, and other philosophical theories presumes a uniting of a metaphysic of substance with an underlying hylemorphism. A substantialist metaphysic establishes a unity of being on the basis of its providing a motive and principle of genesis internal to being itself; it is what constitutes a substance. A theory that assumes the hylemorphic schema is one that takes the individual to result from the encounter between a pre-existent form and matter. In either case, Simondon worries that the principle of individuation is made anterior to the process of individuation itself, thereby promoting the constituted and given individual as the only starting point.

Rather than grasping the principle of individuation in the very event of individuation *as operation*, a hylemorphic schema makes itself indispensable for the operation to exist, that is, one must have either matter or form, one substance or the other (11). The metaphysic of substance and the hylemorphic schema reciprocally sustain one another. In order for the interaction of form and matter to occur, each must presume that the other is a separate and wholly distinct substance. The hylemorphic schema, moreover, furnishes a way to structure knowledge for the benefit of the substantialist metaphysic. Hylemorphism and substantialism aver that "in both cases *an obscure zone*" (11) is where the operation of individuation is recoverable. For it is in this obscure zone that the principle of individuation constitutes itself in action. The critique of the substantialist and hylemorphic schema is meant to clear enough speculative room for Simondon to explicate ontogenesis. We will see later how the obscure zone establishes the space for the subject to emotionally feel herself – in anxiety, in shame – existing as a problem posed to herself.

PLATO AND ARISTOTLE

This critique of the metaphysic of substance in concert with a critique of hylemorphism invites us to ask whether or not Simondon is more Aristotelian or more Platonist. Further, Plato's and Aristotle's diverging conceptions of the Form perhaps most pointedly encapsulate the challenge as Simondon conceives it. He claims Aristotle is preferable to Plato if one hopes to fully explain, ontogenetically, individuation. And yet Simondon rejects Aristotle's starting point – the individual, although he credits Aristotle with making becoming *internal* to the genesis of form or structure. Plato requires a notion of genesis, identical with the process of degradation, endorsing ontological asymmetry to reflect a principle of genesis (as the idea or pure Form) anteriorly situated to individuation in its taking as its starting point the pure and absolute Archetype.

"Form," such as Platonism presents it, maintains a "metaphysical sociology" (FIP 731), an implicit "political theory of the ideal group" established on the basis of its constituting an analogy between the Idea or Form and the ideal city (FIP 730).[2] For Socrates, the tacit contract ("to persuade or obey") is only an amplification of the notion of the Form *qua* Archetype. Simondon takes Platonism as functionally structured by an analogy: the ideal city as an analogue for the invariant *to eidos*, the pure Form. Hence, Platonism, according to Simondon, is nothing more than a "pure sociology become metaphysic."

Certainly, Simondon argues, Aristotle's notion of form is more "eminently operative." It "perfectly agrees with becoming and the individual in its becoming" (FIP 733). However, it is precisely the "implicit or explicit" biologism underpinning the Aristotelian hylemorphic scheme that renders it unsuitable for comprehending the nature of groups. If the first reality for Plato is the group, then for Aristotle, according to Simondon, it is the living individual. Thus, the only option Aristotle leaves to explain the individuation of the group requires an appeal to inter-individual conventions. The individuation of groups, that is, their own specific mode of becoming, is relegated to a secondary characteristic of the individuated individual.

Reading IPC, at various points one gets the impression that Simondon's overwhelming concern is with rescuing Platonism and Aristotelianism from themselves. Or, more to the point, Simondon wants us to see that the notion of form is not the problem, rather it is how Good Form is conceived and the degree to which Platonic and Aristotelian conceptions insufficiently comprehend the successive levels of individuation: from the vital, to the psychic, to the collective, and back again. Indeed, for Simondon, "life" presents Platonism and Aristotelianism with a fundamental challenge, in that it requires addressing anew the vital problem internal to a being's individuation; but, in doing so, it likewise opens thought to its own vitalist principle, to its own problematic or operational being. "This living, which is at once more and less than unity entails *an interior problematic* and *can enter as element in a problematic vaster than its own being*" (IL 29).

In this sense, Simondon looks to the problem of life to give weight to his leveraging the shift of the epistemological and metaphysical grounds of thought to more directly find itself conditioned by its desire to grasp ontogenesis. Indeed, it is precisely his leveraging of the problematic of life which justifies his reconceiving form. Life cannot be packed into the Good Form, the perfectly complete "Form of Forms," the simplest and the most "pregnant geometric form" (IL 26), whether we call it "soul," "good," "evil," "virtue," "object," "subject," "God," "man" or otherwise. But first, how do we describe living – at what level of the biological, physical and the metaphysical? What is its being *as problem* or *problematic*?

THE LIVING PROBLEM OF INDIVIDUATION

Simondon conceives the primary problem of individuation of the living being to be carried forward through its successive and simultaneous acts of psychological and social reformation. However, individuation at the level of the living being operates differently from the operation of individuation at the level of the technical object. The latter is a complete process, yet it is limited to the single moment of its creation. An artisan's hands make a brick, even if using a machine. In either case, a technical object retains a dependency on a degree of exteriority of operation. Living individuation, on the other hand, is never perfectly individuated. It is only ever partial, incomplete, though never potentially lacking, whereas the technical object draws its *ecceity* from the same operation of individuation that constitutes its genesis. Technics produces a more or less stable, partially individuated being: like a "brick that returns to dust after several years or several thousand years" (IGPB 46).

For the living being, on the other hand, "individuation is not produced by one sole operation, limited in time; the living being is itself partially its own principle of individuation." This must be reconciled with Simondon's belief that a living being exists as only always a becoming *between* individuations, not as a becoming after individuation. "The individuant and the individuated are in the living via a prolonged Allagmatic relation" (IGPB 47). It is this Allagmatic relation that reconciles them. For it is a relation that it establishes at once while promoting ontological complementarity between the structure it becomes and the operation of becoming individuating being (IGPB 46-7). This is why Simondon argues that, unlike the technical object, the living being is "at once the individuating system and its partial result." Thus, the principle of individuation of the living being is of an operation comprised of dual resonances of simultaneity and succession, most concretely experienced by us in the terms of memory and instinct. Conversely, ontogenesis for the technical object happens only at the temporal dimension of simultaneity.

In the end, Simondon argues, the principle of individuation is precisely not an object, insofar as it is the mode of being anterior to the subject and object, which, as such, means that being's acquiring a form escapes any attempt to reduce it to a category, "the residue of the knowledge" conditioned by the presumption of the already individuated subject. But might this force us to return to what is revealed about the nature of temporality unique to individuation, so as to more accurately *describe* the being of becoming?

LEVERAGING THE PROBLEM OF LIFE: OPERATIONALITY OF THOUGHT

The penultimate chapter in IGPB, "The Individuation of Living Beings," is effectively the bridge between the two parts that make up *L'individuation à la lumière des notions de forme et d'information*. Specifically, in this chapter Simondon orients his thought around two questions. The first question is *"How is the distinction between the physical individual and the living individual to be conceived?"* How does the distinction of the physical and the vital condition the successive stages of individuation Simondon describes: from the vital, to the psychic, to the transindividual. The second question is: *"What is the relationship between metastability and homeostasis?"* Really, both questions coalesce around the challenge of conceptualizing "metastability," the catalyst for engendering individuation: life.

The critical and speculative aspects of thought reciprocally support and foster one another in leveraging the problem of the individuation of living beings. Both of these aspects of thought come together in Simondon's thesis: one *knows the individual through individuation and individuation through the individual*. The critical and speculative starting point is not the individual, privileged ontologically or epistemologically. The critical dimension appertains to Simondon's criticism of the latent hylemorphism and substantialist ontologies arrogated with variable degrees of self-consciousness by psychologists and sociologists. Left unaddressed in the human sciences, and the primary target of his critique, is how their work, resting on an unexamined hylemorphism, obfuscates the problem of individuation, which, for Simondon, is the only true path for us to follow to a new theory of knowledge and a new theory of life.

> According to this perspective, consciousness would not be considered through an adversative scheme of "all or nothing," of subject or object but, rather, as starting from a more primitive trans-consciousness. Moreover, I don't believe it is possible to maintain the opposing dualism "subject" and "object" but, on the contrary, must consider [this opposing dualism] as expressing the result of a process of form-taking (*un processus de prise de forme*), which is, in this case, the process of individuation. The word "ontogenesis" resumes the question.[3]

Simondon's theory of ontogenesis is, consequently, the speculative and more affirmative response to the critical dimension. In the end, it is what permits us to describe the individual as wholly a product of the creative, inventive, a figment of a process of "form-taking" of the new *in action*. The nature of the problem of individuation as the vital problem is one with the requirement of destabilizing all those categories dependent on a stable ontological and epistemological individuality – either as object or as subject. Seeking to renounce "the factitious unity which the understanding imposes on nature from outside," Simondon speculates that it might be possible to somehow intuit the vital activity, to grasp "that which subsists of the direct movement in the inverted movement, *a reality which is making itself in a reality which is unmaking itself*."[4]

How might we grasp "becoming" in being at the level of thought? This is, of course, a very ancient question likewise asked by thinkers from Heraclitus, Lucretius, and Bergson through Nietzsche and Deleuze. The challenge facing all of them is that such a concept remains fundamentally antithetical to its "object," life; if only to give it an intelligible form, the process of objectification "slows down," stabilizes and, indeed, restricts the movement it objectifies. For this reason the human sciences have misconstrued and misrepresented "metastability," reduced to just a factor in the stage of an object's inertial stabilization; and, in this regard, its significance both as a catalytic principle (in the scholastic sense) and a fundamental phase in ontogenesis is lost, at least from Simondon's perspective. Because it is essential to characterizing individuation, metastable being forces philosophy and the sciences to leap out of those epistemological registers and categories whose imperatives direct the structuring of knowledge. No longer can one assume individuation to be restricted to the physical domain. Individuation must be conceived relationally and, more specifically, as the relation of milieu and individual (IPC 16).

Any attempt at the axiomatization of the human sciences and psychology depends on engaging with the presence of this pre-individual being, particularly as it makes all previous logics inadequate for the purpose. The difficulty in properly *grasping* ontogenetically a living being, according to Simondon, is that to do so requires that one is prohibited from the starting point of homeostasis, nor must one seek to identify it with the self-regulation of a state of perpetually fluctuating equilibrium. For Simondon, much of the physical and human sciences remain crippled by this confusion (the outcome being what he calls "contemplative" knowledge). What is life, after all, but the insertion of indetermination, unforeseeable, in the course of its evolution? So the metaphysical problem of ontogenesis and the problem of how to have knowledge of this movement are inseparable and codetermine one another's paths of individuation. The very problem of ontogenesis or individuation invites a conception of knowledge and a certain metaphysics to imply one another, which, in turn, invites a leap, first out of the immediacy of the "here and now" and into ontogenesis, and then a leap back into *hic et nunc*.

Simondon begins to address the first question by using a "physicalist paradigm" without a "reduction of the vital to the physical" (IGPB 231). One must be careful to not confuse them. To begin with, physical analysis emphasizes the "energetic and structural conditions" nurturing all "meta-stable systems" (IGPB 240). It is undeniable that all physical systems or things (or things as systems) are only the "residue of a vaster process" and, so, appear only *after* the "emergence of the vital" (IGPB 235). In this regard, Simondon's work agrees with the uniquely vitalist strain running throughout French philosophy. We are left with how to describe the vital problem as it extends into the social and political realms, foregrounding the metaphysical justification for the epistemological shift demanded in order to invent the *concept* of life. And so the purpose of "The Individuation of Living Beings," the second part of IGPB, is to establish the relationship between the problem of vitalism and the problem of individuation. Indeed, at the conclusion of this work we are left pondering if Simondon's intention was all along to conceptualize what is most "*vital*" in vitalism.

Sustaining Canguilhem's postulate, Simondon likewise posits that "the nature and value of the concept are here in question, as much as the nature and the sense of life."[5] What this means is that the "concept of life" and the "life of the concept" discover their shared imperative in those operations which direct their distinct if, nonetheless, related individuations, as living individual being and as knowing subject. Seeking to grasp life, the living induces thought to reflect upon its own practice, to inquire into those conditions nurturing the becoming of the living, as well as thought's individuation. In other words, in grasping life we grasp the necessity for being and thought to be structured in parallel individuations to one another. Individuation evades its being known through the mode of objective knowledge but is analogously attributed to known being via a thought, which by *reflecting upon its own practice*, is able to *grasp* it in itself. Rather than concerning itself with satisfying sufficient objective and subjective conditions, knowledge attains the level of the *operational*. This is reflected in the nature of the concept that results, which is no longer a product of a self-constituted, internally coherent *a priori* analytic, but is rather a *technique*. A concept is made to be inseparable from its reflecting back upon the elements and process structuring its genesis. It is *operational* knowledge in action.[6]

THE ONTOGENETIC LEAP

"All philosophical activity, as a result of the reflexivity of thought, is also a reform of the mode of knowledge, and possesses an impact on the theory of knowledge" (MEOT 233). The inner possibility of ontogenetic knowledge, as a reform of knowledge, is evident in the specific totality expressed through the paradigm of crystallization. The crystal invites a mode of understanding as a reform of knowledge, inviting relation with the unity-forming act: as a result, the pure power of transductive operation comes to the foreground, laying the groundwork for what I would call the *ontologization* (or "ontogenetization") of knowledge contemporaneous and in correlation with the ontology that guides and sustains it. In other words, Simondon calls for an "Allagmatic epistemology," one that fundamentally transforms philosophy and the human sciences.[7] An ontogenetic perspective on metaphysics, epistemology, and method offers philosophy such an opportunity. It presents us with the opportunity for grasping being via a kind of "pure intuition," a kind of "comprehension without knowledge," which is, however, useful to guide and sustain knowledge but of a different kind, grounded not by any pretense to objectivity, nor by affirming subjective certainty. It is instead the problem of genesis, that is, individuation, which marks the comprehension of being at the limits of knowledge. Now we must fully appreciate Simondon's resurrecting the ancient problem of individuation, with origins traceable to medieval theology and philosophy. It gives proof of the need for a "reform of fundamental philosophical notions" (IPC 29).

In an incredibly important passage from MEOT, Simondon not only outlines the necessity for the shift from either *a priori* or *a posteriori* knowledge (objective or subjective), but provides the form it will take: from philosophical reflexivity to finally the intuition of being *qua* becoming.

> Knowledge by intuition is a grasping of being, which is neither *a priori* nor *a posteriori* but contemporary with the existence of being that it grasps. At the same level as being; it is not a knowledge derived from idea, for intuition is not yet contained in the structure of the known being; it does not belong to this being; it is not a concept, for it possesses an internal unity that gives it its autonomy and its singularity, prohibiting genesis through accumulation; finally, knowledge truly mediates in this sense, it does not grasp being in its absolute totality, as idea, nor starting from its individual elements and in combination with one another, like the concept, but at the level of the constituting domains of a structured ensemble. Intuition is neither sensible nor intellectual; it is the analogy between the becoming of the known being and the becoming of the subject, the coincidence of two becomings: intuition is not solely, like the concept, a grasping of figural realities, nor, like the idea, a reference to the totality of grounds for the real taken in its unity; it addresses itself to the real insofar as it forms systems in which genesis is carried out; it is knowledge proper of genetic processes. (MEOT 236)

Simondon addresses the problem of genesis by enacting what I am calling an "ontological or ontogenetic shift." What this means is that Simondon "shifts" the ontological perspective assumed by the speculative from that of the individuated individual to a perspective that grounds itself in the act of grasping the being of the individual in the continuum of "dephasing," making up the potentially interminable and inventive unfolding process of becoming individuated.

> The individual would then grasp as a relative reality, a certain phase of being which supposes like it a pre-individual reality[8] and which, even after individuation, does not exist all alone, for individuation does not exhaust at once the potential of the pre-individual reality and, on the other hand, what individuation makes appear is not the individual alone but the individual-milieu couple. (IPC 12)

Hence, this ontogenetic shift is enacted at both the ontological and epistemological levels, in parallel with one another. In a manner similar to Husserl's phenomenological reduction, the ontogenetic "shift" shifts thought from what is given to the *operation* that gives to us what is given as being. Individual must be taken to be relative in two senses: first, it is not all being (*tout l'être*) and, secondly, it is the result of a pre-individual reality of being. Although Simondon uses individuation or "ontogenesis" interchangeably, both denote the *genesis* of the individual. For it is the primary aim of the ontogenetic shift to make grasping "the character of becoming of being" possible, in other words, "that by which being becomes, as being *qua* being (*de devenir de l'être, ce par quoi l'être devient en tant qu'il est, comme être*)" (13).

"Analytic science" is the accepted form of structural knowledge, whereby all being is quantifiable, measurable, and divisible into its basic elements and combinations. Philosophical intuition, conversely, supports Simondon's proposing an Allagmatic epistemology, and orients thinking more closely with the problem of genesis, intuitively guided and sustained by it. With the reforming of knowledge Simondon wonders if an "analogic science" might not result, one that not only fully appreciates that the individual being is "a domain of reciprocal convertibility of operation into structure and structure into operation," but, even more, one that finds the condition for its possibility in the idea that "the individual is the unity of being grasped preliminary to every distinction or opposition" (IL 565). The analogic science is a temporal science.

This is why I claim here that Simondon's use of the crystal paradigm is meant to dramatize the insufficiency of its own use as paradigm; for it points to the epistemological limitations of reducing the vital to the physical, individuation to crystallization. Directing our theoretical gaze beyond itself toward the "theater of individuation," the crystal functions, on the one hand, as a model for the progressive recruiting and transferal of potential energy from a metastable source to a state of final stability, conditioning in turn the change of a local state back to the same metastability initiating the initial transformation; while, on the other hand, the crystal paradigm

inspires Simondon to theorize a new logic and a new epistemology, neces-
sitated by the ontologization of thought – the ontogenetic leap or the leap
into ontogenesis, which *vitalizes* thought in order for us to properly grasp
the problem of individuation, to think through it in responding to the
ontological shift. We orient ourselves *in thinking through this problem*. In
this regard, Simondon's own use of the crystal paradigm plays out for
our benefit the drama of individuation at the level of being and thought,
in comparison to the analogical logic of the general theory it is meant to
describe. We are not leaping, however, beyond philosophy: quite the contrary, philosophy is made synonymous with the leap, once it is made to be
one and the same *reflexive* operation.

FROM THE VITAL TO THE COLLECTIVE

Near the conclusion of the first of the two texts which make up the
"Introduction," Simondon broadly outlines how the ontological and
epistemological terms conditioning his formulation of ontogenesis likewise specify the conditions for a response to what he characterizes as the
psychosocial problematic. However, while composed prior to the first text,
it is the second text (lecture "Form, Information, and Potentials") where
Simondon more concretely details the particular psychological and social
(not to mention, potentially, political) stakes at risk.

Before completing my own exposition of this Introduction in this
chapter, I would like to connect Simondon's more mature position, evident
in the first text, to a certain aspect of the 1960 lecture, the second text:
his call for a "human energetics." I would like to use this opportunity
granted to us by François Laurelle, the editor, to appreciate more fully
Simondon's thought of the process of becoming. The challenge we face in
reading IPC is how we might somehow bridge the two parts comprising
the Introduction. Simondon invites a response to this challenge by enticing
us to ponder if *social reality* might not structure itself and its potentialities
in the same manner as individual beings (62). In other words, might the
operation of individuation at the individual level parallel and be codeter-
minate with the operation of individuation at the social level? This is in
short the psychosocial problem. I would like to suggest that what connects
them is Simondon's displacement of the Theory of Form (his proposing
the Good Form) with a new notion of information.

It is forcefully presumed in psychological and social theory both as
method and metaphysic, explanatorily and descriptively promoted, that
if one is going to achieve a true grasping of the psychosocial the first step
must be to replace the notion of Form with "information," whose primary
benefit, according to Simondon, is that it supposes the existence of any

system as only ever in a state of metastability and, so, always on the cusp of individuating itself. The reason for this is that the only way to conceive information is not as a single term, stable and, as such, uniquely identifiable like a Form. Information displaces form. Information reveals itself through the "emergence of signification" out of a relation Simondon calls the "*disparation*" (28).[9] A Theory of Form (Simondon capitalizes this term) defines form's birth as the resolving of tensions. By necessity such a theory must ignore the very idea of metastability. The primary example of how theories disregard metastability can be found in the different guises adopted by the "Good Form," which are responsible for organizing knowledge, a Form more purely *significative* because it is simple; the perfect state of equilibrating those forces otherwise conflictual, now equalized and made compatible, determine its structure. Simondon reconceives the Good Form in terms of information, consequently, describing it as "that which maintains the energetic level of the system, conserves its potentials in compatibilizing them: it is the structure of compatibility and viability, it is the invented dimensionality according to which there is compatibility without degradation" (29). Deleuze famously draws our attention to Foucault's brilliant analytic of the "Man-Form" in the latter's *Order of Things*.[10] But, on our own, we discern its presence throughout the history of thought: the Soul-Form, Cogito-Form, Ego-Form, Woman-Form, Labor-Form, etc. All of these candidates are but variations occupying the place of the Good Form. Yet beyond the forms taken by the Good Form is the discovery of "*being's* inherent significations," which is to say Simondon seeks to discover this inherence of signification in the very operation of individuation (29).

The primary benefit of Simondon's theorizing ontogenesis is that it provides a speculative perspective that permits the bringing together of psychology with sociology, while evading the tendency to reduce either to the presumptions of the other. It is "ontogenesis that indicates what participation in the collective is, as well as psychic operation conceived as the resolution of a problematic" (20). The living being is only ever "more and less than a unity" precisely because of the pre-individual metastability at its interior, the catalyst for structuring how the individual being might continue striving to exist. An individual's "participation" is catalyzed by its being an element, a singularity, in a vaster individuation, emerging out of the share of pre-individuality, the potentials therein, which the individual interiorizes. This is where the power of an individuation lies, the potential for an individual being to become "an element in a vaster problematic" beyond itself, to be de-individuated, starting internally, psychically, from within. As a result, in order to fully comprehend the psychic activity at the interior of the theory of individuation, we are required to see it as the resolution of a metastable state's conflictual character. What is more, it is necessary to discover the actual ways for institutions to activate these meta-stable systems in life. It is here we begin to speak of the collective as such.

Simondon's displacing the notion of Form with information means that there is a shift from a Theory of Form, permitting our looking back to resituate his earlier lecture (the second text of the Introduction), where, I would argue, his use of information is able to discover its common cause with his developing a non-probabilistic "energetic theory of form-taking." Denying any privilege to stable configurations, he hypothesizes that "we consider what is most important to explain in the psychosocial domain is what occurs when one has to deal with *metastable states: it is the form-taking in the metastable field which creates configurations*" (62–3). A living being's existence is what it becomes, given the potentiality of the share of pre-individuality it expresses. But the being of pre-individuality is itself purely energetic. The relation of a structural germ to the potential energy of a metastable state is precisely what causes the polarization; the spark of individuation is this event of disparity. It is here, therefore, that Simondon argues that we must search for "the foundation of a genesis constituting the individual" (IL 88). The living individual is alive precisely *because* it is the bearer of this polarization, this energetic disparity, which makes it possible but remains unexhausted in its coming-into-being as individual.

The psychic is the "slowing down" of the individuation of the living, an "amplification" of the initial genesis of the living. "There is psychism when the living can't completely concretize itself; it conserves an internal duality," (IL 165) the individuated and the pre-individual. As such, the psychic life maintains within itself what it takes from the living: "a tensed and metastable state, rich in potentials" (IL 165).

> The entrée into psychic existence essentially manifests itself as the appearance of a new problematic, higher, more difficult, which cannot receive any true solution at the interior of the living being properly said, conceived at the interior of its limits as individuated being; psychic life is neither a solicitation nor a superior rearrangement of vital functions, which continue to exist beneath it and with it, but a new plunge into pre-individual reality, coming after a more primitive individuation. Between the life of the living and psychism, there is an the interval of new individuation; the vital is not matter for the psychic; it is not necessarily recovered and reassumed by psychism, for the vital already has its organization, and psychism can barely deregulate it in attempting to intervene in it. (IL 165)

Coming after vital individuation, the psychic individuation occurs in the shape of the action carried out by an element of the problem, as *subject*. Subjectivity, conceivable as "the unity of being insofar as living individu-ated and insofar as being represents its own action through the world as element and dimension of the world" (19), it remains always open as a result of the vital problems conditioning it.

At the same time as it individuates the psychic being containing it, the charge of pre-individual reality correspondingly ensures that it exceeds the limits of the individuated living, likewise incorporating the living into a system of the world and of the subject. In this way, the subject's participation conditions the individuation of the collective. For individuation in the form of the collective likewise individuates the individual, a group individual, associated to the group by the pre-individual reality, which it includes in it and which reunites with other individuals, *individuates in collective unity*.

LOOKING FORWARD

As neither a substance nor the individuated part of a collected individual, the collective intervenes to resolve the individual problematic. What this signifies, according to Simondon, is that the basis for the collective reality is partially contained in the individual. It is pre-individuality in relation to the individuated reality. "The relation, to the world and to the collective, is a dimension of individuation by which the individual participates, starting from the pre-individual reality which individuates itself in stages" (20). But if relationality is a dimension of individuation through which the individual becomes, that relationality is information. And it is as information communicated that it achieves its ontological significance. "Psychism is made of successive individuations permitting being to resolve problematic states corresponding to the permanent putting into communication what is larger and smaller than it" (22).

The two individuations, psychic and collective, are reciprocally dependent upon one another. Together these individuations define the category of the "transindividual," which accounts for the psychosocial unity of interior individuation (psychic) and exterior individuation (collective). Transindividuality is the purest expression of relational being, which is fundamental to Simondon's ontology of ontogenesis. Instead of elements (particles or clouds of particles) as starting points, might we see each starting point only as a singularity, as only already a relation-to another starting, which is then another relation-to, potentially, ad infinitum? Might we imagine that relations come first and not the extremities of these relationships? We are only ever in the intervals between intervals – and so, we exist like *glissandi* in our own aleatory music. Any notion of the singularly unique individual being is put into question (or, rather puts itself into question), for individuation cannot be resolved solely at the level of the individuated being.

Critique of hylemorphism is only ever preparatory to the speculative, to Simondon's desire to found the human sciences on the basis of a "human energetics" (63). One might say that the limit between the structural germ and the *structurable* metastable field modulates the latter's energy, causing the structure, the form, to advance. In this regard, Simondon is not rejecting the Theory of the Form as much as he reformulates it, foregrounding metastability in the constitutive role it plays in the ontogenetic process. Stability is made insignificant by comparison, if we wish to grasp morphologically "the life of social groups."

The composer Iannis Xenakis,[11] for example, heard music in the life of groups, the mass phenomena – not in the discernible individual voices, the intrinsic qualities of the sounds, but in the vaster movement of distribution of these events, engaged in the vaster choreography, producing a unique composite *living* sound. Simondon transposes the form–matter relation, then, into a transductive relation and into the progression of the structuring-structured couple through an active limit, the passage of information. It is the foundation for a participation in a vaster individuation – like the "pre-revolutionary" clamoring voiced by a collective demonstration. Hundreds and thousands of people shouting a slogan that reproduces itself like an organism into a gigantic rhythm, sometimes splintering into cries, sirens, sound, gunfire, silence, and temporalities. Whose voice modulates time's becoming in a crowd? Simondon suggests that we should consider a mass phenomenon to be an event, for it is the accumulation of potential energy in a field, conditioning the creation of a relatively homogeneous field, a re-partition of energetic potentials measure by measure.

Simondon's ontological shift redirects our theoretical 'gaze' from the individuated form to the problem of *genesis*. And genesis is most immediately grasped, writes Simondon, in those "certain moments" when social groups reach a threshold, when they become incapable of conserving their structure's coherence, when their internal incompatibility, psychically, becomes so definite "they de-differentiate and oversaturate themselves" (63). And yet this precisely nurtures the transindividual's nativity and the parturition of a new world.

NOTES

1. Appended to *L'individuation à la lumière des notions de forme et d'information*, once it was finally published in complete form.
2. Bernard Stiegler writes some interesting pages concerning Socrates, which take up this issue. Cf. Stiegler, *Acting Out*.
3. Gilbert Simondon, "Forme, Information, Potentiels," *Société Française de Philosophie* (1960): 765, <http://www.sofrphilo.fr/?idPage=34>.

4. Henri Bergson, *Creative Evolution*, trans. Arthur Mitchell (New York: The Modern Library, 1944), 199, 248, Bergson's italics.
5. Georges Canguilhem, *Études d'histoire et de philosophie des sciences* (Paris: Vrin, 7th rev. edn, 2002), 335.
6. Simondon illustrates this shift to the operational in a fascinating passage from *Du mode d'existence des objets techniques*: "On the contrary, operational knowledge gives itself the possibility of constructing its object; it dominates and makes it appear, governs it; the genesis of its representation originates from the manipulable elements like the artisan who constructs the object which he poses before himself, assembling the pieces into a coherent manner. The concept, the instrument of operational knowledge, is itself the result of a reassembling operation, implicating processes of abstraction and generalization, starting with the given experience the *hic et nunc*, instead of residing in the unconditional totality anterior to all human gesture, even governing the human gestures already conditioned by it prior to coming into existence and being accomplished. For contemplative knowledge, the real is absolute subject, though for operational knowledge it is always object, in the primary sense of 'what is posed in front of it,' like a piece of wood is placed on an workbench, awaiting its incorporation into an ensemble under construction. The real for operational knowledge does not precede the operation of knowledge; it follows it. Even if it appears to precede it according to current experience, it follows it according to real knowledge, since this knowledge only grasps the real when it reconstructs it by the manipulation of elements" (MEOT 235).
7. "The need for *Allagmatic* epistemology is to determine the veritable relation between structure and operation in *being* and, departing, to organize a being's rigorous and valid relationship between structural knowledge and operatory knowledge, between analytic science and analogic science" (IL 565).
8. The first appearance in the text of "pre-individual."
9. Because there is no truly accurate English translation, I have chosen to retain the French.
10. "On the Death of Man and Superman," Gilles Deleuze, *Foucault*, trans. Seán Hand (Minneapolis: University of Minnesota Press, 1988), 124–32.
11. Iannis Xenakis was one of the most important twentieth-century avant-garde classical composers. Having escaped from the German and then British occupations of Greece, during which he was severely injured in street-fighting, he eventually settled in Paris and, after a time, became the first assistant to the groundbreaking French architect Le Corbusier. Glissandi were the primary structural elements in Xenakis' music, inspired by the mass demonstrations held in his native Greece protesting occupation. For an important reference to Xenakis in Simondon's works cf. Gilbert Simondon, *Imagination et invention, 1965–1966* (Chatou: Transparence, 2008), 181.

2

The Individuation of Perceptive Unities and Signification

SIDESTEPPING NOMINALISM AND IDEALISM

In Chapter 1, Part I of IPC, Simondon's starting point and the anchor for his approach to the problem of individuation is the analysis of perception. This might appear at first blush surprising, but a series of questions invite Simondon's analysis. Is something perceivable because it as an individuated individual, that is presumed by the perceiver to have already attained the state of being of the individuated? And if so, might perception be merely a matter of objectifying, of making actual what already exists *virtually* as "object"? Is an object individuated prior to being perceived, or does the perceiver bring about its phenomenal individuation, conditioning it? Simondon invites us to ask if perception might function in dual registers, both as an operation of individuation of the individual who perceives and of the thing perceived. Might the perceiver grant to being the impetus for its becoming individuated, and, in doing so, discover that what compels its individuation is the act of perceiving? In this chapter Simondon targets perception as a way to display his basic claim that an operation of individuation (of which perception is one mode) is not a process limited to one unique domain of reality, psychological or physical, but traverses and transductively connects multiple realities, from the psychological, to the physical, the metaphysical, and the social.

All the questions concerning perception coalesce around the debate between nominalism (or metaphysical realism) and idealism. Nominalism argues for the existence of individuated objects inhabiting an actual spatio-temporal reality, independent of human experience or knowledge. Idealism, on the other hand, makes the claim that whatever reality objects possess is given to them by the mind perceiving them; the "external world," rather than being independent of the perceiving mind, is its representation.

Simondon's theory of individuation (ontogenesis) sidesteps both nominalist and idealist claims concerning perception. The reason is quite simple: both make an appeal to an idea of completeness in the form of the individual, which serves as the grounds for their epistemologies. Both likewise find in their ontologically privileging the individual a support for how they conceptualize human beings' experience and existence in the world. The "objectivity" ascribed to the object designates the individuality for a human being as much as it does the object, for the latter is conditionally reliant on the metaphysical and epistemological unity granted to it by the notion of the individual. Thus, Simondon's focus on the genesis of perceived unities is intended by him to direct our theoretical gaze to the operation of individuation, which brings the perceived object, the unifying of the perceived flotsam and flux, into being. In this regard, perception is a living being's individuation, as she reflects her grappling with the problem of how to live in the world.

For Simondon, perception individuates by establishing a differential bipolar and intensive field. And the perceptive activity mediates the intensities in the relation between world and subject; it elevates the information of the formed system by the subject and the field in which it orients itself to a stable structure. This metastable field or "milieu," with which the particular subject is associated, while always present and always experienced, is not always grasped as such. In it resides the life, the potentiality of becoming.

MERLEAU-PONTY'S LESSON

Undoubtedly, Simondon's most significant teacher while studying at the *L'École normale supérieure*, whose presence is evident throughout IPC (even more than Georges Canguilhem), was Maurice Merleau-Ponty. Merleau-Ponty describes his own project as a "phenomenology of phenomenology." For Merleau-Ponty, philosophy is inextricably tied to the radicalizing of the act of reflection, which he took to be the heart of phenomenological practice, the phenomenological reduction. Once philosophy becomes a problem for philosophy itself, we discover the "invitation to re-see the visible, to re-speak the word, to re-think thought."[1] Phenomenology is a philosophy of perception, as Merleau-Ponty describes it, because perception affords philosophy the means by which to test philosophical reflection, to gauge which perspective permits the interrogation of itself, turning inward to probe our seemingly unwavering "perceptual faith" in a world that exists by what we perceive. It is, in short, the reconquering of the sensible: a "return to the things themselves." In doing so, the phenomenological gaze turns back upon itself, to interrogate the pretenses only half-heartedly admitted, but which it, nonetheless, embraces, so as to grant the world knowledge; even if, in doing so, the world stands revealed "as strange and paradoxical."[2]

> To return to the things themselves is to return to this world prior to knowledge, this world of which knowledge always speaks, and this world with regard to which every scientific determination is abstract, significative, and dependent, just like geography with regard to the landscape where we first learned what a forest, a meadow, or a river is.[3]

Merleau-Ponty writes that perception "is a metamorphosis,"[4] and philosophy gains power from its assuming the functions of an operation that revalues the perceived world by taking perception as the opportunity to reflect on the conditions for its own genesis. This is why Merleau-Ponty argues, "we must consider reflection to be a creative operation that itself participates in the facticity of the unreflected."[5]

Once philosophical reflection becomes conscious of itself, of its own practice, it is able to bring total clarification to the object, transforming its being through its being-perceived. If I might anticipate my claim at this moment before I have fully laid out the proof that Simondon and Merleau-Ponty share the same goal, even if they achieve it by different (and diverging) philosophical paths, the individuation of being cannot be grasped except by a correlated parallel and reciprocal individuation of knowledge. We must confront the problem of genesis in a two-fold manner: at once a phenomenon of the "spectacle of the world" and the means by which the structuring of our existence is changed.

In what he calls "hyper-reflection" (*sur-réflexion*) Merleau-Ponty finds their point of synthesis. For once phenomenology has been transformed through its attaining hyper-reflexivity, it finally accomplishes Husserl's ambition: it becomes a "phenomenology of genesis."[6] Hyper-reflection is necessary in order for the philosopher to suspend faith in the world, to finally *see it*, "to read in it the route it has followed in becoming a world for us; it must seek in the world itself the secret of our perceptual bond with it."[7] Philosophy's conversion into hyper-reflection is for Merleau-Ponty the true task left to philosophy.

It follows that philosophy, being inspired by perception to re-evaluate its own practice, to reform itself in terms of a hyper-reflexivity, brings perception into line with the same vitalist imperatives prompting its transformation into the ontology of ontogenesis. As Merleau-Ponty writes, "I live my perception from within, and, from within, it has an incomparable power of ontogenesis."[8] So we see that what spurs the re-examining of the notions of "object" and "subject" is the need to find a philosophical practice, a mode of knowledge, to grasp (if not to conceptualize) the more ancient "brute being" of relation between the two extremities, anterior to their being individuated "object" and "subject." With the ontological leap into ontogenesis, questions are made to shift from "*What is* the 'object'?" and "*What is* the 'subject'?" to "*How is* the 'object' individuated?" and "*For whom is* the 'subject' individuated?" "An analysis of the physical reality cannot be separated from a reflection on the same conditions of knowledge," writes Simondon (84). Or, as Merleau-Ponty writes, philosophy must "direct toward itself the very same interrogation that it directs toward all forms of knowledge."[9] Only in this way might we find a way to orient our thinking to grasp thought and being as they traverse one another's planes of individuation. Perception elicits philosophical reflexivity by the challenge it puts to it.

> When I turn toward my perception itself and when I pass from direct perception to the thought about this perception, I reenact it, I uncover a thought older than I am at work in my perceptual organs and of which these organs are merely the trace. I understand others in the same way. Here again I have but the trace of a consciousness that escapes me in its actuality and, when my gaze crosses another, I reenact the foreign existence in a sort of reflection.[10]

Accordingly, our grasping individuation via hyper-reflection (*sur-réflexion*) is analogous for Merleau-Ponty, however indirectly, to perceiving oneself in perception. As if for the first time, we stand astonished because we now perceive the world and its things themselves before us not merely as representations whose purpose is to confirm self-individuality, but as problems, engendering our joyous speculations. We grasp the movement of being in individuation, progressing from brute being to individual phenomena, in the same way, really, in the same action, as perception.

The critical justification of knowledge demonstrates the deployment of an ontological function in perception, "of an originary contact with being and with one called experience." There is little doubt, for Merleau-Ponty, that experience is transformed as a phenomenon of scientific analysis, of reflection, explication, which searches within itself for a pre-established, if implicit, understanding. "But from the moment it is placed at the center of philosophy, a question is posed: there is a contact with Being before reflection. How do we comprehend their relationship? Is it necessary for [knowledge] to coincide with a constituting dynamism?"[11]

Each perceptual object (transcendence) is but a mode of coexistence that, to whatever degree and relationship, constitutes at once individuality and otherness. If perception is the operation by which a being opens itself to the world, natural and social, via the perspective it constructs, then equally it opens before us – if we are willing to intuitively grasp it – that which is transcendental, "where the *Ursprung* of transcendences takes place," where time is uncovered "beneath the subject" through a "fundamental contradiction," which puts us into communication with others and on the basis of making knowledge possible.[12] It is by the individuation of knowledge and not by knowledge alone that the individuation of being is grasped, and the transcendental experienced.

So it is, Merleau-Ponty argues, that we are immediately brought to "rediscover" the social world. "We inseparably bear along with us, prior to every objectification," the social.[13] Life "has a social atmosphere just as it has a flavor of mortality."[14] The social carries forward what began in the natural, if at another dimension: the springing-forth or bringing into presence of those transcendences that determine the fashion in which a human being lives her or his individuality.

ASSOCIATIONISM AND FORMALISM

Simondon targets the psychological problem of how to explain the segregation of perceptive unities to support his claim that "individuation is not a process reserved to a unique domain of reality" like psychological or physical reality. Individuation traverses all multiple domains, bringing them into communication with another. And perception is the transductive operation *par excellence*.

But for us to fully appreciate what Simondon takes to be at stake in his designating perception's *operational being*, we must appreciate how his description seeks to evade the opposition between those psychological and sociological theories which he critiques for falling into one of two factions: the "genetic" theory of association or "holistic" formalism.

In either case, Simondon's rejection is made on the grounds that both speak insufficiently to the logical and metaphysical issues at play in perception's operationality, which separates being into perceptual unities, primarily resulting from their presumption that the basis for its synthesis is the notion of the individual, wholly complete, sovereign, and self-compatibilizing. Simondon's foregrounding of perception as operation is at the expense of a presumption of privilege for any anteriorly existent state of being, subject or object. What this means is that substantial individual being created on the basis of the categorical division of "subject" and "object" must be rethought. Simondon writes, "the individual is neither a substantial being like an element or a pure relation." Which is to say, there is only ever "a true individual in a system where a metastable state occurs." He continues: "If the appearance of the individual causes the metastable state to disappear in diminishing the tensions of the system in which it appears, the individual becomes entirely an immobile and inevolutive structure: the physical individual." By contrast, according to Simondon, "if this appearance of the individual does not destroy the system's potential from metastability, then the individual lives, and its equilibrium is that which sustains the metastability: it is in this case a dynamic equilibrium, which supposes in general a series of successive new structurations, without which the equilibrium of metastability could not be maintained" (79–80).

David Hume is the rarely mentioned interlocutor with whom Simondon is in silent dialogue in Chapter 1. Hume's skepticism is the source for the kind of associationism Simondon targets. And yet, more positively, it is also Hume's skeptical treatment of inductive reasoning which is the precursor for Simondon's own destabilizing of traditional epistemological categories and logical reasoning. Hume argues, "we have no reason" to believe the sun will rise tomorrow. All we are left with is the constant conjunction of the experiences, which together suggest the sun will rise again. All we "know" for certain is that it rose today, and yesterday, and the day before. These perceived impressions are associated by the imagination. Indeed, it is precisely the impression's lived vivacity – the intensity of a flame, for example – which constitutes the associated belief in the idea of heat. So it goes that, according to Hume, all ideas are ultimately traceable to habits or custom, most especially the idea of a personal or individuated self, which is no more than a necessary figment of synthesis required by our habits of speaking. No single impression of the "I" exists. As a result, Hume actively avoids the dead-end of the debate between nominalism and idealism.

Finally, we must be true to the fact that, for Simondon, Humean associationism maintains the seeds for the necessity of its own desuetude. It is fundamentally incapable of providing the grounds for addressing the problem of individuation. While associationism, as Simondon allows, is able to explain the genesis of perceptual unities, this same "genetic theory of pure appearance" cannot explain where the internal coherence of the individualized object comes from. That is, how the object's "veritable interiority" emerges, according to Simondon, is irreconcilable with acts of association.

Habit, which Hume invokes because it purportedly guarantees coherence and unity to perception, in fact remains a dynamism, which cannot communicate to perception what it itself possesses, Simondon argues. The appeal to habit, in fact, divulges a hidden "innatism." In other words, the individual remains at the center of relations, even if it is an isolated non-substance. For Simondon, however, "belief in the identity of the self as permanent reality superior to the changing development of impressions and ideas is unfounded" (IL 476). Which is to say, any theory that adopts associationism via contiguity does not fully explain the individualized object's internal coherence in being perceived. Hume's conferring upon habit so great an importance simultaneously grants theoretical preference to the activity of the individual subject and the resulting knowledge of this individual reality. The perceived object exists as nothing more than the accidental accumulation of elements, whose coherence is likewise accidental, given existence by the activity of the subject's imagination.

Deleuze helps us to see how Simondon's shift from the activity of the individual to the activity of individuation, while certainly undercutting Hume's theory specifically, supports more generally the formulation of the empiricist problem. The subject's invention and belief is what constitutes the given itself, synthesizing it into a system. But how is the subject also given? According to Deleuze, the empiricist problematic is one in which "the given is no longer given to a subject; rather, the subject constitutes itself in the given,"[15] even as the given is constituted in the subject. Deleuze looks to Hume for a concept of the subject that is practical, less metaphysical and, so, divorced from any transcendental pretensions.

Sharing with Deleuze the description of subjectivity as a process, Simondon nonetheless finds that adopting a genetic point of view discloses the limits of association. For Simondon, the genesis of the subject and object operate on the same plane of individuation.[16] In the end Simondon criticizes associationism for not being truly genetic,[17] not dynamic enough in how it conceives and values the genesis of the "subject" and the "object" in thought. For Simondon, the perceived object is not merely a unity of parts (*partes extra partes*), passively constituted, as a result of habitual repetition. It is dynamic; it "possesses a dynamism, which permits its being transformed without the loss of unity" (74). Thus, "it is not solely a unity but also an autonomy and a relative energetic independence which makes it a system of forces" (74).

Formalism presents Simondon with a different challenge. He suggests that it is "closer to the point" than a theory of associationism but still it does not explain the genesis of perceptual unities any better. The error lies, he argues, in its conceiving the "Good Form" against which individual beings are said to be true or false when measured against this standard model of perfection to determine how closely they achieve a resemblance to it.

Simondon reconceives the Good Form *energetically*; that is to say, rather than it designating the simplest and most coherent geometric form possible, it symbolizes the state of a system's lowest, non-entropic level of energy. At this lowest energetic state the Good Form represents the highest attainment of stability achievable, which makes it resistant to all exterior forces, alterations, and interferences. The Good Form is said to conserve a system's potentials by ensuring compatibility, in contrast to less perfect individualities and their incarnating ever-escalating degrees of incompatibility, difference, and metastability. There is little wonder that it functions as the ideal paradigm of perfect equilibrium, geometrically pregnant yet meaningfully formal. As a result, it is the image thought gives itself in order to direct analysis; it offers a supporting structure of good sense, leading thought properly, rightly. And, so, it must take on normative value beyond its being a speculative ideal if we hope to truly comprehend, and in comprehending, totalize, the perceived world. After all, the Good Form is created by formalism to act as the structuring image of being and thought, the model for all thought to emulate.

And it is by virtue of these laws of Good Form that the immediate knowledge of a perceived object is possible – the synthesis of perceptual unities is accomplished. Whatever genesis of perceptible object is possible is only because of the categorical representation of the Good Form and the hylemorphic schema associated with it; the latter ensures the former's being as the ideal synthesis of the *a priori* and the *a posteriori*, the concept and the sensible. In this sense, not only Plato, but especially Kant, are formalist. As Kant argues, time and space "dwell in us as forms of our sensible intuition, before any real object. Determining our sense through sensation has enabled us to represent the object under those sensible relations." In order for them to represent this object they must, nonetheless, "presuppose perception."[18]

Too often rendered innocuous by formalist theories, Simondon draws our attention to the paradoxicalness and ambivalence inherent in the notion of the Good Form. Simondon makes a comparison between the simplicity of geometrical forms like the circle and the square, easily wrenched from the "incoherent lattice of lines," to those forms invented by the artist. Simondon argues that it is foolish to argue that the "geometrical simplicity" of the circle is somehow formally superior to an artist's invention – the Greek column is not in any manner a "perfect" cylinder. "[The column] is, on the contrary, a figure of rotation not only of thinning, degraded at the two extremities but, moreover, it is non-symmetrical in relationship to its own center, the largest diameter being placed beneath the milieu of the highest" (77).

However, Simondon writes, "If the form is actually given and predetermined there would not be any genesis, any plasticity, any incertitude relative to the future of a physical system, an organism, or a perceptive field' (74). Perception is important for no other reason than that it offers us the means to counter any reduction of knowledge to the representation of some ideal Good Form; further, it is irreconcilable with any attempt to credit the cohesion of the physical object to the proportional quantity of information. The very nature of information, as Simondon defines it, makes this impossible. "The geometric rigor of contour has often less intensity and meaning (*sens*) for the subject than a certain irregularity. A perfectly round or perfectly oval face, incarnating a geometrically good form, would be lifeless; it would remain cold for the subject perceiving it" (88). If we look to a concrete example, the point can be obviously made if we compare the intentionally banal photos in a family album or the newspaper circular with the art photographs of Francesca Woodman, or Joel-Peter Witkin. The role and intent behind photographs of extreme tonal contrasts, and extreme relationships of clarity to obscurity, have a higher value and greater intensity, according to Simondon, than those of a photograph more uniformly tonal, more "gray," geometrically centered, and without deformation. The baroque photographs of Witkin powerfully express, if somewhat ironically, the demarcation Simondon sets as the threshold separating the living and the lifeless in our perceiving the deformed and the perfectly formed. Witkin's work exploits the idea that life emerges only through deformation, the pure movement of individuation; the equilibrium of death lies drawn in the perfectly individuated contour.

A form like a square, while it can be very stable, very pregnant, nonetheless receives a weak quantity of information in the sense that it can only very rarely incorporate in itself disparate elements. It is difficult to discover the square as the solution of a perceptive problem. "The square, the circle, and more generally simple and pregnant forms, are structural schemes rather than forms" (78). It is possible that these structural schemes, though innate, "are not sufficient to explain the segregation of unities in perception; the human figure with its own amicable or hostile expression, the form of an animal with its typical exterior characters, are as pregnant as the circle or the square" (78). After all, it is difficult – really impossible – to define a lion's or a tiger's form, or for that matter to identify it by the motifs of its coat, solely on the basis of a resemblance to geometric shapes. Nature does not have any geometric shapes, for living nature is not made of perfect angles or perfect lines. These are figures born from human imagination.

Simondon insists that formalism is "closer to the point" than any theory assuming a perspective of associationism because he finds the problem not to be in the notion of the form *per se* but in the way the form has been conceived. He agrees that, like associationism, formalism presents only a false geneticism. If we reverse our perspective and begin our analysis not from the individual to individuation but from individuation to the individual, similar to Deleuze's call for a "reversed Platonism," perception assumes the role of providing the means for reflexively grasping individuation *in the act*. "There is a genesis of forms just as there is a genesis of life" (74). Importantly, Simondon stresses that a state of entelechy cannot be entirely predetermined by the cluster of pre-existing "virtualities" pre-forming it.[19] For this reason his project cannot be said to completely jettison the idea of form *tout court*; it fundamentally reformulates it, beginning with its avowed first principles. For Simondon, "this critical moment" is "where unity and coherence appears."

The reason "laws" or rules predicated upon the Good Form provide an insufficient explanation for the segregation of units in the perceptive field is that, according to Simondon, they do not take into account the character of the solution to the problem presented by perception. Theories adopting these rules can only apply themselves to a false image of individuation, that is, to the transformation and degradation of already individuated forms more so than to the genesis of these forms themselves. What this suggests is that these rules predicated upon the Good Form must presuppose that forms pre-exist fully formed and fully individuated prior to any changes of state. Change is only an "accidental modification" of the perfected Good Form.

Metastability, that is the potentiality that constitutes it, appears as the genesis of forms, putting into question all anterior forms. But what this means is that the very notion of adaptation and, indeed, the suggestion that a form's genesis results from the need to adapt to the vital milieu inadequately projects, for Simondon, a causality to explain individuation. A theory of adaption would seem to Simondon as merely extending the formalist theory. Not every transformation is a genesis of form – for example, the erosion or calcination endured by a crystal. Prior to the crystal's reaching its state of being, there exists a state of tension, of metastability. However, in order for a crystal to grow, a considerable amount of energy must be interjected into the crystalline local milieu *from outside*. As a result, a disparity is created within the crystal. By contrast, only a living being exhibits the genesis of forms.

> There is a genesis of forms when the relation of a living ensemble has its milieu and in itself passes through a critical phase, rich in tension and virtuality, and which comes to an end as a result of the *disparition* of species or by the appearance of new form of life. The entirety of the situation is constituted not only by the species and its milieu but also by the tension of the ensemble formed by the relation of the species to its milieu and in which the relations of incompatibility become more and more strong. (76)

Not only the species alone but the species and its milieu together achieve a new structure. Before perception, before the appearance of the form engendered within it, potential exists in the incompability between subject and milieu. Perception is, therefore, not the grasping of a form but the solution of conflict; the discovery of compatibility, once perceptually accomplished *invents* a form. "This form that is perception modifies not only the relation of object and subject but still the structures of object and that of the subject" (76).

Formalism fails in envisioning the "absolute whole (*l'ensemble absolu*)" (75). It is incapable of accounting for "the collection of forces and potential energies," in other words, "metastability": the state of the oversaturated solution at the moment just before crystallization begins. Formalism, in the form of the Good Form, is useless, in spite of pretending otherwise, at predicting what will happen at this critical instant (at the moment where potential energy is maximum) of relative indetermination. "This state of metastability is comparable to a state of conflict in which the instant of the highest incertitude is precisely the most decisive instant, for it is the source of determinisms and genetic sequences which take from it their absolute origin" (75).

We notice carefully the path Simondon takes from the formalist conception of the Good Form, created to act as a paradigm of geometrical simplicity and axiomatic stability, to his reforming of it to reflect the energetic–informational state, transformed at the macro–level, so as to express the emergence of the individual from the metastable, the asymmetrical, the differential. This new "form" is only ever the expression of the nascent potentiality, which arises not from homeostasis but from the disparity internal to it, operationally and structurally. This culminates in the act of perception.

Perception demonstrates how reality is sensibly structured (or rather structures itself) *transductively*. As Simondon writes, "the individual is neither a substantial being like an element or a pure relation." Which is to say, there is only ever "a true individual in system where a metastable state occurs." He continues: "If the appearance of the individual causes the metastable state to disappear in diminishing the tensions of the system in which it appears, the individual becomes entirely an immobile and inevolutive structure: the physical individual." By contrast, according to Simondon, "if this appearance of the individual does not destroy the system's potential for metastability, then the individual lives, and its equilibrium is that which sustains the metastability: it is in this case a dynamic equilibrium, which supposes in general a series of successive new structurations, without which the equilibrium of metastability could not be maintained" (79–80). A perceptual object's stability corresponds to its integration into the "sub-ensemble" of a considerably vaster "problem." A perception becomes phenomenal once the problem it poses has been resolved. This, however, does not mean that metastability has been completely exhausted, its potential satisfied. Once integrated, its appearance becomes one phase in this vaster metastability, relative to the other phenomena making up the asymmetry characterizing vital processes.[20]

A crystal's fixed structure is only a frozen instant. However, "the successive layers of the microscopic crystalline aggregate network forming around the crystalline germ continues," perhaps, indefinitely (80). What we encounter in a crystal's form is only "the vestige of the individuation formerly realized in a metastable state" (80). Now, if we add the additional aspect of life to what is only physical paradigm, a living being seeks to maintain a "permanent metastability" around it (80). This is the challenge facing every living being: to foster a metastability that nourishes without destroying the individual it nurtures. We only ever live by tenderly negotiating our self-destruction. I am reminded of Artaud: "I surrender to the fever of dreams but only in order to derive from them new laws."

A living being is like a crystal insofar as maintains around itself, in its relationship to a milieu, a permanent metastability. And so its life is endowed with a vaster and more plenteous "indefinite life." This does not mean that life is eternal or somehow defies finitude; on the contrary, its share of the infinitude giving birth to it amplifies finitude. Existence is limited by the tension maintaining itself between a living being's structuration and yet amplified through the permanent metastability of the assemblage shared between the individual and the milieu. The individual little by little loses its "plasticity," its capacity to render metastable situations, to make of them problems to multiple solutions. One might say that as the living individual structures itself more and more, it tends to repeat its anterior behaviors as it moves further away from its birth toward death.

DURATION AND INDIVIDUATION

In IPC the issue of time is a difficult problem. I will wait until a later chapter to fully explore its implications. For now, I would like to draw the reader's attention to what I would suggest is indisputable: from Simondon's perspective, living duration (*durée*) is distinct from the temporality of individuation. And in this manner, Simondon moves very close to Bergson – a philosopher with whom Simondon has a complicated and often ambiguous relationship. It is Bergson who famously defines *durée* or duration as the purest form of time, "the succession our conscious state assumes when our ego lets itself *live*, when it refrains from separating its present state from its former states."[21] Duration and life are synonymous for Bergson; or, rather, the former virtually conditions the actuality of the latter, even as duration constitutes "memory." Bergson writes, "Inner duration is the continuous life of a memory which prolongs the past into the present, whether the present distinctly contains the ever-growing image of the past, or whether, by its continual changing of quality, it attests rather the increasingly heavy burden dragged along behind one, the older one grows."[22] It is the "real time" that nourishes and is nourished by life. "Duration is the continuous progress of the past which gnaws into the future and which swells as it advances."[23] And so, without this ontological "memory" not only surviving but making up the very "substance" of the present, time would be nothing other than distinctly quantifiable and spatialized instants, the complete converse of duration.

Simondon's account of the durational characteristics, which he attributes to individuation, is clearly influenced by Bergson, including assigning it multiple and often simultaneous paths of progress. This is, of course, not too surprising, given that Bergson is really the only near-contemporary philosopher who is mentioned by name in IPC (allusions are, of course, made to Heidegger, Canguilhem, and Merleau-Ponty, as I have already discussed). Still, Simondon maintains an uneasy relationship to his predecessor's thought. This is especially apparent in the few passages in IPC where we note Simondon's engaging the social and political consequences that follow from adopting the Bergsonian metaphysic. For now, let us focus only on the correspondences between Simondon and the Bergsonian conception of *durée* for conceptualizing the temporality of individuation.

Duration must not be confused with individuation. Different individuations have distinctly unique temporalities, distinct speeds, rhythms, and qualities of elaboration, which distinguish them not only from one another but also from a more generalized duration. As soon as an organization's successive behaviors and temporal sequences of acts appear, specifying the individual, there exists a threshold of irreversibility which establishes the limit beyond which death lies for the human individual structuring her progress. Only those beings with little or no differentiated structure have a potentially unlimited duration of life. Of course, they would become immortal. Finitude is the appearance of the individual but the individuation of the individual expresses the eternal. For with individuation we have a direct expression of Nature, the metastable pre-individuality of being, preserved and conveyed through the individuating processes themselves. We will return to this temporal paradox later. For now, I would like to suggest that the degree of structural individuality corresponding to the limit of an individual life, relationship to other beings, as well as interior organization, is situated on the same plane of immanence by the irreversible character of "temporal structuration." Importantly, neither the structural relation to other beings nor temporal structuration in itself is directly the cause of the other. "The common origin of these two aspects of the individual reality seems to be, in fact, processes, according to which metastability is conserved, or augmented, in the relation of the individual to the milieu" (81). Admittedly, this is a difficult and complicated idea. Nonetheless, it is an important statement for opening up a discussion relative to the temporality of the individuation of individual and collective.

PERCEPTION AS SOLUTION TO A PROBLEM: DISPARATION

As we progress through Chapter 2 of IPC, we notice how Simondon's focusing on perception is intended to demonstrate how information becomes significative. However, the final pages of IGPB set the stage for this chapter, for it is in these pages that Simondon appropriates Merleau-Ponty's discussion of binocular vision (*Phenomenology of Perception*), when he takes the two distinctly independent, yet complementary, images that form on the left and right retinas as dramatizing the movement from information to signification.[24] As Merleau-Ponty describes it: in order to focus and see the object, one must first "experience double vision as a disequilibrium or an imperfect vision."[25] Simondon might call this the dis-individuating moment conditioning perception, the tension anterior to vision yet resolved by it. As a result of the superimposition of these binocular images, a single monocular image forms "by means of a certain number of fractioned actions on a number of finite plans, corresponding to simple laws of transformation" (IL 223). Signification, Simondon argues, arises out of difference or a certain *disparation* between the images given by the right retina and the left. It is in this "double vision to normal vision" that we intuit the pre-individuality that conditions our seeing, which is gifted with becoming reflexively conscious, however rapidly, "of progressing toward the object itself and of finally having its carnal presence."[26]

> The relief [or *étagement*: projection from a surface, an elevation of land] inter-venes as signification of this duality of images; the duality of images is neither felt nor perceived; alone the relief is perceived: it is the sense of the difference of the two givens. Similarly, so that a signal receives a signification, not only in a psychological context but also in an exchange of signals between technical objects, it is necessary that a *disparation* exist between a form already contained in the receptor and an information signal brought from the exterior. If *disparation* is non-existent, the signal exactly regains the form and information is non-existent, insofar as it is the modification of a system's state. On the contrary, the more *disparation* augments, more information augments, but up to a certain point only, for beyond certain limits, depending upon the characteristics of the system's receptor, information becomes suddenly non-existent, when the operation by which *disparation* is assumed as *disparation* is no longer able to carry itself out. (IL 223)

In the above passage we get a demonstration of the Allagmatic method at work: the lightning quick, alternating shifts between disciplines and concepts, Simondon's own discourse reflects on its own the operation, foregrounding the process itself as he carries forward a process of structuring an image through a series of analogies. His goal is not only to reveal what makes the transformation of one structure into another possible – the fundamental *disparity* at the heart of his own discourse's operation – it is also to demonstrate it in action. Simondon is speaking of his own discourse, not as a metaphor, as he describes a synchronized oscillator augmenting a signal's different frequencies, establishing a discursive paradigmatic structure with a real ontological significance as the condition for information to be integrated into the receptor's (the human eye's) functioning once the *disparation* establishes the criteria for relating the extrinsic signal and the intrinsic form. For Simondon, this image is analogous to our "looking" at an object.

Simondon's basic point is that increasing the gap (*l'écart*) that structures a stereoscopic shot enhances as well the *disparation* at the heart of the image, increasing, as a result, the perceiving objects in their ever deeper and significative perspective. "*Disparation* is not and cannot be made, for it is not at the level of signals, and does not give birth to a *signal* but a *signification*, which only has some sense in a functioning" (IL 224). The full meaning or significative value an object is said to possess becomes apparent only on the basis of the potentiality put into play in a *disparation*; while, operationally, it is no less real than whatever object is actually touched, actually tasted, or actually smelled, even though presently it is *non-phenomenal*, *in-actual* in itself.

QUALITATIVE INTENSITY OF PSYCHIC INDIVIDUATION

Individual objects are not perceived as if they are indefinite sources of signals, "an inexhaustible reality, like matter, left indefinitely for us analyze." Rather, says Simondon, we perceive only secondarily the individuality of objects. Objects are given meaning via definite "thresholds of intensity."[27] It is important to understand that Simondon defines intensity qualitatively, that is, as information.

> It seems therefore that neither the concept of the 'Good Form' nor that of quantity of pure information is suitable for defining the reality of information. Above information as quantity and information as quality exists what one would like to call information as intensity. (87–8)

Perception is the transductive operation by which "experience" of the physical object occurs through the organization of thresholds and levels, which maintain and transpose via different relations. It activates the intensity of information in terms of the relations it creates, the distances and proximities it reflects in time and space, along an intensive gradient of information.[28] Information and intensity are synonymous along this perceptual gradient. "The physical object is a fasciae of differential relations," Simondon writes, "and its perception as individual is the grasping (*la saisie*) of the coherence of its network (*fasiceau*) of relations" (83).

Kant sought to explain perception via the synthesis of the diverse (*divers*) given by sensibility. Simondon, on the other hand, contests this Kantian form of synthesis as the importing of a secret hylemorphism. In its place Simondon describes two types of diversity: a qualitative (heterogeneous) diversity and quantitative (homogeneous) diversity. We might likewise be reminded of Bergson's defining of two types of multiplicity: one that is non-numerical and continuous and the other that is numerical and discontinuous, one temporal or durational and the other, spatial.[29]

Simondon's primary rival and accomplice, the Theory of Form or Formalism (of which Kant is a variant), explains perception by presuming that it is already the result of a homogeneous diversity: unity is the result of adding another homogeneous kind. However, for Simondon, what must be added is the intensive diversity, "which renders the subject-world system comparable to an oversaturated solution; perception is the resolution which affected this oversaturated system; one might say that every actual perception is the resolution of a problem of compatibility" (91).

This is, of course, not unknown to Kant, who seemed to introduce a concept of intensity in terms of magnitude. And yet to reduce intensity to magnitude is reduce it to space, to the quantitative, to extensive magnitude. This is why he argues that the perception of an object, as appearance, is possible only through the synthetic unity of the manifold, which shares the same conditions being represented, intuition of space and time, as the concept of magnitude. Every appearance is manifested in space and time and, thus, "every appearance is an extensive magnitude, cognizable through successive synthesis (from part to part) in apprehension." Hence, Kant argues that all appearances are intuited aggregates, antecedently given parts, or approximations to negation = 0, in other words, what Simondon calls individuated individuals, whose being is presumed to be given as such. It follows that, for Kant, extensity is the precondition for rendering the intensive possible, first by rendering it as a "magnitude" and, secondly, by reducing intensive magnitude to a wholly negative quantity.[30]

Even the slightest difference of intensity – of light and color – distinguishes forms (degrees of gray, for example). But for Simondon, "it is at the level of different gradients, luminous, colored, somber, olfactive, thermic, that information takes a predominant intensive sense" (88). A perception's potentiality derives from the intensive dynamism fed by the incompatibilities or disparities anterior to it. Fears, intense desire, joyful ecstasy, all increase perceptual intensity, even if (or, precisely because) their causes are unclear.

Simondon reasons that it is necessary for objective quantities and qualities to be grasped not as accidental or secondary properties of some substantive individual thing but, instead, as intensive intermediaries mediating the subject and the world, signals enabling the coupling of the subject and the world (90). Further, different types of modulation converge toward the modulation of intensity, so that perception as differential is a mode of "modulation." Form is displaced by the activity of modulation, the differences of intensities, which perception mediates.

It is the tension or the degree of metastability internal to a system formed by the human being or animal in relation to a determined situation which structures in perception the corporeal schema of the animal. "The perception grasps (*saisit*) here not only the form of the object, but how we orient it in the ensemble, its polarity, causing it to have been laid down or erected on its feet, that makes it face or flee, have a hostile or confident attitude" (79). Perception segregates unities at the same time as it discovers their polarity. "The unity is perceived when a reorientation of the perceptive field develops via the function of the object's proper polarity" (79). It follows that perceptual nascence is actually tied to the dynamic character of the perceptive field. It is not a consequence of the form alone but above all it falls within the range of the solution responding to the "vital problematic" (92).

This is why Simondon can say that the "object is an exceptional reality." *An object is not perceived.* What is perceived is the world, against which the object emerges before us, with sense and objectivity; it appears for us in a polarized manner to make sense of our situation. Only provisionally are intensities signified "object." We are not the adequate cause of all that we are, Merleau-Ponty reminds us. That we are visible, that any thing is visible for that matter, results from "what already sustains us while we traverse it with a look that, in its own way, is part of it."[31] Thus, in speaking about what perception is and how its action exemplifies the best way we might grasp the individuation of a being by its raising the information of a system formed by the subject and its field to a level, we can grasp how a human being orients himself, which commits us to accepting Simondon's thesis that perception is inseparable from the *metastable* stable state *preceding* it (90).

Simondon's reworking of the Kantian structure preserves qualitative diversity as the condition for the possibility of knowledge. Perceptions are, for Kant, sensible representations given to consciousness, which make actual space and time. Knowledge is achieved by an originary act of synthesis, *quantitatively added to* the diversity given by sensibility, so that it is brought to a magnitude and, accordingly, a homogeneous unity ("homogeneous manifold").[32] What is added by way of synthetic unity is, therefore, not a more radical difference but a higher form of experiential continuity, "transcendental apperception," as the grounds for any and all possibility of the objects of experience.[33] For Simondon, the object is only provisionally the stabilizing of a situation's dynamisms in tension with one another. "The system world-subject is an overdetermined or oversaturated field" (91). It is through orienting itself in this oversaturated field like a crystalline germ that the subject brings unity to the qualitative and intensive heterogeneity. In this regard, for Simondon, all perception is "*differential perception*" (90, my italics).

It is important to appreciate that this points to perception as an active gesture, which supposes that the subject is a part of the system in which the perceptive problem is posed. It is as problematic as the object perceived and, in this regard, Simondon makes Kant Humean. For as a result of its own perceptive gesture, without recourse to some form of transcendent *a priori* identity, the subject constitutes the unity of perception in the system formed by the world and the subject. Yet if, for Kant, this is the only goal that matters, Simondon requests that we step back to disclose the underlying ontological presuppositions hidden by adopting this goal. In so doing, Simondon hopes that once again we find ourselves addressing anew less a submission of epistemology to ontology than a ontologization of epistemological categories and concepts, so as to reflect back upon, that is to interrogate, the claim it makes on those conditions credited with the genesis of knowledge.[34]

Despite the critique of associationism, as I previously specified, Simondon's concept of the subject has a direct affinity with Hume's problematizing the legacy of the Kantian subject. For Simondon, perception reflects the intensity of information. It follows that a new concept of the subject is required for orienting the human individual in relation to the informational associated dynamic milieu. Each received perception signals the differential coefficient of possible intensities. Thus, a subject must orient herself, so as to exist in a joyful relationship with the world.

Merleau-Ponty writes (clearly aware of Simondon's work): "I live my perception from within, and, from within, it has an incomparable power of ontogenesis."[35] So, whatever claim made by perception to the benefit of knowledge "is a grasping of being, which is neither *a priori* nor *a posteriori* but the contemporary of the being it grasps, and at its same level" (MEOT 236). If perception prompts the leap into ontogenesis, both critically and speculatively it likewise prepares us for what it discloses by opening us to the vital problem contesting those categories supposedly offering an explanation for it.

CONCLUSION

Simondon contends that the operation by which the segregation of perceptive unities happens takes place in the same way as the genesis of concepts. While accepting Kant's characterization of the concept as reflecting the rational category of understanding, Simondon does not, however, accept that if one hopes to grasp individuation, it becomes necessary to achieve a synthesis of diverse perceptions by placing them beneath an *a priori* scheme, thereby conferring unity on them. Not a synthesis, rather it is an operation of propagation internal to the perceptual field, structuring step-by-step domains, progressively modifying while in operation. No one concept is granted an intrinsic priority over any other concept; rather, it is the totality of concepts, their coming together to make an ensemble present in the logical field, that sustains any one particular concept. The entrance of new concepts into the logical field causes the restructuration of the totality of all concepts, leading to a new metaphysical doctrine as the best possible outcome. Perception's role, therefore, is to modify the intensive threshold distinguishing concepts prior to this restructuration.[36] In order for the formation of the concept to be possible, Simondon suggests, an inter-perceptive tension is just as necessary to structuring the subject's relation to itself and to the world. Neither the *a priori* nor the *a posteriori* can be the starting point for the mediation between a subject, the world, and others. Mediation is not of the same nature as the terms mediated. Mediation "is tension, potential, metastability of the system formed by the terms" (93).

Because Simondon characterizes it to be inextricably tied to the progress of reflexivity in thought, all philosophical activity is likewise a reform of the mode of knowledge. It enforces a rethinking of its concepts, its categories, and its actions on the basis that doing so justifies the use philosophy makes of perception. Once we have an awareness of the ontogenetic character of perception, and as a result of the new manner it offers, philosophical thought is led to pose anew the problem of the relationship between concept, intuition, and idea, and correlatively, to correct the sense of nominalism and realism. This is why Simondon begins with a discussion of perception – for it leads not only to our appreciating the problem of genesis but also to our reconceiving knowledge as operatory, that is, ontological and not merely structurally responsible for universal and objectively necessary apodictic judgments.

NOTES

1. Maurice Merleau-Ponty, *Notes des cours au Collège de France 1958–1959 et 1960–1961*, ed. Stéphanie Ménasé (Paris: Gallimard, 1996), 375. My translation.
2. Maurice Merleau-Ponty, *Phenomenology of Perception*, trans. Donald A. Landes (New York: Routledge, 2012), lxxvii.
3. Merleau-Ponty, *Phenomenology of Perception*, lxxii.
4. Maurice Merleau-Ponty, *The Visible and the Invisible; Followed by Working Notes*, trans. Alphonso Lingis, ed. Claude Lefort (Evanston, IL: Northwestern University Press, 1968), 8.
5. Merleau-Ponty, *Phenomenology of Perception*, 62.
6. Merleau-Ponty, *Phenomenology of Perception*, lxxxii.
7. Merleau-Ponty, *The Visible and the Invisible*, 38.
8. Merleau-Ponty, *The Visible and the Invisible*, 58.
9. Merleau-Ponty, *Phenomenology of Perception*, lxxxv.
10. Merleau-Ponty, *Phenomenology of Perception*, 367.
11. "But then why are we constituted ourselves? And if we are given to ourselves in a blind and global apprehension, if reflection can only enumerate and project discursively on this side of (*en deçà de*) our experience the conditions without which it appears to us it would be impossible, without ever coinciding with the functioning of the whole, then what is this reverse of reflection where reflection is prepared, the hyper-reflection (*sur-réflexion*) that will discover it for us?" (Merleau-Ponty, *Notes des cours au Collège de France*, 369).
12. Merleau-Ponty, *Phenomenology of Perception*, 382, 383.
13. Merleau-Ponty, *Phenomenology of Perception*, 379.
14. Merleau-Ponty, *Phenomenology of Perception*, 382.
15. Gilles Deleuze, *Empiricism and Subjectivity: An Essay on Hume's Theory of Human Nature*, trans. Constantin V. Boundas (New York: Columbia University Press, 1991), 86–7.
16. In Deleuze's later works he will more explicitly adopt this formulation.
17. Deleuze's interpretation of Hume is interesting as a way to delineate a fault-line between himself and Simondon. Deleuze writes: "Empiricism is not geneticism: as much as any other philosophy, it is opposed to psychologism" (Deleuze, *Empiricism and Subjectivity*, 108).
18. Immanuel Kant, *Critique of Pure Reason*, trans. Paul Guyer and Allen W. Wood (Cambridge: Cambridge University Press, 1998), A 373.
19. As I have suggested in the introduction. Here we find what would appear to be a fundamental divergence between Simondon and Deleuze. And yet Deleuze's later formulation of his ontology of the virtual seems to be an attempt at bridging this gap. Simondon distrusts the term "virtual" to the benefit of the more Aristotelian "potential," whereas Deleuze rejects the latter while promoting the former. One wonders if this seeming incongruity is largely a disagreement over terminology, for otherwise both philosophers share metaphysical and epistemological, structural and operational similarities.

20. Gilbert Simondon, *Cours sur la perception: 1964–1965* (Chatou: Transparence, 2006), 222.

21. Henri Bergson, *Time and Free Will: An Essay on the Immediate Data of Consciousness*, trans. F.L. Pogson (Mineola, NY: Dover Publications, 2001), 100, Bergson's italics.

22. Henri Bergson, *The Creative Mind*, trans. Mabelle L. Andison (New York: Citadel Press, 2002), 179.

23. Bergson, *Creative Evolution*, 4.

24. "From Information to Signification" is the title of the specific section to which I am alluding. Gilbert Simondon, *L'individu et sa genèse physico-biologique* (Grenoble: Millon, 2nd edn, 1995), 218–22.

25. Merleau-Ponty, *Phenomenology of Perception*, 241.

26. Merleau-Ponty, *Phenomenology of Perception*, 242.

27. Cf. Deleuze's discussion of "intensity" in *Difference and Repetition*, esp ch. 4. Note also Deleuze's displacement of quantitative by qualitative *qua* difference.

28. Simondon, *Cours sur la perception*, 292.

29. Bergson, *Time and Free Will*, 121–2. Of course, Deleuze will make much of this distinction between multiplicities in his book *Bergsonism*.

30. A 162–76/ B 202–18.

31. Merleau-Ponty, *The Visible and the Invisible*, 61.

32. A162/B202–163.

33. "The supreme principle of all synthetic judgments is, therefore: Every object stands under the necessary conditions of the synthetic unity of the manifold of intuition in a possible experience. The conditions of the possibility of experience in general are at the same time conditions of the possibility of the objects of experience, and on this account have objective validity in a synthetic judgment *a priori*" (Kant, *Critique of Pure Reason*, A158/B197).

34. On this account Simondon extends Merleau-Ponty's "interrogative mode." He writes, "The interrogative mode derived by inversion or by the reversal of the indicative and of the positive, is neither an affirmation nor a negation veiled or expected, but an original manner of aiming at something, as it were a question-knowing, which by principle no statement or 'answer' can go beyond and which perhaps therefore is the proper mute or reticent interlocutor of our questions" (Merleau-Ponty, *The Visible and the Invisible*, 129).

35. Merleau-Ponty, *The Visible and the Invisible*, 58. Recently, with the publication of discovered notes written at the same as he was drafting *The Visible and the Invisible*, illustrating Merleau-Ponty's close reading of Simondon's works, there has been a greater appreciation of the influence the younger thinker may have had on the older philosopher. Cf. "Life and Individuation, with Unpublished Texts by Merleau-Ponty and Simondon," *Chiasmi international publication trilingue autour de la pensée de Merleau-Ponty* 7 (2005).

36. "One can say in this sense that conceptualization is to perception what syncrystallization is to the crystallization of unique chemical species" (93).

3

Individuation and Affectivity

THE PROBLEM OF AFFECTIVITY AND EMOTION

After taking up nearly the entirety of the previous chapter with discussing different approaches to the problem of perception and, in response, devising a philosophy of perception, if only on ontogenetic terms, in Chapter 2, Part I Simondon ostensibly does an about-face and argues that the failures of formalism or what he calls the "theory of Form" are confirmed by the inordinate analytic privilege it gives perception. That is to say, whether self-aware or not, formalist theories favor the analysis of the perceptive relation over "the active relation and the affective relation" (97). While it certainly would not be too surprising for this chapter to begin with a more definitive rejection of formalist theories on the grounds of their prohibiting a proper addressing of the relationship between consciousness and the individual, we are left to wonder, nonetheless, how Simondon intends to reconcile the development of a theory of perception in the preceding chapter with his disavowal of the importance of perception in this current chapter. The answer is that it is not perception but affectivity which permits a true appreciation of how the relationship between the consciousness and the individual comes about. As a result, we must take Simondon's reformulation of perception in the previous chapter to be a propaedeutic for this analysis of affect and affectivity.

Simondon hopes that, by considering all the aspects of the relation between perception and affectivity, "equilibrium" can be re-established between consciousness and individual. Most especially, to his thinking, the subject exists only to the extent that it "carries out the segregation of unities in the object world of perception." According to Simondon, "The individual individuates to the extent that it perceives beings, this constitutes an individuation by the [perceptual] action or the fabricated construction, and belongs to the system including its individual reality and the objects that it perceives or constitutes" (98). If association is credited with providing the subject with its necessary form, then perception provides it not only with its singular content but its expressive rehearsing of the movement of its becoming individuated as such. The subject is defined by this double expressiveness: of structure and of operation. Affectivity adds still another dimension: "The affective state polarizes the living" (115), for what defines the dimension of affectivity is the individuation which occurs there. It is where the relationship between consciousness and the individual progressively and brusquely structures itself. It is where the subject experiences it most directly and individually. Structure and operation come together in affectivity.

By placing affectivity and emotivity at the center of the individual's individualization, Simondon takes his analysis to be in agreement with the findings gathered by biological research. Or rather, it would be more accurate to say that Simondon finds the justification in the biological sciences for his placing affectivity and emotion at the heart of the individual's individualization. In either case, an example would be pathology's showing how a tumor in the mesencephalon or the "mid-brain," the oldest layer of the nervous system, and the part of the brain most responsible for vision, hearing, and motor capacities, contributes to what has been described as the profound "dissolution of individuality." Simondon writes: "It seems these [affectivity and emotivity] are the very basis for personality." Thus, he stresses, "while a weakening of functions of representative consciousness or capacities of action alter the personality without destroying it, often in a reversible manner, the alterations of affectivity and emotivity are very rarely reversible" (100). This is to suggest that they function and have a place at a different level, more subconscious than representatively conscious. (I will speak more to this later.) Before turning to the specific definition which Simondon gives to "affect" or "affectivity," first it might be helpful – if I might be permitted to mimic Simondon's method – to designate against whom he positions himself.

Simondon refuses the two primary explanations, as I see it, governing the apprehending of "psychism." The first explanation says that an assemblage of psychic characteristics, which together compose "personality," explains consciousness. The second explanation, made famous by Henri Bergson and William James, is that psychic reality is a pure indissoluble and continuous unity, a "stream of consciousness." Simondon, contrary to both explanations, seeks a principle that is neither the "residue of analysis that fails before the indivisible (*insécable*), nor is it the first principle that contains everything in its unity from whence everything ensues" (98).

Simondon proposes a notion of psychism for the purpose of replacing both: neither pure interiority nor pure exteriority, it is, instead, the "permanent differentiation (*différenciation*) and integration, according to associated regimes of causality and finality," which he calls "transduction" (98). It is a kind of psychism without a psyche or, at least, a vacant psyche, an empty form, in itself formless. It is only ever a process, an operation, a structuring movement. For Simondon, the psychic is transduction, and transduction is the motivic structure of movement conditioning the development of causality and finality. Transduction sets the parameters of individuation or ontogenesis. While the psychic assumes a transductive form through affectivity and emotivity, they are the "permanent liaison of individual to itself and the world, or rather the liaison between the relation of the individual to itself and the liaison of the individual to the world" (98). Simondon shifts the grounds for explicating the individual's psychic interiority from pure consciousness or organic unconscious to the level of the affective-emotive sub-consciousness.

THE AFFECTIVE PROBLEMATIC: AFFECTION AND EMOTION

In spite of the fact that pleasure and pain constitute the primary dimensions in the polarity of affectivity by which the subject orients itself in the world, the subject is not reducible to these dimensions alone. Pleasure and pain, Simondon writes, "are the rooting of the actual experienced in the existence of the living, in the structures and potentials which constitute it or that it possesses" (115). Nor will we reduce affectivity to sensation. Certainly, sensations provide the "field of movement, which agrees with itself," as pleasure and pain "are the field of insertion into living being of affective qualities" (115). The sensations garnered from perception 'put being into question' by rendering being vulnerable to an interrogation that problematizes it, disclosing being as a problem only ever to some extent unresolved. But this does not mean a resolution is not possible, only that sensation puts its challenge to the subject, for an individuated being's sense organs leave it exposed to the need for orienting itself in the world (or a plurality of worlds) according to diverse polarities. Sensation and affection present two ways by which the being of the world can be made questionable (116).

Something in the margins of thought appears before us, however fleetingly, anterior to every consistency applied to our conceptualizing the object. Contrary to phenomenology, in sensation there is not any "*intention* to grasp an object in itself in order to have knowledge of it, nor the relationship between *an object* and the living being" (118). Orientation is primary: what does it mean to orient oneself in thinking? Thinking orients itself on the basis of a series of emerging affective differences, intensive and qualitative (hot/cold, heavy/light, somber/clear, outside/inside, right/left, height/depth, etc.) (117). Importantly, each set we grasp from the center of its emergence, rather than at its extreme terms: "is not synthesis but transduction" (118). This phrase "not synthesis but transduction" must be emphasized, for this explains how Simondon takes us beyond Kantianism, beyond phenomenology and, indeed, upturns a good deal of the psychological and cognitive theories fixing on perception. Sensation "is *transductive* more than relational" (118), for it offers us that by which the affected living being adjusts to its place within such a transductive reality.

Our sensible reality is *tropistic*, lived by grasping it as a series of sensible gradients, intensities, rather than as objects: "movements, of which we are hardly cognizant, slip through us on the frontiers of consciousness in the form of indefinable, extremely rapid sensations. They hide behind our gestures, beneath words we speak, the feelings we manifest, are aware of experiencing, and able to define. They seemed, and still seem to me to constitute the secret source of our existence, in what might be called its nascent state."[1]

Affection translates these intensive sensations, transforming them into its associated milieu, which is experienceable. Sensations and affections remain "incomplete realities" beyond the sub-ensembles – the other sensations and affections and milieus – they are associated with and in which they operate. Pleasure and pain, yes, but also cheerfulness and sadness, happiness and unhappiness, exaltation and depression, bitterness and felicitousness elaborate the affectivity of individual being.

SARTRE'S EMOTIVITY

The non-coincidence of affections pushes toward emotion in the same way that the non-coincidence of sensations pushes toward perception (120). While Simondon never explicitly references it, it seems clear that he theorizes a conception intended to fundamentally disagree with Jean-Paul Sartre's theory of emotion. The distance between the two is set by their relative approaches to situating affection within the psychosocial.

In this regard, Simondon completely displaces Sartre's characterization of emotion as a "pure transcendental phenomenon," at least in the sense that it is taken to elucidate the essence of an organized type of consciousness. As Sartre describes emotion, "it expresses from a definite point of view the human synthetic totality in its entirety."[2] Explicitly refusing to reduce emotion to affectivity, at least from the phenomenological perspective, he defines it as "an existential mode of human reality."[3] Sartre's affective neutrality obviously conflicts with Simondon's depiction of a dynamically bipolar world, only ever in tension and oversaturated with affective singular intensities. Affectivity is but the effect of a more profound act of giving meaning; it describes the texture objects acquire, the substantializing quality an object acquires once it becomes emotionally meaningful for my psychic life.[4] Thus, to ascribe emotion a significative function for Sartre requires a concept of consciousness determined by the phenomenological notion of intentionality, which directs the individual toward the object. "We live emotively a quality that penetrates us," Sartre writes, "which we suffer, and which exceeds us on every side; at once, the emotion ceases to be itself; it transcends itself; it is not a trivial episode of our daily life; it is intuition of the absolute."[5] But what is the absolute from the Sartrean perspective?

It is this question that draws my attention, where a point of coincidence between the two thinkers might be discovered. We recall Sartre's essay "The Transcendence of the Ego" and its powerful characterization of an impersonal consciousness: "This absolute consciousness, when it is purified of the 'I,' is no longer in any way a *subject*, nor is it a collection of representations; it is quite simply a precondition and an absolute source of existence."[6] If we acknowledge that consciousness, by its very nature, transcends itself, so that it knows itself only by an ego's projecting its intention on the world, then Sartre's fascinating passage discloses for us two related, if nevertheless divergent, paths that might be taken for rethinking emotion. On the one hand, emotion permits us our glimpsing of the wholly ontological source, impersonal and pre-individual, anterior to intention credited to a consciousness in experiencing an object. The fact of consciousness derives from an operation anterior to it, which gives the forms of the object and the subject as *"transcendents."* On the other hand, the absolute is "magical," according to Sartre, insofar as consciousness in relation to it is degraded and rendered passive. The "magical-ness" exemplifying the world for us results from our passivity and impotence, from our naive faith in what appears before us, in first finding ourselves immersed in it, particularly in the "inter-psychical relations of men in society."[7] Others appear for us out of the necessity of our consciousness; only in this way do we participate in this world. Emotion confirms our perceptual faith, our belief, in the existence of this magical world, this faith which poignantly makes this world phenomenal to the extent that some part, some aspect of this world, however transfigured by our relationship to it, continues to be inexplicable.

SIGNIFICATION OF THE AFFECTIVE SUBCONSCIOUS

According to Simondon, affection is a "subjective transductive reality," for it belongs to the very activity structuring the subject. This is in contrast to sensation or rather the outcome of perception, which is an objective transductive reality; that is, it results from an already individuated subjectivity encountering the world and orienting itself to it. In either case we identify the modes of a living being. Affections realize each lived moment of a life as one in a series of "polarizations," changes in the equilibrium of potentialization, which divide and separate into smaller heterogeneities. Any one particular and singular affect poses a unity of integration in a being's life. And this affective unity is itself a temporal unity, a coalescence of times, separately individuated only with the vaster whole implicated in their passing. This is why Simondon describes any one affect as a "gradient of becoming" (119). Becoming is the whole, the affect belongs and is expressed through it.

Both perception and emotion accede to other perceptions and emotions only through the "rupture of this metastable equilibrium" (121). In the case of emotion, Simondon describes it as "a kind of internal caesura" (122). And yet, if perception unveils the world's unity to the subject, then, as a correlate, emotion discloses the unity of the living encountering the perceptible world. Both modes are in their own way "psychic individuations" that perpetuate living individuation, bringing it to some degree of wholeness (120). Still, more integrative and richer than affection, Simondon characterizes emotion as an "insular temporal unity" and structure. It guides the living, conveying meaning (*sens*) by assuming affectivity and unifying it. As such, far more completely and radically than affectivity, that is, how one is affected by the world, emotion provides the means to interrogate being, to put it into question. Emotions without content are impassive; affects without emotions are directionless. Emotion modulates psychic life, while affection is what is modulated (123 n.3).

Simondon's characterization of the affective-emotive dimension as "sub-conscious" is meant to be explicitly anti-Freudian and chiefly intended by him to counter not only the psychoanalytic topography of the psychic but, just as importantly, the covert metaphysic accompanying its conceptualization.[8] The "unconscious" serves for psychoanalysis as a kind of transcendental faculty by which to establish the limits of consciousness. However, the mechanism of repression is inseparable from Freud's particular conception of unconsciousness. It is this connection that explains the central role repression has in Freudian theory. As Freud describes it, whatever idea representing a drive that is prevented from becoming conscious exists in the unconscious state. Thus it is that the unconscious system is comprised of acts that are distinguished from conscious acts *solely* on the basis of their being temporarily latent, neither actual or conscious; the repressed acts or ideas, if they are to become conscious, would stand in stark contrast with other conscious processes. Without negation,

71

that is, any sense of contradiction, the unconscious is purely a process of displacement and condensation. Yet inseparable from the unconscious is repression. The function of repression, as Freud theorizes it, is to inhibit the drive impulse, transforming it into an emotion. We note Freud's adoption (like Simondon) of an energetics for describing the drive mechanism, which profoundly transforms his conception. An emotion or sensation corresponds to the energetic discharge originating from an unconscious system's fecundity. Thus, any emotion repressed, once restored, points back to its previous "unconscious" being. An emotion's development is attained, equilibrium achieved, once it has acquired a form of representation in consciousness.

Contrary to the Freudian unconscious, Simondon maintains the existence of a more fundamental "sub-conscious" layer at the limit between consciousness and unconsciousness. Where Freud adds the "pre-conscious" as a kind of intermediary between the unconscious and conscious, in truth it is a property of consciousness, for it exists as only a capacity "for" consciousness. The Simondonian sub-conscious, on the contrary, is essentially affective-emotive; it is a true intermediary between consciousness and unconsciousness, insofar as it is wholly relational. And it is this "relational stratum" which constitutes the center of individuality (99). Advancing through brusque leaps, while only obeying a "law of thresholds," affectivity and emotivity enact as *relation* what joins the continuous and the purely discontinuous, consciousness and action. Consciousness is only an epiphenomenon of the constitutive roles played by affectivity and emotivity.

In IGPB, Simondon illustrates how the structure of a living organism is this "instauration of a transductive mediation of interiority and exteriority going from an absolute interiority to an absolute exteriority through a series of different mediating levels of relative interiority and exteriority" (IGPB 227). Each level enacts differentiating energetic polarities, within which potentials exist, latently, awaiting transductive mediation in relation to other levels, other polarities. Thus, life provides a dynamic topology that maintains within itself a fundamental degree of metastability.

For this reason, Simondon assigns to emotion and affect an ontological significance beyond psychological states. Or rather, one might more accurately say, as psychological states they express the individual's strivings, impulses, appetites, and volitions, insofar as the dispositions they reflect are but effects of the individual's essential constitution as it strives to preserve its existence, to increase its power of acting, and to supplement the force of its existing. Simondon, in this regard, abolishes the barrier between the psychological and the ontological by reconceiving them as attributes, whose power stems from the operation of individuation. Accordingly, the analysis of individuation, which Simondon proposes, centers on affectivity and emotivity. He writes, "Psychoanalysis acted with accuracy without always employing a theory adequate to its operational accuracy, for it's very much in fact on the affective-emotive regime which psychoanalysis acts when it addresses itself to the individual" (IPC 99).[9]

AFFECTIVO-EMOTIVE VERSUS IDEOLOGY

> If one can speak in a certain sense of the individuality of a group or of that a people, it is not by virtue of a community of action, which remains too discontinuous for it to act as a solid foundation, nor an identity of conscious representations, too large and too continuous to permit the segregation into groups. It is at the level of affective-emotive themes, mixtures of representations and actions, which constitute collective groups. Inter-individual participation is possible when affective-emotive expressions are the same. The vehicles for this affective community are then not only symbolic but efficacious elements of group life: sanction and re-compensation regimes, symbols, arts, objects collectively valorized and devalorized. (100)

A group's "individuality" – which is to say, how an individuated group comes to be distinguished, individualized, from other individuated but not yet individualized groups – is neither a matter of "community of action" nor an "identity of conscious representations." What does this mean? In the instance of the "community of action," actions by one or more individuals, even if directed by shared goals, remain subject to the vagaries and idiosyncrasies of the time in which they occur and the actors which carry them out.

The second instance, "identity of conscious representation," Simondon renders inconsequential. His doctrine of communication (inter-subjective) and expression discloses a reality he calls the "communication of sub-consciousness" (101). Simondon points to an often-cited example of the profound relationship between two laboring oxen, which is so strong that the accidental death of one causes the death of its companion. Simondon discovers that the Greeks have named this "solid, if wordless, relationship." They refer to this relationship of *lived sympathy* as the "community of the yoke" (συζυγΥια).[10]

"Ideology," more strictly defined by the Marxist tradition, is the "identity of conscious representations." The function of ideology is, on the one hand, to establish cohesion in society, while, on the other hand, a society is overdetermined by ideologies, with the goal of securing a specific group's domination over other groups and their ideologies. At once a relatively autonomous objective social operation and a reflective subjective structure, ideology is responsible for subjecting all individuals to the dominant system, thereby imposing a particular temporal continuity. However, Louis Althusser, the important Marxist philosopher, argues that ideology has less to do with consciousness than the unconscious. Largely accepting psychoanalytic topography, he finds ideologies to be profoundly unconscious, and consciousness more a product or construct of ideological operations.[11] Consciousness is, therefore, a *function* of ideology, not vice versa, insofar as its goal is the "representation of the imaginary relationship of individuals to their real conditions of existence."[12] The ideological "interpellation" of individual being brings her *and* the group to which she now belongs to individuality. Ideology constitutes the individual, who becomes a subject that accepts her or his role as a part of the system of productive relations.

According to Simondon the failure of any ideological critique or attempt to use ideology to explain the psychosocial has been predetermined because it takes for granted certain psychological and social premises. Ideology, conceptually, paints "too broadly" for it to be theoretically useful. It shifts the question of individuation to representation and, finally, to consciousness, as if it were enough for it to be confirmed theoretically to guarantee its substantial existences. From Simondon's point of view, ideology leaves unaddressed how the group comes to be individuated and individualized. If it speaks to the individual subject, it ignores or merely takes for granted, as Althusser argues, that "ideology has always-already interpellated individuals as subjects, which amounts to making it clear that individuals are always-already interpellated by ideology as subjects, necessarily leading us to one last proposition: *individuals are always-already subjects.*"[13] We will see later how diametrically opposite this is to Simondon's position. For now, we are confirmed in appreciating what Simondon identifies as the great error infecting the discourse of the human sciences: the ontological and epistemological privileging given to the individual. Lost is the problem of individuation, that is, the problem of genesis, which is all the more surprising given Marxism's avowed desire toward collectivism and a broader social and political analysis. And here, perhaps, Simondon's critique is at its most interesting, as it takes us beyond a critique based in the physical and physiological to the realm of the affective-emotive, in order to respond to the problem of the *individualization* of the group.

BEYOND RELIGION: TRANSINDIVIDUAL SPIRITUALITY

Simondon's foregrounding of the "spiritual life" introduces what is certainly the most central and far-reaching concept developed in IPC: transindividuality. It is important for us to recall that Simondon understands spirituality to be distinct from, indeed perhaps even opposed to, religious dogma. One might say that religion becomes spiritual, however briefly, *prior* to its being individuated in dogma, that is, institutionalized, and by some act risking its being called it into question, dis-individuated: as is the case with martyrdom, the Protestant Reformation, or the "Arab Spring." Spirituality is the supreme moment of supreme powerlessness, where religion is forced to confront its central collapse, the threshold of formlessness – the pre-individual as the *genitality* of religiosity. This is why we might call a spirituality without religion more truly powerful than strictly speaking religion itself.

This is why the supreme inducement to Simondon's addressing the problem of the individualization of the group is religion. Indeed, Simondon has little doubt that there is no more powerful dramatization of the emotive-affective than religion – either in the instance of its providing a model for other social and political forms or joining with them in a theocracy. Religions subsist on the affective-emotive, which in turn provides it with motive and a practice. Consequently, Simondon points to religion as the most complete act of transindividuality: "Religion is the domain of the transindividual; the sacred does not at all have its origin in society; the sacred is fed by the sentiment of the perpetuity of being, precarious and vacillating perpetuity, depending upon the living" (103–4). Sacred rites do not originate from the fear of death. "Death appears to become hostile when it is abandoned, not as death but as living in the past, whose perpetuation is confined to posterity" (103). Christian theology fixes death before us, providing it a substantial identity, so that we might again and again experience ourselves as eternal, in anticipating our eternal salvation by reliving it through our repeating prescribed rites and practices. "It is only by illusion, or rather by the demi-vision that the spiritual life gives the unique experience of the eternity of being" (105).

While certainly refusing Nietzsche's more hysterical pronouncements, Simondon exploits the philosopher's resources to clarify a shared rejection of the substantialist metaphysics, which serve theologically to justify the eschatological notion of eternity. Well-known is Nietzsche's diagnosis and critique of religion and morality; less appreciated is how they are woven together round the notion of eternity. The role of God as creditor-judge has significance only to the extent that the guilt we, the debtors, carry for a debt that can never be paid must be insured.[14] Eternity is for Nietzsche a "torture without end," the true hell where immeasurable punishment is carried out to satisfy the impossible debt of "sin," the most imperfect act. The individual being becomes synonymous with the interminable guilt formalizing this debt.

A theistic spirituality creates the fundamental norms that must be followed if one is to have any hope of living a religious life based on the

Gospels, or any sacred text. Simondon finds this most evident in Jesus' instruction to his disciples "to love God and your neighbor." This norm served to extend a model for the early church community in Jerusalem to follow: "And all that believed were together, and had all things in common" and "Praising God, and having favor with all the people" (Acts 2:44, 47). To love Christ is to love the Church, the body of Christ. It is this love, this affective-emotive act, which is the spiritualizing force, according to Simondon. So, whomever becomes a member of the Church equally becomes Christ, that is to say, a participant in the community of God and the entire human race. Spinoza takes this further, of course, and sees Jesus' command as essential both to Christian doctrine and to the social and political conservation of the sovereign authorizing this edict for the public. "No one can behave piously toward his neighbor according to God's decree, unless he accommodates piety and religion to the public interest."[15]

It quite clear that Simondon's interest in religion has nothing to do with a direct critique of theological doctrine. He doesn't make any explicitly irreligious comments at all. His interest lies in religion as a mode of the structuring of being, as it operates as a mode of individuation relative to its own specific domain of pre-individual reality – spirituality. And for this reason, Simondon's perspective shifts our focus from religion more properly to how it discloses the more important dimension of the affective-emotive, where the spiritualizing emerges to determine the relationship between the individual and the collective. More to the point, for Simondon, religion presents us with the opportunity to theoretically examine this relationship on affective-emotive grounds. Why? For what purpose? We might have the opportunity to reformulate spirituality as a consequence, so that one is capable of grasping transindividuality in giving birth to the "subject-being," otherwise left unthought-of by what he refers to as "onto-theistic doctrines and norms." Simondon's formulation of a *non-theistic ontogenetic spirituality* is purely and immanently psychosocial because the "psychosocial is of the transindividual." (Though whether or not it is non-deistic must remain for now an open question that we should ask again, later.) For this reason, we must see spirituality as less the preserving of religious doctrine than wholly and directly revolutionary and creative, which should be, in truth, one and the same: "Spirituality is not only what stays put (*demeure*) but also what shimmers in the instant between two indefinite densities (*épaisseurs*) of obscurity and conceals itself forever; the desperate gesture, unknown, of the slave's revolt is of a spirituality like the work of Horace" (105). The subject at this affective-emotive level implements "this ascending of the undetermined toward the present that is going to incorporate it into the collective" (106). As such, not only a new temporality but, as well, a new spatiality is created, both associated with the individualization of the individual and the collective. The individuated being is at once alone and not alone; in order that the collective can exist, it is necessary that the separated individuation precede it and continue still from the pre-individual, which the collective will individuate itself in reattaching the separated being (105).

THE PROBLEM OF ETERNALNESS OF LIFE AND DEATH

As we saw in Chapter 1, an individual's desire to obey something beyond itself opens us to the possibility that at some level the *living* individual, constitutively, must remain unfinished. It follows that a living individual, as Simondon describes it, *amplifies* its incompleteness, which calls for a new idea of eternity, one that denies the notion of a perfect eternity, closed absolutely upon itself. As we saw in the first chapter, such a condition is contrary to the very idea of life. So, let us ask another question: "What is the nature of eternity, or perhaps, that *kind* of eternity that conceives of itself as interminably open, partial, incomplete, necessarily and essentially unachievable?" If the idea of eternity is not incompatible with life, then might the latter be reformed by the former's imperatives? Might we ask, as Simondon invites us: "if I experience my finitude, might I, therefore, experience my eternity?" I ask this question to emphasize that when he speaks of eternity, one should not confuse it with "immortality."

Immortality is the "sensible symbol" of belief in eternity. Such a belief instills in the individual a faith in his or her capacity to surpass their limits. As such, according to Simondon, it is the obverse of the finitude that individualizes being. But it does not itself individualize. Offhandedly Simondon makes a reference to Spinoza's phrase "*sentimus, experimurque, nos aeternos esse*" ("we feel and know by experience that we are eternal"),[16] which illustrates, he suggests, an experience of eternity at the level of the affective-emotive.[17] At once, the affective-emotive surpasses the individuated being in carrying out the eternal, but only by reflecting on itself, by disclosing the principle *within* individuation, which provides the individuated being with the impetus for its coming into existence. Psychic and collective individuation incessantly and persistently creates being as it advances, maintaining in each created or individuated scope of being, *hic et nunc*, an operation of individuation. After all, an individual exists and is only capable of individuating as a result of the relations it establishes with others and that others establish with it. This individuation is founded on a transindividual relation; affectivity and emotion at once express and prepare the way for this relation to compose itself. The individual as "subject," as the summative outcome of the individual with its associated pre-individual nature, receives the power of perpetual individuation. It is precisely the charge of pre-individuality brought to the subject by this dimension of transindividuality that fosters individuation.

"If some reality is eternal, it is the individual, inasmuch as it is a transductive being, and not as a substantive subject or body, conscious or active matter" (102). That reality that is eternal is "the individual insofar as transductive being." Transduction is the ways and means by which the operation of individuation is carried out, "an operation, physical, biological, mental, social through which an activity little by little propagates within a domain's interior . . . each region of constituted structure functioning as the principle of constitution for each subsequent region," so that a modification is carried forward (transducted) to each subsequent region, which then registers its propagation with a change of state, a conversion of energy to a higher or lower magnitude for the next region to propagate through converting its structure, progressively extending further alongside the structuring operation (24–5). Such is the nature of the meaning Simondon gives to the "eternal." To be eternal is to be operationally "a being-related" through the structuring operation of individuation. Eternity designates the transductive temporality fostered by the recurrent process of providing its own permanent condition, which individuation gives itself in carrying itself out, potentially indefinitely: "a continuation of access for individuation" (20).[18] It is metastability that grows itself (*se grossit*), enriches itself, creates itself indefinitely, that maintains within the living the potentiality for becoming. In this obscure realm, we find the eternalness of the living: a notion of time as mediation, operative in the process of ontological transformation on the grounds of which is enacted a transvaluation of values, including "spirituality," where the eternal and innovation come together indissolubly, *becoming* co-substantial in the creation of new being.

But how do we then reconcile what is eternal in the individual being with its essential finitude? What is death? After all, doesn't our finitude define our human being? If we think human being through the problem of individuation, we are forced to rethink the very notion of death.

No longer is death the annihilation of the individual. For death to be absolute, not only the individual but also the pre-individual reality associated with it would have to be totally exhausted. Instead, the dying individual becomes what Simondon calls an "anti-individual." She changes "sign" but perpetuates herself, nonetheless, in being transformed into an "individual absence." What does this mean? It means that any experiencing of the world's presence is mediated by the absence of the individual, now dead. Simondon describes a world constituted by actually living individuals and "gaps of individualities," "actual negative individuals" of amalgamations of affectivity and emotivity, which exist as symbols: Buddha, Jesus, Muhammad, Michael Jackson, Elvis Presley, as well figures like the Ayatollah Khomeini and the Eternal President Kim Il-Sung. The moment an individual dies, leaving to whatever degree an incomplete life, other individual beings take on the responsibility for "re-actualizing this active absence, the seed of consciousness and action."

Simondon invokes the Greek funeral rite to provide a concrete example for how the memorializing of the dead illustrates a kind of eternalness; Moreover, the ancient Greek funeral oration (*epitaphios*), as Simondon reads it, was itself a technic whose mediation of the multiple dimensions of Athenian society (social, political, cultural, psychic) brought the individual Greek to the signification of the idea of Athens, the city. These values were then transductively amplified throughout the regions of ancient Greece. "In the fine death it is still the city that conquers nature. The political oration seeks to go beyond the common fate of mankind, and it is significant that the Athenians chose the setting of the public funeral to reaffirm the omnipotence of the polis: to replace man with the citizen, even in death, is certainly the ultimate achievement of the civic imaginary."[19] An oration's joining the individual's death with the eternal life credited to the *polis* reaffirms the omnipotence of the individuated Greek subject together with the eternal life of the group (Athenians) to which the individual belongs, even after death. In fact, the funeral rite makes possible the overcoming of a final death; nature is overcome. Every religious funeral rite together with social and cultural evocations of the dead, from *El Día de los Muertes* to the commemoration of the tomb of the Unknown Soldier, reincorporates the dead individual's absence into the surviving milieu; the individual continues to exist and is often a more active participant in a society "after death" as a symbol. "Hence, it is possible that something of the individual is eternal, and can be re-incorporated, in some way, to the world" (102).

An action carried out by the subject expresses spirituality through its establishing an "objective eternity," creating, if you will, "a monument more durable than bronze in language, institution, art, oeuvre," writes Simondon. An emotion expresses spirituality to the extent that it permits this union with action to penetrate the subject, "flowing back into it and filling the subject up, rendering the subject symbolic in relation to itself, reciprocal in relation to itself, comprehending itself via reference to what it encroaches upon" (110). It is the reciprocity of the relationship between the "humanism of constructive action" and the interiority of a retreat into emotion which opens for us a way to grasp the conditional reality of the collective. In doing so, Simondon argues we genuinely grasp transindividuality "in its real form."

Simondon formulates his notion of the transindividual to contest the impoverished image of emotion, which science "deposited in monuments of indifferent eternity" to oppose religious faith. Simondon postulates that science has gone too far, depriving emotion of its active positivity when it separates it from what conditions its genesis, the individuating collective. Once this is done, emotion is deprived of action, while the collective becomes enslaved to emotion in the form or rite of spiritual practices (110). Simondon contests the image spirituality has been forced to assume to free it ontologically from the rupturing of action and emotion, which has led to two separate and irreconcilable existences: science and faith. This is "the debris of spirituality." True spiritual unity, conversely, Simondon writes, "is in this transductive relationship between action and emotion" (110).

SIMONDON'S SPINOZISM I

As we progress through IPC, Bergson is one of the philosophers (Spinoza and Nietzsche are the other two) with whom Simondon maintains a continuous, if often oblique, dialogue. And, so, I feel justified in recalling Bergson's letter written to H.M. Kallen, who worries that Bergson confuses duration (*durée*) with eternity. Bergson responds, "I do not reduce duration to the 'eternity' of ancient philosophers; on the contrary, I seek to make the 'eternity' of the ancient philosophers descend from the heights where it sat to bring it back to duration, in other words, to something that enlarges itself (*se grossit*), enriches itself, creates itself indefinitely."[20] If life is a series of resolution to problems (as I described it in Chapter 1), a characterization that most certainly agrees with Bergson, then it is in each resolution successively connected to another, each anterior resolution reprised and reincorporated in ulterior resolutions, that we grasp the eternity of becoming. Eternity is one with the *necessity* that compels the totality of its movement. In other words, we speak of the necessity of the motive abetting its singular event, provided by the potentiality that is metastability.

It is time to admit the postulate, which has informed my reading of Simondon's work to this point and will direct my interpretations going forward: Simondon is fundamentally Spinozist. Not only are there direct allusions and borrowings (as I have tried to show repeatedly) but Simondon shadows important aspects of Spinoza's approach. A case in point is this discussion of eternity.[21] Spinoza does not restrict eternity to its being solely necessity; it is instead a certain conjunction of existence and necessity. In fact, Spinoza argues that the idea of eternity has less to do with time than with the capacity to strive to exist. Not simply the cause for something to exist, eternity is the affirmative plentitude of existence.

However, it is still crucial for us to determine how forms realized by this articulation allow us to think about the status of different modes and, notably, in the case of Simondon, the being of the individual. One must reject whatever tendency one might have – either in Spinoza or

Simondon – to see immortality (of the individual) and eternity (as ante-rior to the individual) as identical. Indeed, the important Spinoza scholar Pierre-François Moreau's primary argument supporting the possibility of a "metaphysical experience" is one that grasps eternity, if only because it is brought to the surface by the "feeling" or "emotion" (*sentiment*) of finitude. Such an experience is impossible if the significance of eternity and immortality are rendered the same. Moreau writes: "The feeling of finitude is the condition for the feeling of eternity and even, in a sense, it *is* the feeling of eternity." Moreau believes that it is this same movement which in Spinoza permits the soul's acceding to necessity while conscious that not everything is immediately necessary; as a result, it confronts its powerlessness, cultivating the aspiration for an escape from contingency. "In its very limitation, finitude plays therefore an intensely positive role: it lays out the necessary features and provokes its being assumed as eternal."[22] For this reason, every soul, every individual soul, is part finite and part eternal; but, importantly, according to Moreau's reading of the *Ethics* V, not every soul possesses the feeling of finitude and, hence, the experience of eternity.

What this means is that necessity is manifested in "each of the moments of our affective life." For Moreau, Spinoza's geometrical method, which uses proofs of demonstrations, operates both epistemolog-ically and ontologically to formulate a world that is so violently dissimilar to the inconstancy and insecurity that we feel in *this* world that we long for the eternal. And in our longing or striving to exist we feel the power of the eternal. In other words, it is powerlessness, inconstant and perishable, yet nonetheless compelling our strivings for existence that necessitates a kind of knowledge sufficient for grasping the feeling of eternity – for it provides the "aspiration to develop from the latter, which is the desire for blessedness."[23] Spinoza writes: "All our strivings, *or* Desires, follow from the necessity of our nature in such a way that they can be understood either through it alone, as through their proximate cause, or insofar as we are a part of nature, which cannot be conceived adequately through itself without other individuals."[24] Moreau argues that Spinoza's is an "ontol-ogy of positive finitude," where the finite is positively founded in the infinite, so that "our power to think (as well as to act) is the same power of God" or Nature.[25]

Moreau's interpretation of Spinoza is relevant on several counts. First, the "positive ontology of finitude" provides support for our exposition of Simondon's affective conception of anxiety, implicitly meant to contrast with Heidegger's more famous account in *Being and Time*. Second, in anticipation of our exposition of Simondon's ethical position, Moreau's disclosing of the finitude-eternity problem lays the groundwork for us to connect via Spinoza the ontogenetic project with moral problems emerging from the antagonism between the collective life and individual blessedness, civic self-sacrifice and individual destiny, which are dramatized for us nearly every day. Whatever ways we affectively experience finitude when mollifying powerlessness in the face of eternity, we affirm at the same time the opposite, and bring finitude and eternity to their unguarded unity, to "spirituality," in responding to the necessities demanded for a collective life to exist. "This antagonism leaves space to a possible compatibility so the *individual,* instead of being known as a substance or a precarious being aspiring to substantiality, is grasped as *the singular point of open infinity of relations. If* relation has value of being, there is no longer opposition between the desire for eternity and the necessity of the collective life."[26] And so, when Moreau (*qua* Spinoza) writes, "I experience my finitude, therefore, my eternity,"[27] let us read, "I experience my individuality, therefore, my transindividuality." What connects them is the problem of individuation.

Finally, we look to Spinoza for the engendering postulate compelling Simondon's structuring ontologico-epistemological parallelism: "The order and connection of ideas is the same as the order and connection of causes" argues Spinoza.[28] Simondon calls for a parallel individuation of knowledge – that is, the "idea." "In order to think the living, it is necessary to think life as a transductive series of operations of individuation, or still as an enchainment of successive resolutions, each anterior resolution being able to be reprised and reincorporated into ulterior resolutions" (IL 214). The problem of individuation necessitates as its correlation a kind of comprehension that reflexively grasps the individuation of that knowledge responsible for adequately comprehending being and being-thought. To grasp individuation is to experience it. As in Spinoza, Simondon situates this movement between the undetermined natural and the *hic et nunc* of actual existence at the experiential affective-emotive level. The level of the affective-emotive registers the tension active within the relationship of the individual and its associated milieu; and, subsequently, the subject acquires the capacity to orient itself to the world it thinks and within which it strives to exist.

THREE POINT OF COINCIDENCE WITH HEIDEGGER'S ANALYTIC

During the time when Simondon wrote *L'individuation à la lumière des notions de forme et d'information,* Heidegger's thought was nearly ubiquitous at every level of post- Second World War French intellectual life.[29] The near total absence of any reference to Heidegger baits us, does it not? I would, however, claim that we are only slightly risking an exaggeration claiming that Simondon's analysis of anxiety is a covert negotiation w.... Heidegger's famous account in *Being and Time*.

Like Simondon, Heidegger's anxiety or *angst* is not reducible to a mental state but reflects the ontological status of a human being-in-the-world. As such, anxiety designates the way human *Dasein* (human 'there-being') becomes attuned or adjusted to this worldly existence. It is a mode by which the world becomes meaningful and, for Dasein, achieves its factical (actual) phenomenal being, preparing the way for the disclosing of the meaning of being more generally. Dasein's anxiety stems from the burden of its existence, that is to say, those possibilities left to it for existing. We find echoes of Simondon here, the individual bearing the share of pre-individual being. Similarly to Simondon, for Heidegger anxiety discloses to Dasein more positively those possibilities for being in the world left to it, authentic and inauthentic. In this regard, anxiety acts as a fundamental attunement for Dasein's being-in-the-world. Anxiety individualizes Dasein. How one is anxious discloses how the world is individualized, relative to those possibilities belonging to their Dasein. Anxiety conditions human Dasein for freedom and, thus, individualizes being to make a decision, to make choices, by permitting the human Dasein to grasp itself, standing anxiously before all its possibilities. Anxiety discloses to human Dasein how being comes into being. With its individuating being, anxiety individualizes Dasein.[30]

Death is, as Heidegger describes it, "the ownmost, nonrelational, and insuperable possibility" of Dasein.[31] Which is to say, death is the only true, final, and absolute possibility by the simple fact that Dasein exists. Anxiety discloses to Dasein that it only ever exists as "thrown being-toward-death," even while most of us (the "they" or the "public"), in our everyday preoccupations with living, are consumed with trying to flee from this fact. Anxiety does not permit this failure of courage. It fosters resoluteness before death. And it is this stance toward death, toward the inevitability of it, that makes Dasein what it is, that *individualizes* being. For once Dasein lays claim to this fate, in anticipation of the death to come, or avoids it, surrendering to "lostness in chance possibilities," in either case, Dasein finds itself for *who it is, who it will become*, authentically or otherwise. Anxiety individualizes Dasein insofar as it serves to disclose its absolute potentiality of being: being-toward-death.

As I look forward to Simondon's own conception of anxiety, I would like to speak to three points of correspondence which I find connect Heidegger with Simondon. First, anxiety individuates Dasein by disclosing its own specific potential for being-in-the-world. Because it is an emotion, an affect, it serves as a kind of understanding of being; it is reflexively ontological in that it belongs to the ontological structure of Dasein, while providing grounds for it to become attuned to understanding the possibilities of existence open to it. Only a reflexive act of *grasping* (*not knowing*, that is, without preformed categorizing or reducing to concepts in knowledge) can correspond with a genesis, not analytically but in the total collaboration of being as it becomes individuated as "knowledge" (that is, as knowledge undergoes its own corresponding process of individuation). Simondon, like Heidegger, accepts that whatever operation of thought results from the need to grasp, to intuit, but not have knowledge, shifts thinking to a different epistemological register. There is no possible knowledge of individuation in the usual sense of the term. "Individuation as such (of an exterior being to the knowing subject) cannot be grasped via the mode of objective knowledge but it is analogically attributed to the known being by a *thought* that *grasps* in itself, by *reflection*, the individuation of its own knowledge."[32]

Second, Heidegger draws a clear if subtle distinction between individuation and individualization. "Anxiety individuates Dasein": it becomes an individual being in being individuated, distinct from other individual beings; and, so, it achieves its "*ownmost* being." This would seem to be in conflict with my statement above ("Anxiety individualizes Dasein"). And yet Dasein "can be individualized in individuation." To be individualized, individuation must have already happened, so that Dasein can be individualized *in* it. Which is to say, individuation is *anterior* to individualization, as the latter makes the former not only possible but actual. Simondon draws a terminological distinction between individuation and individualization. On the one hand, *individuation* is "genesis or ontogenesis." It describes *at all times* the genesis of the determined or individuated from undetermined and pre-individual being to individuated being. It is being as the operation by which it becomes; it is the being of becoming and, therefore, ontologically distinct from what Simondon calls *individualization*, which is the individuation of an already individuated being.

The third and last point of coincidence between Heidegger and Simondon relates to the temporality anxiety is given to enact. Anxiety individualizes Dasein by disclosing its essential finitude so that it becomes difficult (though not impossible) for it to be irresolute in the face of being-toward-death. What this means is that finitude lends Dasein, most particularly once it achieves its subject-being, a certain structural (ontological) *precariousness* inseparable from the constancy won by achieving a state of individuality. In the end Dasein exists for the sake of itself; crucial for it is "being ahead of itself," that is, projecting itself into the future. And so the temporality of Dasein's finitude ultimately and not surprisingly derives from the potentiality-of-being, as it determines the end toward which it sees its existence in the future.

SIMONDON'S NOTION OF ANXIETY

Simondon's own formulation and analysis of anxiety is unique. It is not Heideggerian, though it is formulated, undoubtedly, with the full awareness of him. Anxiety is an "emotion without action, a feeling without perception," Simondon writes. It is, in short, "the pure echoing of being within itself" (112). What does this mean? How are we to understand this description? As this definition makes clear, anxiety is an *ontological* event as much as it is psychological. It does not simply reflect the state of an individual's inner life. More profoundly, it draws theoretical attention to the ontologically significant act of an individuated being's detachment from what makes it what it is; it is individuated "nature." The individuated being "is burdened by its existence," Simondon writes, "as if it had to suffer existence itself (*comme s'il devait se porter lui-même*)" (111). We can hear Heideggerian echoes. Having become individuated with and through a constitutive relationship with other beings, a subject feels itself to be a "subject" but only insofar as its existence is denied, confirming indirectly that it is "more-than-individual." It is the feeling of necessity that compels the subject to pursue its individuation and, likewise, the feeling that acknowledges the failure of individuation to ever complete itself, to be not yet completed in the collective. The subject, as a result, conserves within itself an unresolvable incompatibility brought before us by anxiety. As an existential mode, anxiety reflects the burden of and liberation from existence. "In anxiety, the subject feels itself existing as problem posed to itself, and it feels its being divided into pre-individual nature and individuated being" (111).

This "here and now" – *hic et nunc* – is precarious. The stability and the transcendence that lends this world coordination are fleeting, for in both instances a debt is owed to the pre-individuality, the Nature that conditions it. As a condition for its genesis, some aspect of the subject's nature must remain undetermined (απειρν) and will never become actualized *hic et nunc* (111). Pre-individuality does not deteriorate into harmlessness, nor does it become inert, hidden or squirrelled away somewhere silently in the sub-conscious. Anxiety marks the state in which the subject's being is "painfully dilated," at risk of losing interiority to the pure immanence of being, a "universal elsewhere" of pre-individuality, which overwhelms and disorients the subject. Anxiety more directly opens the subject to its pre-individual conditioning. Simondon writes, it is "like a night that constitutes the same being of the subject in all its points" (112).

Simondon is at odds with Hegel, who dismisses those like Spinoza and Schelling who would define the Absolute in a manner that dissociates it from consciousness. And doing so, Hegel argues, these philosophers plunge being into purely undifferentiated beingness, which he famously describes as a "night where all cows are black." Because such a night denies a role to negation, individuation is rendered impossible. Without negation, Hegel believes, there can be no true determination. Unlike Hegel, who shudders before this Absolute, not because it is real but because it exemplifies a failure of conception, Simondon conceives it as the pre-individual and, therefore, the catalyst for individuation. At this point where the self dissolves, at once anguished and liberating, we glimpse the eternalness possible, however indirectly, in the mortal individuality of the *hic et nunc*. As a result, an anxious "subjectivity" is born contrary to that promoted by idealism and phenomenology: "*universel contre-sujet*." Rather than celebrating unity, an identity gathered from transcendence in the manner of idealism and phenomenology, subjectivity finds itself clinging "to everything in the same way it clings to itself." Anxiety is the affective-emotive response to "this immense swelling of being." Or, as Simondon writes, "the individuated is overrun by the pre-individual" (113).

A finite subject is incapable in itself of arriving at the level of a unity alone, that is to say, without mediation, by directly resolving pre-individual being and individual being. But here we discover the paradox of anxiety: it reminds us directly that to become individuated is to gain being from sacrificing oneself to the pre-individual and, eventually, to a new individuation. "If the experience of anxiety could have been supported and lived enough, it would have led to new individuation at the interior of being itself, a veritable metamorphosis" (113).

We recall the pivotal passage in IGPB where the successive levels of individuation are described: from the vital, and the psychic, to the transindividual. In particular, Simondon distinguishes the two modes of existence of the simple life and psychism by the respective roles affectivity plays in each. In life, the affective serves a regulative role, meaning that it is dominant over other functions for the purpose of assuring life's permanent individuation. In psychism "affectivity is overflowing" (IL 165), meaning that affectivity poses problems rather than resolving them, and in doing so, leaves unresolved other problems resulting from perception. The entering into psychic existence essentially manifests a new problematic, which, because of its difficulty, is not resolvable, confined within the psychic interiority of a living being. Instead, this new psychic problematic newly plunges into the pre-individual reality, "succeeding a more primitive individuation" (IL 165). I would call it an ontological plunge into the interval of the new individuation between the life of the living being and psychism. Bergson, admittedly under different but not complete conflicting circumstances, refers to this as the "leap into ontology."

Psychism appears as a new stage of individuation of being, which has for a correlate, ontologically (*dans l'être*), an incompatibility and a vital dynamism of decreasing oversaturation and, outside of being, insofar as a limited individual, an appeal to a new charge of pre-individual reality capable of supplying a new reality to being; the living individuates itself much earlier, and cannot individuate by being its own matter, like the larvae metamorphosizes by feeding on itself; psychism expresses the vital, and correlatively, a charge of pre-individual reality. (IL 166)

And so the relation between the vital and the psychic further confirms the validity of Simondon's critique of hylemorphism. Psychism's appearing is conditioned by a relation, neither form or matter, but from individuation to individuation. As Simondon writes in these pages, which line up with IPC's description of the painful dilation of being, made real in the psychic phase of anxiety: "psychic individuation is dilation, a precocious expansion of vital individuation" (IL 166). But in its appeal to pre-individual reality, psychic individuation is itself but a phase, a transition, to the order of transindividual reality. "The psychic is the incipient transindividual" (IL 166). Upon this reality being grasped in a new individuation readied by the living, it conserves immanently within its own development a relation so that each psychic being participates in connecting to other psychic beings.

In conclusion: Simondon states that all those structures and functions resulting from the individuation from the pre-individual reality to the living individual can only be accomplished and stabilized in the collective. Anxiety is preparation for the leap into the "ontological beyond" (*un au-delà ontologique*) of collective being. Structures and functions are unsettled as a result of their being animated by a pre-individual force that renders them incoherent, although disposed to being transformed. In short, for this "new birth" of individuation to take place requires the old structures and functions to be dissolved and reduced. And for the latter to happen the periodic (transductive) annihilation of individuated being, its "dis-individuation," is required. Anxiety compels this action by demonstrating the individuated being's stake in the pre-individual reality out of which it emerges, while, at the same time, threatening always its own self-destruction. Still, like Heidegger, Simondon's purpose in discussing anxiety is not merely negative; there is a positive dimension to it. The individual being is freed to think on a collectivist foundation, encouragement for contriving another unknown individuation. This is our reward for accepting and, indeed, encouraging the destruction of individuality. Hence, when Simondon writes that anxiety "is the departure of being" (IPC 114), he means this in the most positive and affirmative sense.

EXCURSUS

In this final section Simondon defines "spirituality." As one reads IPC, there is a danger of becoming confused by Simondon's tendency to circle back to previous concepts, certain structures and descriptions. But what might seem repetitious (and certainly there are instances when this is the case) is in actuality his attempt to address the same problem of concept from a different perspective. This is certainly the case with spirituality. Simondon will return again and again to this notion. However, each return is done from a different perspective. This is the case for nearly all of Simondon's major terms and principal definitions. In this chapter's next section Simondon discusses spirituality and collectivity within the context of establishing a definite relationship between emotivity and affectivity (the affective-emotive). Later, in Chapter 6, I will shadow his placing of the discussion of spirituality within the more direct discussion of transindividuality and the individuation of the collective. One of the most difficult challenges when reading Simondon is to remain aware of the occurrence of a discursive change of context relative to the problem to which Simondon's terms are being applied.

THE SPIRITUALITY OF BECOMING-COLLECTIVE

"Spirituality" designates the cultural dimensionality in which the individual and a collective are individualized; in tandem, though without subsuming one to the other, it is the achieving of an "individualized collective." Signifying "a superior life," spirituality is the meaning given to being "as separated and reattached, alone and as member of the collective." The collective exists only if the separated individuation, which precedes it, includes within itself the pre-individual. For it this pre-individual metastability that the collective draws from in order to individuate itself in reattaching the separated being.

> Spirituality is the signification of the relation of individuated being to the collective and, therefore, as a consequence, the founding of this relation – that is, of the fact that the individuated being is not entirely individuated but still contains a certain charge of non-individuated, pre-individual reality, with which it preserves, respects and lives. (105–6)

The only thing preventing the collective from restricting itself to the "false aseity of substantial individuality" is its awareness of the constituent pre-individual share it preserves in itself. But how does the individual remain cognizant of the part it plays in bringing the individual to the collective individuation?

We can grasp the significance of spirituality only if we understand what are affectivity and emotivity. "Pleasure and pain, sadness and joy," Simondon writes, "are the extreme divergences concerning this relation between the individual and the pre-individual" (106).[33] Non-representational modes of thought signal the path taken from the pre-individual to the individual and, perhaps, back again. Spirituality names this path; it is unconscious until made affectively and emotionally apparent. As in Spinoza, for whom affect defines a continuous force of existing, ontologically reflecting a certain capacity or power to exist, likewise the affective-emotive modes have acquired meaning in the accomplishment of the relation between the pre-individual and the individual: the positive affective states indicate "the synergy of constituted individuality and the actual movement of the individuation of the pre-individual" (106). Those negative affective states, on the other hand, according to Simondon, indicate a conflict, an unfavorable event arising out of the conflict between these two domains.

However, we must not speak of affective states as if they were distinct units of being; instead, there are *affective exchanges* between the individuated and the pre-individual. The affective-emotive is a movement of exchange between the undetermined nature and the *hic et nunc* of actual existence. The subject is the product of this ascent from the undetermined to the present, by which it becomes incorporated into the collective. The affective-emotive is not merely the result of action in the interior of the individual being. It is a "transformation." It has an active role in expressing the relationship between the two domains of the individual and pre-individual, which together constitute the subject-being, while modifying the action in the functioning of this relationship, harmonizing with it, and harmonizing the collective. "The expression of affectivity in the collective has a regulative value," as it has a primary role in the pre-individual's individuating of itself within different subjects in order to establish the collective (106).

Neither emotion nor affectivity is, strictly speaking, a psychological act. Emotion "is this individuation *midway* in the process of self-effectuating in the transindividual presence" (107, my italics). Yet emotion serves as an entry point for affectivity to determine the unity of signification consigned to an individual being. The charge of pre-individual nature is translated and propagated in the form of affectivity, which, in turn, provides the impetus for collective individuation. Each subject-being is the agent of affectivity. Composed as it is of both realms, each individual subject-being, consciously or not, exists as a mediator between the pre-individual and the individual. Emotion, on the other hand, announces to other subjects and to a world that would put it into question, the presence of the subject.

Emotion resolves the affective problem. In this regard, the relationship between emotion and affect functions in a manner parallel to the way perception resolves action. "Action is to perception what emotion is to affectivity," Simondon writes. Hence, we see the relevance of the discussion of perception in the first chapter. In both instances of perception and emotion there is a "discovery of a superior order of compatibility, of a synergy, of a resolution by the path to a more elevated level of metastable equilibrium" (107).

Without doubt, Simondon intends, by focusing on emotion, to direct the theoretical gaze toward those affective conditions that make possible an individual's participation in the collective. Emotion and action are brought to reconciliation within the unity afforded by the collective's "superior individuation." But there is an additional purpose driving the "affective turn" that happens in this second chapter: it provides a justification for the *distinction made between the individual and the subject*. If the formative problem for the individual is that of perceptive worlds, the problem for which subject is the response is that of the heterogeneity of the perceptive worlds to the affective worlds. The subject *qua* subject is constituted by an incompatibility internal to it: "the subject is individual *and other than* individual" (108, my italics). The subject is only able to coincide with itself through the mediation that the individuation of the collective provides, because the individuated being and the pre-individual being, which are the elements making up this process, cannot coincide directly with one another. This internal disparity constitutive of the being of the subject becomes apparent only in the dimension of affectivity.

Spirituality is neither pure affectivity nor the pure resolution of perceptive problems. Rather, their reciprocity within the incipient collective creates the conditions for the unifying of what Simondon calls a "genuine action" and "genuine emotion." He writes, "Action and emotion are born when the collective individuates itself; the collective is, for the subject, the reciprocity of affectivity and perception, reciprocity which unifies these two domains each in itself in their giving a further dimension" (109). To be more concrete, this world is given a "sense" as a result of its becoming oriented; and "it is oriented because the subject orients itself according to its emotion" (109). For emotion is not merely an internal mental state of change, it is also "a certain *élan* through which a universe acquires a sense; it is the sense of action" (109). Emotion is as much an attunement that brings about an existential change or transformation as it is a wholly psychological outcome. Emotion orients being for us who experience it. This is why Simondon claims – building on Sartre and, especially, Heidegger – that emotion topologically *structures* being. Emotion prolongs itself in the world in the form of action, as action prolongs itself in the subject in the form of emotion: "a transductive series going from pure action to pure emotion" (109).

90

Instead of separate and distinct isolated psychic states of operation, emotion and action participate in the same reality. We grasp them as distinct only by abstracting them into these two terms – the extreme ends of an operation, which we then award, as a result, full self-sufficiency. Only then do we have confidence, to whatever degree it might be displaced insecurity, in their worthiness as objects of study. In fact, Simondon argues, to genuinely grasp them *hic et nunc*, one must overcome the abstract partitioning of the two, and grasp 'emotion-action' where it exists at the limit between subject and world, for that is where it operates – at the limit between individual being and the collective. And so we return to Simondon's definition of "spirituality," the reunion of these "two opposed sides ascending toward the same summit" (109).

NOTES

1. Nathalie Sarraute, *Tropisms, and the Age of Suspicion*, trans. Maria Jolas and A. Calderbook (London: Calder & Boyars, 1963), vi. Is it possible that Simondon admired Sarraute's work? They were contemporaries.
2. Jean-Paul Sartre, *The Emotions, Outline of a Theory*, trans. Bernard Frechtman (New York: Philosophical Library, 1948), 17. Undoubtedly, existentialism as a kind of humanist anthropology is at fault. "This anthropology is realizable, and that if one day it is realized, the psychological disciplines will have their source there" (19).
3. Sartre, *The Emotions, Outline of a Theory*, 18.
4. Sartre, *The Emotions, Outline of a Theory*, 91.
5. Sartre, *The Emotions, Outline of a Theory*, 81.
6. Jean-Paul Sartre, *The Transcendence of the Ego: A Sketch for a Phenomenological Description*, trans. Andrew Brown (London: Routledge, 2004), 51.
7. Sartre, *The Emotions, Outline of a Theory*, 83.
8. In his lectures on *The Question of Lay Analysis*, Freud questions the usefulness of retaining the term "subconsciousness" given that both topologically and qualitatively it invites a lack of clarity. Freud asserts: "The only trustworthy antithesis is between conscious and unconscious." He continues: "If someone talks of subconsciousness, I cannot tell whether he means the term topologically – to indicate something lying in the mind beneath consciousness – or qualitatively – to indicate another consciousness, a subterranean one, as it were. He is probably not clear about any of it. The only trustworthy antithesis is between conscious and unconscious." Sigmund Freud, *The Question of Lay Analysis; Conversations with an Impartial Person*, trans. James Strachey (New York: Norton, 1978), 19.
9. Carl Jung's analysis of the "unconscious (or sub-conscious)" is given credit by Simondon with discovering the primary affective-emotive themes. Simondon's preference for Jung over Freud is both illuminating and, from our contemporary perspective, perhaps a bit odd. Still, we must remember that Deleuze

91

and Guattari likewise speak admiringly of Jung: "Jung is in any event more profound than Freud" (Deleuze and Guattari, *A Thousand Plateaus*, 241).

10. Simondon translates this Greek term as "communauté de joug." The Greek does not have a true English equivalent, so I have chosen to translate Simondon's French. However, it should be noted that Simondon's French translation might not be all that accurate. A few English options would be "spouse of the yoke," "partner of the yoke" – which is to say, the Greek has a meaning that is significantly more restricted than that of the community.

11. Louis Althusser, *Writings on Psychoanalysis: Freud and Lacan*, trans. Jeffrey Mehlman (New York: Columbia University Press, 1996), 116.

12. Louis Althusser, *Lenin and Philosophy, and Other Essays* (London: New Left Books, 1971), 153.

13. Althusser, *Lenin and Philosophy*, 175–6, Althusser's italics. Translation is slightly modified.

14. Friedrich Wilhelm Nietzsche, *On the Genealogy of Morality*, trans. Carol Diethe (Cambridge: Cambridge University Press, 1994), 68.

15. Benedictus de Spinoza, *Theological-Political Treatise*, trans. Michael Silverthorne and Jonathan Israel (Cambridge: Cambridge University Press, 2007), 243.

16. *Ethics* VP23Schol.

17. Curley's translation of this pivotal and difficult passage has a footnote that supports Simondon's interpretation: "This sentence illustrates well the kind of difficulty characteristic of this part of the *Ethics*. On the face of it, Spinoza implies that we (who are here identified with parts our minds; cr. IIP13C) not only will *after* the body, but did exist *before* it (though he denies the Platonic doctrine what we can come to recollect our preexistence). But in the same breath he asserts that we are eternal (cf. IIA1 and ID8) and that the eternal has no relation to time." Benedictus de Spinoza, *The Collected Works of Spinoza*, trans. and ed. E.M. Curley (Princeton: Princeton University Press, 1985), I, 608.

18. "To say the living is problematic is to consider becoming as a dimension of the living: the living *is* according to becoming, which operates a mediation. The living is agent and theatre of individuation; its becoming is a permanent individuation or rather *a continuation of access for individuation* advancing from metastability to metastability" (20).

19. Nicole Loraux, *The Invention of Athens: The Funeral Oration in the Classical City* (Cambridge, MA: Harvard University Press, 1986), 337.

20. Henri Bergson, *Ecrits Philosophiques* (Paris: Presses universitaires de France, 2011), 480. My translation.

21. Here I would like to borrow aspects of Pierre-François Moreau's brilliant analysis in order to illustrate the complementary relationship between Spinoza and Simondon on the basis of eternity. Cf. Pierre-François Moreau, *Spinoza, l'expérience et l'éternité* (Paris: Presses universitaires de France, 1994). All translations are mine.

22. Moreau, *Spinoza, l'expérience et l'éternité*, 544.

23. Moreau, *Spinoza, l'expérience et l'éternité*, 545.

24. Benedictus de Spinoza, "Ethics," in Curley, ed., *The Collected Works of Spinoza*, 588B.

25. "What appears as limitation, and what, under the effect of determined law, is truly limitation, is only the limited form of a resolutely affirmative power. The effects of this limitation are lived as powerlessness, misery, contingency. But they are moreover, as such, carriers of a positivity, which manifests itself in the separation they provoke and the path they create leading toward other forms of the same power" (Moreau, *Spinoza, l'expérience et l'éternité*, 547).

26. Gilbert Simondon, *L'individuation à la lumière des notions de forme et d'information*, ed. Jacques Garelli (Grenoble: Millon, 2005), 506, Simondon's italics. I will return to this passage again.

27. Moreau, *Spinoza, l'expérience et l'éternité*, 548.

28. *Ethics* IIP21P7.

29. Dominique Janicaud, *Heidegger en France*, Bibliothèque Albin Michel Idées (Paris: A. Michel, 2001).

30. "Anxiety individuates Dasein to its ownmost being-in-the-world which, as understanding, projects itself essentially upon possibilities. Thus, along with that for which it is anxious, anxiety discloses Dasein as *being-possible*, and indeed, as that, solely (*enzig*) from itself, can be individualized in individuation (*Vereinzelung*)." Martin Heidegger, *Being and Time: A Revised Edition of the Stambaugh Translation*, trans. Joan Stambaugh (Albany: State University of New York Press, 2010), 182/187–8.

31. Heidegger, *Being and Time*, 241/251.

32. Jean-Yves Chateau, *Le Vocabulaire de Gilbert Simondon* (Paris: Ellipses, 2008), 21–2, Chateau's italics.

33. "Joy" and "sadness" are the two primary affects for Spinoza's *Ethics*: "By Joy, therefore, I shall understand in what follows that passion by which the Mind passes to a greater perfection. Sadness is that passion by which it passes to a lesser perfection" (IIIP11Schol.).

4

Problematic of Ontogenesis and Psychic Individuation

Simondon begins Chapter 4, "Problematic of Ontogenesis and Psychic Individuation," by stressing the importance of distinguishing "signal" and "signification." A signal *stands for* something else. Its function is to transmit or convey information. Like a symbol, it is an *expressive* structure that references something anterior to it. But it is not responsible for creating meaning or signification, it merely carries meaning into presence. Signification is a distinct and expressive act that confers meaning, as Husserl carefully posits.

Beyond the initial individuation carried out by perception, the individual is further individuated through the establishment of a relationship to exterior objects. Yet where Husserl saw the fulfillment of meanings confirming the psychical ("consciousness-of") – however transcendentally re-conceived – for Simondon, the reverse is true: information's progressing toward signification is the genesis of the psychical individual paralleling and expressive of the operation of individuation. While certainly keeping aspects of Husserl's thought, one might say that Simondon *ontologizes* Husserl. For Simondon, the event of meaning, in other words signification, is an ontological event, synonymous with the operation by which the *individuated is individualized*. An individual's existence lies in its making actual "a real process of individuation, in other words, when significations appear; *the individual is this by what and in what significations appear*, though between individuals there are only signals" (125). In other words, the individual is the phenomenal form signification assumes – it is what being becomes in becoming-individualized. When Simondon speaks of individualization he is speaking of the being of the individual as only ever a problem that seeks a resolution, all the more difficult because this incompatibility is internal and, indeed, prompts its own genesis.

> The individual's genesis corresponds to the resolution of a problem which could not be resolved as a function of anterior givens, for they did not have a common axiomatic: *the individual is the auto-constitution of a topology of being that resolves an anterior incompatibility through the appearing of a new systematic.* (126)

The individual becomes knowable precisely once it acquires phenomenal being, that is, spatial-temporal being. "Topology and chronology are not *a priori* forms of the sensibility but the very dimensionality of the living individuating itself" (IGBP 228). The individualized individual achieves signification in conveying the mutual convertibility of order according to space (structure) and order according to time (becoming, tendency, development and aging), thereby making any prior incompatibilities compatible. Yet, even though signification reciprocally determines individuals, it achieves this by divulging, sometimes as only a glimpse or flashing moment, its relationship to the vaster functional becoming. There remains, always, some portion that escapes what is designated "individual."

TRANSCENDENTAL SUBJECT, EMPIRICAL SUBJECT

Simondon insists that the fundamental Kantian opposition between the empirical subject and the transcendental subject, which Husserl molds to his own phenomenological purposes, has been used to obfuscate what are in reality the two actions of individualization and individuation, which operate in concert with one another, constituting the "subject." Because it clarifies for us Simondon's struggles with Kantianism this is an immensely important passage:

> The subject, as the result of an individuation that incorporates it, is the milieu for the *a priori*; the subject, as milieu and agent of the progressive discoveries of signification in the signals originating from the world, is the principle *a posteriori*. The individuated being is the transcendental subject and the individualized being, the empirical subject. (128)

The "subject," for Simondon, is the convergence of the actions of individuation and individualization – their coordination, always questionable and self-questioning, of the transcendental and empirical. It is not a synthesis but a field, a singularity really, in an operation of individuation that marks the emergence of this difference. This is why the individualized subject is "always more-than-one," for resonating *within* it is this relation to other singularities, other fields.

However, while they codetermine one another, this does not mean they are not distinctly thinkable. The empirical is the milieu and agent of signification for itself and its being in the world, in other words, individualization. Simondon claims that once we adopt the perspective of the transcendental the subject has no other "choice" than to think through individuation. This means that, for Simondon, individuation is the transcendental plane, which provides the condition for the possibility of the knowledge of being. "It is itself choice, the concretization of a foundational choice of being; this being exists inasmuch as it is a solution . . . it is the ensemble, the system, out of which emerged [the transcendental subject] and in which it did not pre-exist as individuated" (128). The empirical, conversely, presents the subject with the "choice" to think through individualization. The transcendental plane is the plane of individuation; the empirical plane is the plane of individualization.

Problems emerge through the transcendental subject. To grasp the transcendental requires a shifting of thought from the individual to the milieu of individuation, those transductive relations conditioning one individuation after another. As such, it demands a specific experience. The transcendental is a problematic and problematizing field, whereas the empirical offers a "composite of solutions to these problems" in the form of schemas for directing how problems are to be resolved. "Personality" is everything that reattaches the individual being *qua* individuated being to the individual *qua* individualized (128). The synthesis of individuation and individualization – i.e. 'personality' – is, for Simondon, the principle of the differentiated and asymmetrical relation with other individualized beings. "The concrete human is neither pure individuation nor pure individualization but a mixture of both" (129).

We might interpret sexuality as Simondon conceives it: a distributive combination of the transcendental and the empirical. Sexuality, on the one hand, constitutes itself at the level of individuation, but it is at the level of individualization that sexuality brings into play everyday experienceable contingencies, which determine our sexuality in other ways: in the ways we find ourselves to be specifically sexually attracted to the other, from hair color, to height and weight, dimples, freckles, fetishes, whatever your tastes. Of course, this means that Simondon designates sexuality to be a structural invariant, not a matter of choice, predetermining the being of the individual individuated as homosexual, heterosexual, bisexual, or otherwise. Simondon characterizes a being's sexuality as being individuated but not individualized. This would seem to put Simondon at odds with theorists like Judith Butler, who characterize sexuality or sexual identity as largely a performative affect.[1] Yet, according to Simondon, the integration of individuation (sexuality) and the anecdotal happens at the level of personality. Perhaps, then, it might be said that sexuality is *performative*, if only in a restricted sense.

How can a being individuated to be sexually attracted to the same sex communicate with someone who is sexually attracted to the opposite sex but only when dressed in a bunny costume? If communication is to be possible, it cannot occur at the level of individuation, only at the level of individualization, interpersonally. If sexuality is a product of individuation, which exceeds our choices, signification is totally a reflection of personality, of personal desires acting upon. Personality is "a relational activity between principle and result; it is what causes the unity of being, between its foundation of universality and the particularities of individualization" (129).

"Consciousness" is only the "epiphenomenon" of what conditions any possible communication: transindividuality. Simondon argues, "the relation to the other puts us, the individuated, in question *as* individuated beings" (131). The transindividual integration of individuation and individualization puts into question the individuated individual, at the level of the modifications of individualization. But he is careful to stress that it is not merely a relationship of opposition, the reducing of relationship to the negation of one term or subject existing absolutely in relation to another. It is more purely *relational*.

"AIN'T I A WOMAN?"

Simondon writes:

> To perceive a woman as woman is not to enter into a perception in some already established conceptual framework but to situate oneself at once to individuation and individualization in relationship to becoming a woman. This interpersonal relationship includes a possible relation of our existence as individuated being in relation to oneself. (131)

What if we take Sojourner Truth as an example? Does Sojourner Truth in 1851 not invite us to move beyond the empirical individual that we "know" – though we begin there – to look at *this* being here, before us, and in looking disclose a transcendental plane of communication *beyond* the empirical, as a result of the challenge her presence makes? Look at her.

> Look at me! Look at my arm! I have ploughed and planted, and gathered into barns, and no man could head me! And ain't I a woman? I could work as much and eat as much as a man – when I could get it – and bear the lash as well! And ain't I a woman? I have borne thirteen children, and seen most all sold off to slavery, and when I cried out with my mother's grief, none but Jesus heard me! And ain't I a woman?[2]

Only then might we make sense of the individuation of *this* human being, *this* black woman. How must knowledge be rethought to accommodate its grasping this *haecceity* (*this* woman here), the individualizing difference that, nonetheless, grasps the relational coincidence between individuation and individualization? Signification (of a black individual) materializes the expressed being of this individualized individual (*this* woman). "It is a certain expression, a certain signification, which makes this woman *this* woman" (132), Simondon writes. And the coherence established across these two orders of reality of individuation and individualization comprises signification.

The psychic and somatic, consciousness and the body, are modes of the single vital individuation, expressed affectively through several actions and ideas. Simondon lets us consider "psychic contents as the resolution of a series of problems which are posed to the living, and that it had been able to resolve in individualizing itself; the psychic structures are the expression of this fractioned individualization that had separated the individuated being into the somatic and psychic domains" (133). Individuated being, therefore, expresses itself in successive, partially coordinated, somato-psychic combinations. It is these combinations that reflect the second form of individuation, individualization. "Individualization of the living is its real historicity" (134).

THE TWO MISTAKES: TRANSCENDENCE AND IMMANENCE

Philosophical thought, before anteriorly posing the critical question to all ontology, must pose the problem of complete reality, anterior to individuation, from which the subject of critical thought and ontology emanates. The true philosophy is not first that of the subject, or that of the object, or that of a God or Nature pursued according to a principle of transcendence or immanence; rather, it arises from a real anterior to individuation, a real which can neither be sought in the objectified object or in the subjectified subject but, instead, in the limit between the individual and what remains outside of it, according to a mediation suspended between transcendence and immanence. (137)

This passage is immensely important for appreciating what Simondon believes is at risk as a result of his foregrounding the problem of individuation. Cleverly mimicking Kant's famous phrase, he states that the individuated being can no more account for itself nor all that is in itself than he can account for his "emotion before the starry sky, the moral law within, or the principle of true judgment" (135–6).[3] This is because the individuated being has not retained the entirety of the real that birthed it; "it is an incomplete reality" (136). The genesis of the individual is not a creation of the absolute advent of being but "an individuation *within* being" (136).

For Simondon, transcendence is destined to fail because it contains a fatal contradiction: it presupposes the genesis of what it claims to explain. That is, it presupposes as a condition for its achievement what it claims to discover: individual being. The concept of transcendence confuses anteriority with exteriority. Hence, he suggests that the very notion of a supreme being is incoherent "because it is impossible to make coincide or even to make compatible the personal character of the supreme being, with its ubiquitous character, the positive eternity that provides its cosmological existence" (136).

Simondon identifies three quasi-mythic personae of transcendence that, either by challenging or acquiescing to the gods, symbolize the halting of the movement of the infinite: the Sage (Socrates), the master of using representation in pursuit of wisdom; the Hero, the figure of action (Achilles); and, finally, the Priest or the Saint (Joan of Arc), the vessel for the affective power of holiness. These three figures of transcendence ("*transcendences*") are inhibiting and inhibitory, for they bear "a certain sense of inhibition." The Sage, the Saint, and the Hero alike, for example, prepare themselves for action with the aid of ascetic practices. Nietzsche might refer to them as symbols of the ascetic ideal. At best, according to Simondon, they offer a kind of "negative revelation" of transindividuality without it actually being the case, placing "the individual in communication with a superior order of reality to that of the stream of life" (159). It is precisely by means of the inhibitory exercises "that being surpasses itself, either according to a request of transcendence, or in 'immortalizing itself in the sensible'" (IL 282). The Hero is immortalized by self-sacrifice; the Sainted Martyr's final testimony guarantees eternal salvation; and the Sage wins immortality through his soul-"children."[4] For this reason, these personae, throughout Western culture's history, have come to symbolize the "eternal dimension to the individual life." Nietzsche argues that morality's inhibiting and eventual denial of life originates in the ascetic ideals symbolized by these figures.[5] There is little doubt that here Nietzsche informs Simondon's thinking.

Immanence, like transcendence, falls victim to "the same last failure" of granting ontological privilege to the constituted and individuated individual being (136). Once again borrowing Spinoza's terminology (*the* "philosopher of immanence" for Simondon), he writes:

> Individuated being finds itself, thus, in a double relationship to the world, first, as a being that comprehends *Nature as naturing* [*Natura naturans*] and, secondly, a mode of *Nature natured* [*Natura naturata*]. The relation of *Nature naturing* and *Nature natured* is as difficult to grasp in the pursuit of immanence

at the interior of individuated being, as that of God as personal agent and as omnipresent and eternal, i.e. endowed with cosmic beingness. (136–7)

Individuated being, in whatever name, God or Nature, is still a form that ontologically privileges the individual and, thus, prevents us from escaping the habitual logic that calls for the principle of haecceity either to be intelligible in the form of a universal idea, a category, some relationship of form and matter, or conceivable as a principle of sufficient reason. So it goes that if Kant is the prime representative of transcendence, Spinoza is taken to be the prime philosopher of immanence, as we notice above when Simondon borrows Spinoza's language (*Natura naturata / Natura naturans*), if only to turn these terms against Spinoza. In his critique of immanence we must also factor in how Simondon conceives the uses and disadvantages of Spinoza's ontology for orienting the relationship between the psychological and vital, in order to properly grasp the transindividual. Simondon's work, particularly in IPC, carries out a furtive dialogue with Spinoza, at once structurally mimicking his ontology, oftentimes borrowing logic and paraphrasing terminology, even while Simondon indicts him on the ancient charge of pantheism. This will become more obvious in the next section.

Simondon trusts that neither the idea of transcendence nor the idea of immanence is able to fully account for the relationship of the transindividual to the psychological individual, specifically the auto-constitution of transindividuality. From the ontogenetic perspective, the insufficiency of both derives from the fact that these terms are applied *after* individuation, while, nonetheless, they are "defined and fixed *before* the moment the individual becomes one of the terms of the relation in which it is integrated but for whom the other term is already given" (156, my italics). In the instant of its auto-constitution, the transindividual overwhelms the individual entirely in prolonging it (157), and therefore whatever terms might be applied to it: "transcendence" or "immanence." "The transindividual is neither exterior nor superior; it characterizes the true relation between all exteriority and all interiority in relation to the individual" (157).[6]

THE WORRY OF IMMANENCE

Immanence is the thornier issue. It is Deleuze – the unapologetic Spinozist – who writes: "Immanence can be said to be the burning issue of all philosophy because it takes on all the dangers that philosophy must confront, all the condemnations, persecutions, and repudiations that it undergoes."[7] And Spinoza's thought, in particular, illustrates Simondon's own conflictual handling of it. Over and over again, Simondon rejects

Spinoza on the basis of the latter's metaphysical and epistemological goal of immanence; then, just as suddenly, we find Spinoza's terminology and formulations co-opted (often with attribution) to support Simondon's metaphysical descriptions and speculations. I have noted these instances in previous chapters and we will notice more instances going forward. Still, the problem remains: How to reconcile Simondon's rejection of immanence, an explicit critique of Spinoza and, yet, acknowledge his obvious Spinozist orientation.

Simondon's critique of Spinoza would seem to bring him to the side of Hegel. But Hegel rejects Spinoza on the grounds that real determination is impossible if one posits an absolute positivity of indeterminateness, anterior to the determined being.[8] Is that not exactly what Simondon's conception of a psychic individuation does, as it ultimately supposes the existence of a pre-individual reality, a metastable system rich in potentials and, indeed, conserving and indeed nurturing this seemingly indeterminate reality within itself? Deleuze calls this the realm of "pure immanence." Would not Hegel find Simondon to be too Spinozist?

One wonders if it is a deceptive feint that Simondon deploys by restating the clichéd and not particularly accurate critique of Spinoza, which takes immanence and pantheism to be more or less synonymous. Might this criticism be a way to blunt Spinoza against attacks of the most obvious kind? Simondon's apprehension concerning pantheism is not that it invites anthropomorphism; it is that the unique individual is "dilated to the dimensions of the cosmos." Absolutely privileged, ontologically and epistemologically, it serves both as condition *and* what is conditioned. The individuality of this individual has a unique substance identical with an eternalness, which conserves itself through a potentially infinite expansion, itself made possible by an analogical relationship that joins together the micro-cosmos and the macro-cosmos. What is "oppressive" in this pantheism – Stoic and Spinozist – "is the valorization of the cosmic law as rule of thought and the individual will; now, this valorization of universal determinism intervenes because there exists an implicit proposition: the universe is an individual" (161). As a result, Simondon's concern is that the relation between the biological individual and the transindividual can no longer be interposed by means of a dis-individualization of the individual. The great error that a theory structuring itself on the grounds of immanence commits is the tendency toward pantheism, the threat of "the individualization of the transindividual always inherently apart from immanence" (161). This path of immanence, Simondon suspects, will eventually take us down the path of the individual's re-emergence at the level of ontological superiority.

SIMONDON'S SPINOZISM II

Pantheism's failure lies in its inability to develop a notion of freedom. Simondon writes, "Doubtless, it is because of this inexpungible individuality incarnated in the soul that every pantheism leads to a difficult conception of freedom at the interior of necessity, whose Spinozist form, while 'infinitely subtle,' recalls, even so, the Stoic image of the dog tied to the cart,[9] enslaved inasmuch as his will is not united with the very rhythm of his equipment, and free when he realized the synchronism of his will's movements with the stops and starts of the cart" (161). Pantheism is symptomatic of a too rigid determinism, Simondon believes. It is not that Simondon wants to rescue free will; it is just that pantheism leaves us trapped in a Manichean logic and wholly beholden to a metaphysics that turns becoming into a pale reproduction of individuated being. Genesis would seem to be unintelligible.

Spinoza's formulation of "free necessity" contests the accepted notions of freedom and free will. Spinoza argues that a thing is free only if it exists and acts from the necessity of its own nature; otherwise, it is compelled by something exterior to it, to act and exist contrary to its nature. Hence, God exists necessarily and, so, it exists freely because it exists from the necessity of its own nature only. And so, too, to grasp the being of something from the Spinozist perspective is to acquire knowledge of the necessity that follows from a thing's nature, determining how it exists.

So it is that a thing *strives* to exist, to persevere in being, by being conscious of those appetites, if ignorant of how those appetites are determined. In this way, human beings remain ignorant of the causes of things and, as a result, believe themselves to possess freedom when they do not. But even so, to be conscious of appetites is to grasp them as desires. Still, it is through desires that the individual gains the power to act in support of persevering in one's existence. This is why Spinoza calls desire "the essence of man." "The man's power, therefore, insofar as it is explained through his actual essence, is part of God *or* Nature's infinite power, that is of its essence."[10] What this means is that freedom emerges out of the necessity of the exigency of being, producing "individuality" from relationships that empower (or perhaps dis-empower), thereby expressing the individual being's constitution.

Radically extending Descartes' assertion that either the creator's act is unintelligible *or* it is necessary, Spinoza claims that only an intelligible act offers the possibility for clear and distinct knowledge. The creator's act must be necessary, for the soul is the creation of God's *necessarily* free will and, thus, the "individuality" that defines the soul necessarily follows from God's essence. If this creative act necessarily follows from God, then the soul's existence, as granted by the divine will, assures itself the continuity of its existence. "This individual's transcendence or immanence in relation to the world does not change the fundamental scheme of its [the supreme individual's] constitution, which has as a consequence to confer value to each determination" (161). The existence of the perfect Being is affirmed. The soul is a part of the substance of God; therefore, the soul is in God. Ultimately, the infinite absorbs the finite; the personal dissolves in the eternal being of supreme individuality.

Simondon's ambiguous relationship with Spinoza comes into view when, after he willingly accepts and then dismisses his ontology because of its supposed betrayal of its pantheism, he finds the germ for conceiving transindividuality at a more personal psychological level. Surprisingly, it is his acceptance of "desire," though without acknowledging the source of impetus, which offers Simondon a way to contest the substantial character of the individual "soul." We saw above how this logically leads to paradoxical "free necessity." The problem for Simondon is that the substantiality of the soul is the product of the hylemorphic logic and substantialist ontology, which prohibits raising the problem of individuation; it obligates us to presuppose the existence of an infinite being, reattaching soul to what grants its existence. This is why Simondon claims, "the notion of the soul must be revised," in response to raising the "most delicate question" of the "personal" character of psychological individuality (157).

If we closely follow Simondon's text, we notice how his descriptive claims become clearer. The appearance of psychological individuality elaborates itself in elaborating transindividuality. This elaboration is carried out in two seemingly opposite, though reciprocally codependent directions: it occurs through interiorizing the exterior, while, at the same time, exteriorizing the interior. Again, we remind ourselves, the transindividual is the event of this *transductive* movement in either direction, interiority to exteriority or vice versa. "Now, beyond the notion of the substantiality of the soul and equally beyond the notion of the inexistence of all spiritual reality, there is the possibility of defining a transindividual reality" (157). The psychological individual is the effect or byproduct of the transindividual process.

TRANSDUCTIVITY OF DESIRE

Although never explicitly admitted, Simondon's proposing that "all research simply demonstrates the existence of the *desire* for eternity" has a Spinozist impetus, insofar as it is a revision of the notion of the soul to disclose what is most personal in psychological individuality. Simondon asserts that it is the notion of desire which best offers a fundamental revision of the soul, disclosing the psychological individuality as a domain of transductivity. This is all the more surprising once we acknowledge that Spinoza's entire psychology is oriented around the notion of "desire" for eternity (the desire to experience being *sub specie aeternitas*). Each individual thing, relative to its specific power or capacities, strives to persevere in its being (*conatus*). It is this striving that defines the actual essence of the individual.

To the degree that a being perseveres in its striving, it expresses its power (*potentia*), which is the capacity or potential for it to act. It is this power or striving that is the essence of the individual itself. Or, rather, "desire" is the very essence *or* nature of each human individual, insofar as it is conscious of how something affects our power. And, so, desire reflects how the individual is determined, from any given affection, to do something, to act. Desires are the strivings, impulses, appetites, and volitions which vary relative to the particular constitution of each human being. The human being's capacity to act, therefore, reflects the degree to which it is either encouraged to act or restrained from acting by whatever affects it. Desire, as a result, is not a finished state which completes the individual. An "affect' is that by which the individual body's power to act is increased or diminished, aided or restrained.

The body, relative to how it allows itself to be affected, dynamically regulates an individual's power. Power is an affection of desire. Desire is purely operational, not normative; it is nothing but striving itself. Norms are the products of desire's operation. As each human individual is affected differently by joy and sadness, love and hate, so too these are less final states than they are operations *in process*, structuring elements of its striving that involve, as we saw in the discussion of anxiety, the dis-individuation of the individual as well as the individuation of being. These emotions are ontological and emotional as they register how or to what extent a being is affected by causes external to it relative to their respective constitutions. The power that expresses an individual's being as it strives to preserve its being is the power itself of God, *or* Nature, not because it is infinite; rather, because it can be explained through the individual's actual essence. The individual's power, therefore, insofar as it is explained through its actual essence, is part of God or Nature's infinite power, that is, of its essence. To the degree that it exists as a share of Nature, the individual is eternal.

Simondon's choosing to focus on the single element that grounds the personal characteristics of any particular psychological individuality is not accidental; rather, it reflects a fundamental ambivalence regarding Spinozism. His call for a revision of the soul initiates a shift from the "false simplicity" of the soul to a focus on "the existence of the desire for eternity," which is, as he suggests, "a reality as Desire" (157–8).

"Now, beyond the notion of the substantiality of being and, likewise, the notion of the inexistence of all spiritual reality," Simondon writes, "there is the possibility of defining a transindividual reality" (157) – which is to say, how the affections of the body and the idea of things affecting it increase or diminish an individual's power, expressing transindividual reality via the potential ("more-than-individual") present in every individual striving to preserve its being. Desire stages "the emergence of a dynamism of being, of transindividuality, a dynamism that causes transindividuality to exist in valorizing it" (158). Desire permits us to more directly grasp because the dynamism of transindividuality appears as it takes place in the form of an indefinite propagation. As a result, a virtual immortality is conferred on desire (158).

AN ABERRANT MONISM

Any theory that would suggest a materialist or spiritualist monism Simondon rejects on the grounds that both ultimately return us to the kind of substantialist metaphysic which posits a principle of individuation anterior to individuation itself. Both impose "a mutilation of complete individual being" (142). This is, of course, not surprising. What is surprising is Simondon's suggestion that his philosophy of individuation is putting forward a "true monism." "The only true monism," Simondon claims, "is that in which the unity [of being] is grasped at the moment where the possibility of a diversity of functioning and structure is suspected" (142). It is a monism which is defined by the moment just prior to the subject and object being structured. In other words, it is a "genetic monism." "This monism is genetic, for alone genesis assumes the unity containing plurality; becoming is grasped as a dimension of the individual, starting from the time where the individual did not exist as individual" (142).

The genetic monism Simondon embraces is an aberrant monism. It is the reinstating of a "renewed concept of the One." A dialectically conceived monism depends on accounting for the identity of the One and the multiple, to confirm their substantiality. As a result, the multiple is merely formal, whereas only the One is real. All being is reduced to some equivocal being of the One.[11] More insidiously, this would seem to suggest that Simondon is trying to sneak transcendence through the back door under the guise of immanence. And, what is more, for us it would seem to contradict the contemporary tendency in philosophy toward difference and multiplicity. How are we then to take Simondon's embracing monism, especially given his avowed refusal of it? Since Simondon himself does not mount a defense, let us try to provide him with one.

"The magic formula we all seek – PLURALISM = MONISM."[12] In a

1973 lecture Deleuze argues that "the only enemy is two" and that monism and pluralism are "the same thing." Opposition between terms occurs the moment they are given a substantive being; otherwise they are only ever multiplicities, arrangements of multiplicities. Hence, Deleuze constructs a monistic field, inhabited by multiplicities, impersonal singularities, potentialities, out of which individualities emerge which are assigned a substantive being after the fact. "There is nothing that is one, there is nothing that is multiple, everything is multiplicities," Deleuze argues. Yet, in achieving its form, one must not give credit to a dialectic which only yields a "false monism." So we see that Deleuze, like Simondon, proposes a truer monism, an aberrant monism. "At this moment, one can see the strict identity of monism and pluralism in this form of immanence . . . The process of immanence is also a multiplicity, i.e., to design a field of immanence populated by a multiplicity."[13]

In overturning the false monism, a path is set for a reconceiving of desire and the inventing of concepts like the "Body without Organs," which for Deleuze in responds to the problem of the unconscious. I guess the only thing left to ask is: does Simondon refuse the very idea of immanence or only a "false" immanence (in the same way he rejects "false monism")?

The only way pluralism and monism achieve compatibility is by our viewing the psychological individual through the lens of an Allagmatic point of view.[14] "In reality, as in every domain of transductivity, there is in the psychological individual the entailment of a reality at once continuous and multiple" (148–9). Ontogenesis offers Simondon "true" immanence: an individuated being not as a given substance but as *becoming, relation, operation.* This conception is contrary to the more common conception, which implicitly finds in monism and dualism a substantiality of one or two "substances," thus ensuring that the retrieval of an effective genesis is not possible. Rather than an implicit pluralism, which it sets up only to refuse, a true monism contains "the dimension of possible pluralism but on the basis of the being that is not able to slip away." Simondon is referring to pre-individual being as the being incapable of "slipping away." Therefore, one postulates a dualism or a pluralism only if either is grasped within a "phase of being anterior to individuation" for the purpose of "relativizing individuation in situating it among phases of being" (142).

THE DANGER OF IMPLICIT SOCIOLOGY

What is Simondon concerned about in relation to the "implicit sociology" he finds comprising normative judgments made by psychology and modern psychopathology? What does "implicit sociology" mean? And why should this be of any concern at all? These disciplines advocate and defend

> EXCURSUS
>
> If I might, I would like to pause for a moment. I have tried to mirror as closely as possible the path Simondon's thought has taken in IPC. Much of the early chapters of his work focuses on questions that are methodological (critique of hylemorphism, theory of transduction), metaphysical (critique of substantialist ontology), psychological (perception, affection, emption), and epistemological (analysis of empirical/transcendental). It is at this point in Simondon's work, however, that we discern a shift toward the more overt engagement with what he calls the "psychosocial." And as Simondon reminds us: The "transindividual is the psychosocial," in that it describes the means by which the systematic unity of interior (psychic) and exterior (collective) individuation is achieved. While the grounds for this shift are laid once he introduces this term "transindividuality," it begins to be more clearly discernible first when he introduces the distinction between individuation and individualization. However, it is most evident when, second, Simondon claims as the justification for his detour into psychology the examination of those ontogenetic conditions and circumstances which have led to the invention of normative social values. The key for the reader, a signal that Simondon is making this shift from overt metaphysics to the analysis of the psychosocial, is when he introduces the problem of "spirit" or "spirituality." So, although Simondon seems to fall victim to repetition and redundancy when he begins to repeat many of his basic concepts and structures already outlined in the "Introduction" within the first three chapters, it is important to remind ourselves that his repetitions are done within a new problematic, registering a different point of engagement.

normative judgments on the basis of their classifying behaviors or states of being. Simondon's goal, therefore, is not the refusal of normativity; it is to disclose the internal mechanism and the *real* ontological conditions which make normative judgments possible. In short, the goal is to disclose those conditions designating "objectivity" in the normative. As he reviews the theories of his contemporaries, particularly the cyberneticist Lawrence Kubie's work on adaptation, he argues that it is precisely the "implicitness" of normativity that directs us to the dynamism implicitly at work in a theory's supposed objectivity. The universe is polarized, with every particle and molecule gravitationally, electrically, and magnetically charged by disparate forces, of "all degrees of the vast domain of transductivity which it constitutes" (146). According to Simondon, one is able to accurately pose the problem of physical individuality if one takes this image of the universe, composed not of neutral particles but of polarized elements in polarizing and polarized relationships of difference, as a basis for thinking it through. What Simondon is proposing is a transductive transcendental critique, one that brings to light the ontogenetic conditions of knowledge. His is not – as Simondon describes it – a "genealogical project." It is the dramatization of what I might call "transcendental transductivism."

Simondon worries that the knowledge of objectivity promises more than it can deliver. An implicit sociology smuggled into a psychological theory does not guarantee its objectivity; knowledge cowers beneath the illusion it promotes. Once the content of the dynamic notions employed by modern psychology are analyzed, notions like the "normal" and the "pathological," we find that these categories, especially normativity, harbor an implicit mistrust of sociology, that is to say, a social theory with its own epistemological and normative presumptions, and even a socio-technique, unnecessary and, perhaps, unwanted by our clarifying psychology's explicit foundations (143).

THE NORMAL AND THE PATHOLOGICAL

The grievous mistake committed by psycho-sociological theories is identical to the one science makes when it tries to define physical individuality: it presumes an ontology of absolute substantialism leading to pure stasis, to conceiving reality and the change defining it, to an ever progressively degrading comparison of states of being (pathologies) relative to the original perfect plentitude (the "normal"). This is supposedly opposed to an ontology of absolute dynamism, of pure chaos, limitless change. Lost is the importance of the fundamental role relation plays, ontologically and epistemologically, operationally and structurally, in constituting individual being. Simondon's challenge to any attempt to implicitly appeal to sociology is on the basis of its rendering relation "inessential" (148).

Certainly it is useful to distinguish structure as the thematic domain of objectivity typified by knowledge like biology, physiology, and chemistry. One cannot define an operation apart from either the structure converted or the structure resulting from the conversion. The operationality of this structuring process foregrounds *relationality*, thereby permitting our determination of the existence and knowledge of the claimed structure of objectivity, in whatever forms it might assume.

Psychological individuality is the "chiasm" between the biological and the physical. A "superimposition" between these domains as they relate to one another, the psychological does not impose itself between them as if from the outside; rather the psychological domain of individuality "reunites them and, partially, comprehends them in being situated *in* them" (152, my italics). The psychological individual attains its structure via the operation of transduction. Thus, it is impossible to pretend that one is able to divide some mental state of behavior into any simple opposition, in particular the "normal" versus the "pathological." Instead of offering a critique of Georges Canguilhem's argument, advanced brilliantly in *The Normal and the Pathological*, Simondon (implicitly) amplifies the essential point that:

> We cannot say that the concept of the "pathological" is the logical contradictory of the concept "normal," for life in the pathological state is not the absence of norms but the presence of other norms. Rigorously speaking, "pathological" is the vital contrary of "healthy" and not the logical contradictory of "normal" . . . Disease – the pathological state – is not the loss of a norm but the aspect of a life regulated by norms that are vitally inferior or depreciated, insofar as they prevent the living being from an active and comfortable participation, generative of confidence and assurance, in the kind of life previously belonging to it and still permitted to others.[15]

The normal–pathological dualism is only a logical feint that distracts from the definite problem of identifying what engenders a multiplicity of norms, whose restriction to two cannot hide what remains most vital: to invent norms that promote rather than restrict the capacity to act, to strive to exist. For Simondon, this is similarly the primary challenge facing his thought. Normal and pathological are not merely normative categories that regulate the action of the individual in relation to its milieu; they are social. Simondon's agreement with Canguilhem's questioning the distinction between the normal and the pathological permits him, similarly, to enjoy the benefits of reconsidering the normative categories underlying the psychological; it becomes clear to what extent these categories – the normal and the pathological – are evidence of the implicit sociology worrying him. This dualism, in particular, is the normalizing of social identities, given psychological significance.

Any attempt to reduce psychic life to a simple duality – normal and pathological – reduces too completely the structuring vital activity of living from the *operation* that brings it to life.[16] But as Canguilhem argues, "Man is truly healthy only when he is capable of several norms, when he is *more than normal*."[17] Simondon theorizes the Allagmatic precisely to address Canguilhem's concern relative to this too thorough separation between structure and operation; as a "general theory of the exchanges and modifications of changes of state" (233), as a "general theory of transformations" (284), it has the goal not merely of bridging this separation, nor solely of describing the nature of their relationship, but as well the rehearsal of that "domain of reciprocal convertibility of operation into structure and structures into operations" (IL 565). The struggle is not over the validity of applying the categories of normal and pathological, who or what concepts or operations are given the freedom *to create* norms for determining value, and who or what has the capacity to put them into practice. If an epistemological shift from the dualism to the question of health is invited, one is granted the normative power, ontologically, to question other norms credited with physiological explanation, inviting new ways of structuring the relationship of the living as it adapts to a given milieu without denying that it carries the risk of illness.

"So it seems to us," Canguilhem continues, "that the norm in matters of the human psyche is the reclamation and use of freedom as a power of revision and institution of norms – a reclamation that normally implies the risk of madness."[18] In other words, in revealing the inadequacy of reducing the psychic to opposing norms, we realize that the true reality of the psychological individual is transductive and, thus, a multiplicity, "at once continuous and multiple" (148–9).[19]

PSYCHOLOGICAL DETOUR TO "SPIRITUALITY"

Procedurally, Simondon's "psychological detour" is not meant to reduce life to the status of a supplement to consciousness (as if this were possible), nor, more realistically, does it lower its ontological value to that equal with the psyche. Instead, it is "an act by which the psychological reality is pitched off center in relation to the biological reality" for the purpose of grasping its problematic: that is, to disclose how the relationship of the world and the "I," the physical and the vital, in being decentered, constitutes itself as transduction: "The psychological reality deploys a transductive relationship of the world and the 'I'" (152).

The psychological detour which Simondon carries out in this chapter reveals itself to have two main purposes: first, to demonstrate that rather than a direct communication between the world and the self, there is a complex act of mediation between them, with each supposing the other; and, second, that in doing so, they come together, to mutually put into question the reflexive consciousness of self (152). Reflexivity bears within itself the germ for its own overcoming: its necessity lies in those mediations that deploy it, endowing the subject and object with reciprocity. As we previously said, the domain of reflexive consciousness is relation, not possession, Simondon asserts. And as such, it can only be constituted by what it constitutes, subject *or* object. To describe this continuous unfolding of reflexivity via a series of transductive reciprocal mediations, Simondon retrieves and reconceives the word "spirit."[20]

Psychological individuality superimposes biological individuality without destroying it, for the spiritual reality cannot be created by a simple negation of the vital. We must note that the distinction between the vital order and psychological order manifests particularly by the fact that their respective normativities constitute a chiasm: it is at the time that biological calm reigns that the inquietude manifests itself, and it is at the time that pain exists that spirituality commutes into defensive reflexes; fear transforms spirituality into superstition. (160)

The psychological individual is responsible for norms that otherwise would not exist at the biological level, responding to the unachievable possibility of biological equilibrium, to the degree of indetermination ever present to the living being.[21] However, the norms created by psychological individuality are not the result of an act of de-vitalization or the inhibition of those tendencies that structure a life's rhythms. A spiritual reality is achievable only once psychological individuality grounds itself in bio-logical individuality without destroying the latter; spiritual reality is born without sacrificing the vital.[22]

Spirituality is the operation that *transductively amplifies* the initial individuation brought forth by the vital, life. As Simondon repeatedly describes it, transduction is the transfer of information little by little, supplied with energy by the changing of the local state to the very place where transformation is produced. Again, Simondon takes the crystal to be the paradigmatic example: a crystalline germ (an "incidence of information") is introduced into a solution with a metastable state, and its introduction begins the process of a change of state (a "phase"-change), causing the solution to pass from a metastable state to a stable state (the crystal). "Amplification" is the indefinite iteration of this initial operation, this initial transformation (CI 161–2). Spirituality expressively grasps the internal problematic acting as the ontogenetic wellspring for living individual being, without exhausting its nascent metastability, that is, "the internal tensions remaining constant in the form of being's cohesion in relation to itself" (IL 206).

Spirituality, in this specific ontogenetic sense, must not be confused with religion or religious belief. Simondon goes to great pains to dis-tinguish them. Spirituality is wholly psychosocial; religion, while psy-chosocial in terms of its source, is, nevertheless, only a deficient form of spirituality, at least in the way Simondon defines it. Spirituality provides the conditions for religion's emergence, but religion cannot provide the conditions for spirituality. Spirituality is expressive of individuation; religion, a phase of individualization. Indeed, it is important to recognize that Simondon equates religion with "superstition," which configures for itself a social form, the "Good Form," such that religion and the Good

Form cannot be dissociated. God, so invented by religion, is an example of the Good Form, which a culture[23] invokes in order to bring realities into a complementary relationship with one another. This is accomplished either directly by establishing a direct liaison between a community and the divine plan (the Old Testament with the notion of the elected people), by the constitution of a final virtual community for the elected beyond the terrestrial experience (Christianity), or by an indefinite possibility of progress or withdrawal on the path to the discovery of God (Saint Paul on the road to Damascus or Simone Weil) (249).

IN THE SPIRIT OF TRANSINDIVIDUALITY

Transindividuality is spiritual, not religious, in the sense that it exceeds biological life; as I described it previously, it shepherds individualized reality into a greater intimacy with the pre-individual, revealing to the subject its being "more-than-individual," more than identity, more than any unity might grant to it, undeniably "incompatible with himself" (108).[24] "Transindividuality is the experience of this excess" constitutive of the subject, while at same revealing of its internal disparity. This is why Muriel Combes, possibly the best commentator on Simondon's work, alleges that his "greatest innovation" is his situating of a "divergence within the subject being, the place where the insufficiency of the individual life appears at the point of the power 'more-than-individual' *in relation* to how the individual experiences the subject."[25]

"It is the transindividual and not society that is the source of all religion," writes Simondon. "Unlike what certain sociological theories wanted to demonstrate. It is only afterwards that this *force* is socialized, institutionalized; but it is not social in its essence" (155, my italics). It is his uneasiness concerning the "implicit sociology" infecting theories supposedly created for the purpose of analyzing the psychosocial that spurs Simondon's creation of the concept of the transindividual. For example, sociology begins its analysis by already assuming a socialized being, which it then reads back into the phenomena it claims to explain. Bergson would seem to fall prey to this error when he insists that "the social underlies the vital."[26]

For Simondon, it cannot be a simple matter of reversal, so that the vital somehow "underlies" the social. It is that individuation is carried out at different and successive levels via the operation of transduction. Accordingly, the vital is amplified rather than exhausted by the movement from the pre-individual to the living individual to the transindividual reality. "Between the vital and the psychic exists, therefore, when the psychic appears, a relation which is not matter to form but one individuation to another individuation; psychic individuation is a dilation, a matured expansion of vital individuation" (IL 166).

As Simondon details in IGPB (and as is foundational for IPC), the psychic problematic constitutes itself in the appeal to the indeterminate pre-individual reality associated with any and all individuated living organisms. It is this share of pre-individuality or Nature which provides the living with the source for potentially new individuations. And subsequently, each new individuation, throughout its successive operations, conserves a relation of participation that attaches each psychic being to other psychic beings. In this way, "the psychic is the nascent transindividual" (IL 166). The living, on the other hand, "cannot borrow from the associated nature of potential producing a new individuation without entering into an order of reality that causes it to participate in an ensemble of psychic reality exceeding the limits of the living" (IL 166).

The vital impetus foments moral obligation – "the necessity of the whole, felt behind the contingency of the parts."[27] For Bergson, "that obligation is the force of an aspiration or an impetus – the very impetus which culminated in the human species, in social life, and in a system of habits which bears a resemblance more or less to instinct."[28] If Bergson characterizes the *élan vital* as a force, not an already individuated substance, Simondon characterizes "transindividuality" or the transindividual as a non-substantializing force, an aberrant monism, equally dynamic and creative.

ZARATHUSTRA'S SOLITUDE

At the heart of Chapter 3 is an extended interpretation of a passage from Nietzsche's *Thus Spoke Zarathustra*. It is a fascinating moment in IPC, not the least because it is the only time Simondon affirmatively engages, to a significant degree, with a philosopher's specific work by name. Here we find Simondon a confirmed Nietzschean. But this moment in IPC is crucial more generally, for it is when Simondon identifies the transindividual as the realization of the psychic life.

Culture is made up of multiple mental and behavioral schemes. It is where the normativity of values is established, beyond any one particular choice that the psychological individual has to make among the different predetermined values and behaviors available to it. An even greater choice must be made between culture and transindividual reality. A culture's role, as Simondon describes it, is to neutralize the tendency of the subject to put itself into question. Transindividuality requires exactly the opposite. "There is in the transindividual relation a demand for the subject to put itself into question because this putting into question is yet begun by others; the decentering of the subject in relation to itself is effectuated in part by others in the inter-individual relation" (154). Still, Simondon notes that the inter-individual relation often masks the transindividual relation. One might, for example, find this to be the case in Husserl's *Cartesian Meditations* insofar as the existence of the "Other" individual is only a pretense for the self to reflect upon itself, to reconfirm the coherency of its individuated existence.[29]

Solitude divulges the contrivances of the transindividual in a manner left unsatisfied by inter-individual relationships, both theoretically and practically. As Simondon writes, it presents a test for the individual to navigate: "the individual finds the universality of the relation in terms of a trial that it imposes on itself, an ordeal of isolation" (155). Simondon proposes that religion offers only one kind of solitude, "or, rather [solitude] is anterior to the whole religious context and is, instead, the common basis for all religious forces, when it translates itself into religion" (155). But what is *philosophical* solitude?

Simondon takes "the example of Nietzsche's Zarathustra to be prescient, for it shows us that the ordeal itself [of solitude] is often commanded and nurtured by the clarity given by an exceptional event, which provides man with consciousness of his destiny and brings him to feel the necessity of the ordeal" (156). In other words, an "exceptional event" reveals for us the power of solitude to reveal to ourselves, not what we are but what we must become, to push us beyond our individual selves toward the transindividual being: the collective. In this regard, solitude is the preparation for a tormenting *disindividuation*. Of course, before we reach this point, the challenge must be faced of grasping this "exceptional event" as it happens. "The Tightrope Walker" dramatizes such an event for Simondon.[30]

Descending from his mountain cave where he had lived for ten years, undergoing a trial of solitude, Nietzsche describes Zarathustra as "transformed." "I need hands that reach out," he says.[31] He feels joy because he is bringing to mankind a "gift," the teaching of the "Overman" (*Übermensch*). Human being "must be overcome." We must seek to move beyond our own self-sanctification, the tendency to make human being the only important and lasting being on the earth. We must resist the tendency to put human being in the place of God. Human being is not substance, it is movement, becoming. Zarathustra speaks of this, of course, more poetically: "What is great about human beings is that they are a bridge and not a purpose."[32] Zarathustra enters the town preparing for the performance of the tightrope walker. Significantly, the tightrope walker's solitude echoes Zarathustra's own.

However, the particularities of Nietzsche's philosophy are, ultimately, taken by Simondon to confirm his own purpose, the defining of transindividuality. And death? While it confirms its affective power, it is not the consummation of solitude. This is important to remember. After the tightrope walker falls and lies shattered on the ground, the crowd in the market place abandons him, where just moments before it had cheered him and impatiently jeered Zarathustra. The crowd only concerns itself with the tightrope walker for as long as he carries out his function of entertaining. Once he fails, falling to his death or at least nearly so, the crowd loses interest. His suffering makes him incompatible with the crowd's beliefs and morality, which in turn protects the crowd from witnessing the tightrope walker's fate.

"For mankind I am still a midpoint between a fool and a corpse," Zarathustra suggests.[33] The fool must be laughed at, cheered; it is his function. The corpse, dismissed, ignored; that is its function. It is therefore important that the tightrope walker, once he falls, is neither corpse nor fool; he is rather, at this moment, "between" these two individualized states, purely a relation, a bridge and without a purpose in becoming-corpse. Zarathustra feels an "absolute and profound fraternity" with the tightrope walker and sits beside him through the night while he dies. Zarathustra then carries his corpse out of town, pursued by the jester who ridicules him, until he finds a hollow tree, a "sepulture" in which to place the dead body. Then it dawns on Zarathustra: "I need companions, and living ones – not dead companions and corpses that I carry with me wherever I want." He seeks companions, fellow creators "who will write new values on new tablets."[34] Simondon writes, "it is with solitude, in Zarathustra's presence to this dead friend abandoned by the crowd, that the trial of transindividuality begins" (155).

What Nietzsche describes as the aspiration "to climb on his own shoulders" is, in fact, the act of all men who look to the trial of solitude as the test for discovering transindividuality. "Now, Zarathustra does not discover in his solitude a creator God," Simondon writes, "but, instead, the pantheistic presence of a world under the control of the eternal recurrence" (156). Embracing the eternal return requires Zarathustra to call into question the signification that determines the human being's coherency as subject facing the world; it is an ontological entitlement fixed in our consciousnesses by knowledge, morality, and the prevalent social norms of the market place. And so, when the animals speak to Zarathustra, they call for a new teaching: "You teach that there is a great year of becoming, a monster of a great year; like an hourglass it must turn itself over anew, again and again, so that it runs down and runs out anew."[35] In teaching this lesson, Zarathustra is continually tested. Solitude rehearses Zarathustra's becoming-earth, for the self-overcoming of the individual being, affirming, as a result, his need for companions who embrace their destiny. *Ünbermensch* is a transformed form of transindividuality realized.

Igor Krtolica argues that what draws Simondon's attention in the encounter between the tightrope walker and Zarathustra is the devaluation of functionalism, its being revealed as more harmful than beneficial for determining relations between individuals, resulting in Zarathustra's "painful disindividuation." Still, disindividuation is not primarily negative. Indeed, quite the contrary; Nietzsche's parable shows us its positivity and, indeed, as provisionally implicated in the transindividual event, "it constitutes the condition of a new individuation in the collective."[36]

As I previously mentioned, Simondon argues that inter-individuality hides the fundamental role of pre-individual reality in effectuating the transindividual. Indeed, he calls inter-individuality a "function of mis-recognition." Thus, we can say, "a first encounter between the individual and transindividual reality is necessary, and this encounter can only be an exceptional event, exteriority presenting aspects of a revelation" (156). And so, for this reason, only an exceptional event like the tightrope walker's fall can reveal the inter-individual relation for what it is: a social function imposed on the subject, concealing its "more-than-individuality."

Although the inter-individual relationship pretends that constituted individuals or the socially instituted group defines it, in reality it is the effect of the pre-individual nature persisting but not yet effectuated in them. Here is where we find a being's "more-than-individuality." And only the transindividual domain, which exceeds the inter-individual identities and the culture that conserves them, provides the condition for its being recaptured: disindividuations, which "consist in a positive emotion that assures the passage to the transindividual."[37] How? With disindividuation the individual is de-substantialized and nakedly stands before the potentialities constituting its being, its "more-than-individuality," beyond its subjectification, once it realizes the stake it has in the pre-individual. Solitude, therefore, is the necessary and purely positive affect for this passage to transindividuality, defined by its being provisional, for only once traversed might the transindividual be achieved; and so, in this sense, *solitude is meant* to be overcome, its role is preparatory, to ready the individual for *subjectivation* by inviting an antecedent disindividuation, priming the movement into the collective. "Beyond the individual, solitude; beyond solitude, the collective."[38] Solitude prepares Zarathustra for the never-ending task of searching for "fellow creators."

SPLIT PERSONALITY: FROM COGITO TO SOUL

An odd moment occurs near the conclusion of Chapter 3, Part I of IPC. Here appears, with little or no preparation, Simondon's extended discussion of dissociative personality disorder, colloquially known as "split personality" disorder. Why? Initially, it is difficult to know what to do with it, especially given that it follows his fascinating "tightrope walker" analysis. We must be careful here. We must fight our first inclination to blame its placement on a lapse in editorial license. If we compare IPC with the larger IL, it is clear this is unfair and inaccurate. Despite the fact that this discussion seems to appear out of nowhere, in fact it is anticipated by his investigating the problem of the normal and the pathological; but, additionally, his rethinking of Descartes' method and the formation of the cogito and, finally, his criticism of Bergson, whose thought he argues remains incapable of addressing mental disorders (148), lay the ground-work for his addressing philosophically "split personality." The question we need to ask ourselves is how the psychological formulation "split personality" overlaps with Simondon's research on transindividuality. In other words, might this disorder provide psychology and philosophy with a point of coincidence to speak to the transindividual?

Although Simondon acknowledges that the split personality is a "very clear pathology," there exists, nevertheless, "an aspect of research of spirituality which cannot help but be considered splitting," that is to say, the very act or process of what it means to split, to double. Spiritually, the Manichaeistic separation of good and evil into angel and beast morally and socially symbolizes in external form, according to Simondon, the internal duality constitutive of the psychological self. Self-hatred transmutes itself into hatred of the Evil Demon.

Simondon's preference for Pierre Janet over Sigmund Freud is based on his belief that the former remains closest to the reality of the "transindividual nature of the unconscious" and is able to more accurately formulate the split personality disorder, as a result, by grasping, *as an operation*, the unconscious more dynamically. From Janet's perspective, rather than a personality "split," it would be better to speak of *doubling* or even the multiplication of personality. Janet asks us to consider the split personality as the creation of "personality-phantoms." "It is not actual personality which splits itself but another personality, an equivalent of personality, which constitutes itself outside of the field of the 'I' as a virtual image constitutes itself beyond a mirror, for the observer, without it being real" (166). This genesis of the pathology is not a defensive reaction to the feeling of alienation, it is the reflection of "the absence of the transindividual," Simondon writes (162).

Rather than a subject's personality splitting, there is a "decentering" of the referential system, forcing the subject, as a result, into recentering itself around new values to match the more base level of existence (162). "Here we find an essential asymmetrical relationship, and the substantialist ideas of two natures (good and evil) are still too close to a symmetrical scheme" (163).

DESCARTES' MEMORY AND SOUL

In the light of Simondon's adapting Janet's formulation of the problem of split personality, Simondon does something quite surprising: he takes this reformulation of the split personality and applies it to his interpretation of Descartes. We recall, of course, that Descartes' meditations are predicated on demolishing all prior epistemological and metaphysical foundations which are found to be inadequate for establishing the definite stable basis for constituting clear and distinct ideas. This is what motivates his method of hyperbolic doubt: to test received opinions, beliefs, and unexamined judgments, to open oneself to reason's true light. On this basis only is a true "first philosophy" possible. Simondon makes no pretense nor feigns false modesty when he, subsequently, couples the goal of ontogenesis with the challenge put to Descartes (and rationalism more generally): "According to this perspective, ontogenesis would be the point of departure for philosophical thought; it would truly be the *first philosophy*, anterior to the theory of knowledge and to an ontology that follows from the theory of knowledge" (163, my italics).[39]

Simondon's primary objective in interpreting Descartes is to illustrate the genesis of the conditions of validity of thought in the subject, which are not identical to those of the genesis of the individuated subject. The human subject's genesis, thus, is separate and anterior to the genesis of thought. The cogito, including the methodological doubt preceding it and "I think therefore I am," which results from the application of this doubt, does not constitute a "true genesis of the individuated subject: the subject of doubt must be anterior to the doubt" (164). The cogito "approaches" but never fully grasps the conditions of individuation since it makes the condition for ending doubt the subject's turning inward: "the subject grasps itself at once as doubting being and object of its own doubt" (164).

Simondon crucially points out that doubt is not simply a method. It is the privileged "operation" that "objectifies in the operation of doubt the doubting subject" (164). Between doubt doubting and doubt doubted, a relation of distance is constituted through which the continuity of the doubting operation is maintained. The subject recognizes its responsibility as subject of the doubt. And yet this doubt, once it achieves a new objective reality, detaches itself in becoming the object of a new doubt.

Memory incarnates this operation's continuity: it is simultaneously an operation of distance and reattachment.[40] As an operation, doubt must be transductive.

> Memory is the realization of distance, gaining of objectivity without alienation. It is an extension of the limits of the subjective system, which gains an internal

duality without cutting or separation: it is alterity and identity progressing together, forming themselves, and distinguishing themselves in the same movement. The memory's content becomes symbol of the present "I"; it is the other part; the progress of memory is an asymmetrical splitting of the subject being, an *individualization of the subject being.* (164, my italics)

Interpreting Descartes' conception of memory in terms of its providing the present "I" with its "associated milieu," for Simondon, "is the unity of the being as totality." Memory provides the "I" with the means for integrating this doubling of the personality that happens in psychological disassocia-tion disorder so that unity can be re-subsumed into the being. Descartes, not Janet, not Freud, more usefully addresses this disorder. How? Because it is Descartes who conceives memory, so that it ensures that the "I" is already "more-than-individual."[41] Descartes' privileging of nascent memory on the basis of its more directly revealing the subject's existence proves, according to Simondon, that the subject's substantial unity is established through the relationship of reciprocity between the doubt that *has just been* (*vient d'être*), just occurred, and *actual* doubt, "which *is* pres-ently (*actuellement*) in the middle of constituting itself" (166).

It is well known that the most damning criticism leveled against Descartes is the charge of logical circularity of argument. Simondon neither ignores nor seeks an apology for Descartes' logically irresolvable error. Instead, he ingeniously argues that if the imperative for clear and distinct ideas is to be satisfied, directing the unique relationship Descartes sets up between the operation of thought (the activity of doubt) and its structures (cogito, God, truth, *res cogitans* and *res extensa*), then the circu-larity of reasoning provides the basis for its own indispensability. And so, it is not a criticism of Cartesian circularity that Simondon offers but, rather, the disclosing of the fact that its operational (and thus, *substantializing*) imperative is required by the internal circular logic of its project.[42]

The return to a purely reflexive subjectivity is accomplished via a method of doubt unequivocally beholden to its being conditioned by and, indeed, reaffirming the consistency and unity of individuated being – that is, the cogito. And it is here that Simondon locates the "failure" of Cartesian circularity. No allowance is made for the "nascent distance" between *actualized* doubt, becoming the object of memory, and the ante-rior *actualizing* doubt (167). It is the difference between doubt as structure and doubt as operation which, as we have seen, is a fundamental relation-ship in Simondon's philosophy. Hence, for Simondon, individuation is never completed, it is only ever in the midst of making itself: "there is still more than the actual subject, insofar as there is distance between *doubt* and '*I*'" (167). For Descartes, this is not the case; the problem of individuation is avoided by the simple fact that it is prevented from being raised from the beginning. It is precluded from being raised because it is formulated from the beginning as originating from the individuated being. There is nothing left, nothing is left over, it has already been fully individuated. The Cartesian circle presumes this distance closed by the reflexive nature of the cogito. Reflexivity forms homogeneity and unity at the very center of the soul.

Yet, despite his critique of Descartes' substantialist metaphysic and the privilege granted to the individual epistemologically and ontologically (in the form of the cogito), Simondon finds a precursor in Descartes. In "L'histoire de la notion d'individu," more so than in IPC proper, Simondon reveals his admiration for and mistrust of Descartes more directly. We are able to see how closely Simondon wants to situate his own philosophy relative to Descartes when he claims that his most profound and novel contribution lies in his employing a mode of thought that raises to the level of actual being what "we would call today information." Simondon suggests that what we call information Descartes calls "the objective reality of the idea." As it was defined previously, information is that by which the incompatibility, the tension between at least two disparate realities of the non-resolved system, reaches the resolving organizing dimension. It is at that point that information becomes signification, emerging through the operation of individuation. Information is the form time assumes in the operation of individuation, the time it takes for signification to emerge. Further, Simondon continues: "In making of information a reality, Descartes gives to the individual the role of an operator (*ouvrier*) of information; this operator has limited forces, and recognizes an anterior and superior being to himself when he discovers a work of information that he cannot have made himself" (IL 440). Descartes' overarching method foregrounds its own limitation, but this is only because it places the greatest emphasis on its own operational being. "Descartes privileged in the individual the operatory aspect of constructive thought, and more generally everything operatory" (IL 441). The operation of thought, at least in the case of Descartes, takes the form of the activity of reflexivity.

Whether Descartes intended it or not, by the emphasis he places on the operationality of thought he requires thought to reflect upon the temporality that its own action commands. What is consciousness except the temporality of the operation of individuation, which determines its existence? In the operationality disclosed by Descartes in thought, time and the "I think" no longer stand incompatibly and incomparably at odds; they are brought together transductively.

"[Time] applies to ontogenesis and is ontogenesis itself" (IL 33). It is because of the memory and the imagination that the individual becomes individuated. These two faculties bring about and express the temporality of this individuation: the pure soul is the "present," while the pure body is "the soul infinitely past or infinitely distanced into the future" (169). Body and soul are the emerging figments, only partially revealing time but, nonetheless, intimating the vaster and more indeterminate temporality of their individuation. Idiosyncratic, admittedly, but nonetheless brilliantly suggestive, Simondon interprets Descartes' enacting of the radical estrangement of the body from the soul as, in fact, the precursor to a "new somatic reality."

> Consciousness is thus the mediation between two corporeal becomings – the soul and the body's ascending movement toward the present and the descending movement starting from the present. One could say that this movement of becoming, proceeding stage by stage, is transductive. The true scheme of real transduction is time, passage from state to state which is made by the very nature of the states, by their content and not by a scheme exterior to their succession: conceived thus, time is movement of being, real modification, reality which modifies and is modified, being at once what it leaves and what it takes, real, insofar as relational to the milieu of two states; to be of the passage, passing reality, reality as it passes, such is the transductive reality. (169)

"Individuated being is the one for which exists this ascent and descent of becoming in relationship to the central present. *There is only the living and psychic individuated being insofar as it assumes time*" (169, my italics). Time is the movement of being. The "I" modifies and is modified, transformed. The nature of this movement is transductive. Transductivity is the form of movement the operation takes and, as such, is synonymous with time. The relation of the individual and the milieu justifies rejection of any attempt either on the part of Cartesians (or, for that matter, Descartes himself) to give to the soul substance, "for the soul does not possess in itself all its reality" (171). The individuated being has a "soul," it expresses time as internal to the outcome of any one particular living individuated state of being. For "the present is the operation of individuation. The present is not a permanent form; it occurs as form in operation, it finds form in individuation" (171). The present, therefore, achieves "presence" as the event's signification or meaning emerges; the transductive operation reaches the phase constituting the relationship between the past and the future. Simondon refers to this event as a "double symbolization," where a unitary form (no less precariously impermanent) is presented as both the effective individual and its catalytic milieu. Simondon revises the notion of the soul (as was suggested earlier in this chapter): it is "the presence of the organism" (171–2) – that is to say, it is wholly and completely purely expressive of the temporality of individuation; it *is* time.

The soul is conceived as what perpetuates the first operation of individuation that the being expresses and integrates because it results from it, but contains it and prolongs it, so although the genesis that made it being is truly its genesis, the soul intervenes as extension of this unity . . . [the soul] is presence to this symbol of the individual; it is at the very center of the individual, but it is also that by which it remains attached to what cannot be individual. (172)

There is no organism to which individuation is first; rather, one is only able to live "in being an organism which organizes and organizes itself in time" (171). Again, the issue is time or the temporality *constituted in* and *constituting of* individuation. "To live is to have a presence, to be present in relation to oneself (*soi*) and by relation to what is outside of self (*hors de soi*)" (171). The temporality of individuation determines the psychosomatic to be both somatic and social, for the relation of the present to the past and to the future is, for Simondon, analogous to the somato-psychic and "this other vaster relation of the complete individuated being to the world of other individuated beings" (171).

NOTES

1. Cf. Judith Butler, *Gender Trouble: Feminism and the Subversion of Identity*, Thinking Gender (New York: Routledge, 1990). Also, Judith Butler, *Excitable Speech: A Politics of the Performative* (New York and London: Routledge, 1997).
2. This is part of the text of a speech Sojourner Truth delivered at a woman's convention in 1852. Shirley W. Logan, *With Pen and Voice: A Critical Anthology of Nineteenth-Century African-American Women* (Carbondale: Southern Illinois University Press, 1995).
3. "Two things fill the mind with ever new and increasing admiration and awe the more often and more enduringly reflection is occupied with them: the starry heavens above me and the moral law within me." Immanuel Kant, "Critique of Practical Reason," trans. Mary J. Gregor, in *Practical Philosophy*, ed. Mary J. Gregor (Cambridge: Cambridge University Press, 1996), 269.
4. Plato, "Symposium," trans. Alexander Nehamas and Paul Woodruff, in *Plato on Love: Lysis, Symposium, Phaedrus, Alcibiades, with Selections from Republic, Laws*, ed. C.D.C. Reeve (Indianapolis: Hackett, 2006), 208e–209e.
5. Cf. particularly the third essay "What Do Ascetic Ideals Mean?" in Nietzsche's *On the Genealogy of Morality*.
6. Simondon borrows from St Augustine the Latin expressions to support the assertion that an appeal is made sometimes to a superior and exterior force and sometimes to profound depth of interiority, illustrated by *In te redi; in interior homine habitat voluntas* (Truth is indwelling is us) (*De Vera Relig.* XXXIX) and by *Deus interior intimo meo, Deus superior superrimo meo* (God who is more interior to me than I am to myself) (*Confessions*, III.6.11).

7. Gilles Deleuze and Félix Guattari, *What Is Philosophy?*, trans. Hugh Tomlinson and Graham Burchell (New York: Columbia University Press, 1994), 45.
8. Pierre Macherey, *Hegel or Spinoza*, trans. Susan M. Ruddick (Minneapolis: University of Minnesota Press, 2011).
9. Cleanthes, "the wicked man is like a dog tied to a cart" – an image of moral determinism.
10. *Ethics* IVP4Dem
11. Here I am essentially borrowing Badiou's critique of Deleuze's metaphysics. Cf. Alain Badiou, *Deleuze: The Clamor of Being*, Theory out of Bounds (Minneapolis: University of Minnesota Press, 2000).
12. Deleuze and Guattari, *A Thousand Plateaus*, 20–1. Simondon's presence is explicitly and implicitly apparent throughout this work.
13. Gilles Deleuze, "Dualism, Monism, Multiplicities," lecture, March 26, 1973.
14. Chateau writes, "we catch a glimpse of how the allagmatic point of view leads to considering all reality not only as structure but as *self-individuating being*, and all individuated being not as a given substance, statically subsisting, but as becoming, relation, operation, ontogenesis." Chateau, *Le Vocabulaire de Gilbert Simondon*, 14.
15. Georges Canguilhem, *Knowledge of Life*, trans. Stefanos Geroulanos and Daniela Ginsburg (New York: Fordham University Press, 2008), 131–2.
16. Therefore, rather than a duality of the normal and the pathological, which imposes a logical and social categorization on the vital, Canguilhem proposes an organism's "health." Simultaneity and successiveness are brought into relation, leading to the engendering of new norms: it is "the capacity to tolerate variations in norms on which only the stability of situations and milieus – seemingly guaranteed yet in fact always necessarily precarious – confers a deceptive value of definitive normalcy." Canguilhem, *Knowledge of Life*, 132.
17. Canguilhem, *Knowledge of Life*, 132, my italics.
18. Canguilhem, *Knowledge of Life*, 133.
19. "In reality, as in every domain of transductivity, there is in the psychological individual the entailment of a reality, at once continuous and multiple" (148–9).
20. "The dialectical relation of the individual to the world is transductive because it deploys a homogeneous and heterogeneous world, consistent and continuous but diversified, which neither belongs to physical nature nor life but to this universe in the midst of its constitution, which we might call 'spirit' [*esprit*: mind]. Now, this universe constructs the transductivity of life and the physical world by knowledge and action; it is the reciprocity of knowledge and action which permits this world to constitute itself not only as a mixture but as a veritable transductive relation" (152–3).
21. "The inquietude in vital security marks the advent of psychological individuality, or at least its possibility of existence" (160).
22. Simondon argues, as a result, that the nature of psychological individuality is essentially "dialectical." Does this mean that we must relegate the psychological to the role of negating action? In other words, must we see the psychological

as wholly negative? Yet it is the *anteriority* that Simondon assigns it that must give us pause, for this invites us to question whether or not he understands the dialectic in an orthodox manner. Simondon's conception of a psychic individuation supposes the existence of a pre-individual reality, a metastable system rich in potentials and, thus, conserving and indeed nurturing within itself, though indeterminate, the primordial individuation of being. Hegel rejects Spinoza on the grounds that real determination is impossible if one posits an absolute positivity of indeterminateness, anterior to the determined being. Simondon's "dialectic" denies the negative any functional role; his dialectic is without synthesis. Simondon's dialectic is of the problem, of the irresolvable *problematic*; it must be distinguished from the opposing of representations, made to coincide in an identity as the final act of negation. Problems are not givens but ideal "objecticities" that find within pre-individual reality their own sufficiency and acts of constitution, their pure potentiality for becoming.

23. Simondon gives a strict definition of "culture" in IPC 250.
24. Muriel Combes, "La Vie inespérée: vie et sujet entre biopouvoir et politique," these de doctorat, Universite Paris 8–Vincennes Saint-Denis, 2002, 171, 206–31. Combes brilliantly develops Simondon's conception of "spirituality" and compares it with Foucault's later work.
25. Combes, "La Vie inespérée," 172.
26. Henri Bergson, *The Two Sources of Morality and Religion*, trans. R. Ashley Audra and Cloudesley Brereton, with the assistance of W. Horsfall Carter (Notre Dame, IN: University of Notre Dame Press, 1977), 119.
27. Bergson, *The Two Sources of Morality and Religion*, 55.
28. Bergson, *The Two Sources of Morality and Religion*, 55.
29. "The only conceivable manner in which others can have for me the sense and status of existent others, thus and so determined, consists in their being constituted *in me* as others." Edmund Husserl, *Cartesian Meditations: An Introduction to Phenomenology*, trans. Dorion Cairns (Dordrecht and London: Kluwer Academic, 1999), 128.
30. Friedrich Wilhelm Nietzsche, *Thus Spoke Zarathustra: A Book for All and None*, trans. Adrian Del Caro (Cambridge and New York: Cambridge University Press, 2006), 11–12.
31. Nietzsche, *Thus Spoke Zarathustra*, 3.
32. Nietzsche, *Thus Spoke Zarathustra*, 7.
33. Nietzsche, *Thus Spoke Zarathustra*, 12.
34. Nietzsche, *Thus Spoke Zarathustra*, 14.
35. Nietzsche, *Thus Spoke Zarathustra*, 178.
36. Igor Krtolica, "The Question of Anxiety in Gilbert Simondon," trans. Jon Roffe, in *Gilbert Simondon: Being and Technology*, ed. Alex Murray, Arne De Boever, Jon Roffe, and Ashley Woodward (Edinburgh: Edinburgh University Press, 2012), 84.
37. Krtolica, "The Question of Anxiety in Gilbert Simondon," 85.
38. Krtolica, "The Question of Anxiety in Gilbert Simondon," 85.
39. This brief paragraph is more thoroughly addressed in the introduction.

40. The distinction between memory and imagination resides in the fact that the principle of the encounter between the "I" and the symbol of the "I" aligns itself on a dynamic tendency of the "I," in the imagination, while in memory the principle of their encounter is in the symbol of the "I": in both instances, there is a symbolization, but in the operation of memory, the symbol is the complement of the "I" for the individual and "I" for the milieu; whereas, in the imagination, it is the "I" that is individual and the symbol of the "I" that is milieu (165).

41. "The being that remembers is more than the 'I'; it is more than individual; it is the individual more than some other thing" (165). And so Simondon finds that Descartes, if read ontogenetically, has a way to "cure" the problem of split personality, to invent a doubled non-actual or *virtual* "*contre*-moi" (counter-"I") (165).

42. "Circularity is a limit-case; already the distance exists necessarily for the circularity to exist; but the circularity recovers and dissimulates the distance; this is why Descartes is able to substantialize what is not properly speaking a substance, to know (*savoir*) an operation: the soul is defined as *res* and as *cogitans*, supports of operation and operation in the midst of completing itself. Now, the unity and homogeneity of this being constitutes a support and an operation that can only be affirmed as far as the being–operation ensemble continues to perpetuate itself according to the same mode. If the activity stops or appears to stop, the permanence of the identity of the substance thus defined is threatened: hence, the problem of sleep and ruin of consciousness in Descartes, relative to the conception of the nature of the soul" (166).

5

The Individual and the Social, the Individuation of the Group

SOCIAL TIME AND INDIVIDUAL TIME

A society does not originate with the individual. Society is composed neither of an ensemble of individuals nor some kind of "substantial reality superimposed over individual beings." Rather, Simondon describes a society as that which permits being to come into presence. For this reason, Simondon describes society as a form of pure time. It structures the temporality of individualized being; it gives to the individual a *presence present* in the world. For Simondon, a society establishes a correlation between the past and the future. As a result, it projects upon the individual a sense of existential permanence; as Simondon writes, "permanence is the stability of a becoming" (175). And as such, the societal individual is only ever a repetition of a society's past deeds and future possibilities: "it bears within the past burden and reticulates future burdens." The individual being attains his or her present presence ("here and now" – *hic et nunc*), therefore, from the society he or she belongs to, as a result of that society's temporalizing the individual being, giving to him or her a temporal structure which ensures a presence in the world now (in the present). Further, whatever feeling of permanence and durability a societal individual has society donates to the individuated individual, as a result of its prolonging and perpetuating the operation of individuation, preserving within a share of pre-individual reality. Society *renders the individual present* through the system of states and roles through which its behavior must pass, even as the individual furnishes that self-same system with a presence. According to Simondon, "the agreement of the individual and society is constituted by the coincidence of two reticulations, and the individual is obliged to project his future toward this social network which is already there" (176).

126

Accordingly, Simondon has two senses in mind when describing the "operationality" of individuation: first, it describes the temporality of individuation, its movement *in time*, as being is formed into presence "here and now." Secondly, because the operation is responsible for structuring a temporal dimension, it provides the condition necessary for bringing into presence more complex beings than the individuated being. Indeed, Simondon claims that now we have finally reached the point where to say individuation is operational is to say that the primary mode for disclosing individuation is societal or, really, a "more complex mode of presence": in other words, the transindividual.

The individuation determining the society does not exhaust the entirety of pre-individual reality. The society and the individual maintain themselves within a regime of metastability, so that a share of pre-individuality is transported by the individual and constitutive of the society. This pre-individuality associated with individual acts Simondon identifies as the source of future metastable states and the potential engendering of new individuations. Time is internal to every living individual being; it is the internal sense, reflecting externally the interior problematic. "The living is at once more and less than the unity comports *an interior problematic* and is able to *enter as an element into a problematic vaster than its own being*" (IL 28–9). Time constitutes the very structure of the human individual's subjectivity. The "interior problematic" Simondon describes is, in fact, time, which is internal to every living being and "vaster" than the human individual's own being. Only our grasping of the operation of individuation lets us glimpse the form time gives itself. What is that form? Simondon has labeled it transduction.

The socialized subject, therefore, is a category of the transindividual – the vaster problematic. For the subject is nothing more than the operation of relating two individuations, psychic and collective, reciprocally determined and, as such, *in time* and *of time*, conditioned and conditioning, "a veritable operation of individuation beginning from a pre-individual reality, associated with individuals and capable of constituting a new problematic having its own metastability" (IL 29). A society is living time; its share of pre-individuality ensures revolutionary potential and promises ontological transformation. Society is wholly a temporal figment, the threshold between the individual and the group.

BERGSON'S OPEN AND CLOSED SOCIETIES

Before continuing my analysis of IPC, it might be useful to summarize the main points of Henri Bergson's *The Two Sources of Morality and Religion*. It is my contention that Simondon's IPC takes Bergson's work to be its philosophical antecedent, but not a totally agreeable one. Bergson's work affords Simondon the opportunity to speculate and produce his own concepts against it, although he agrees with the primary and directing goal of creating a more expansive and profound notion of humanity. It is a notion that transforms the idea of the human to reflect the initial ambition "more metaphysical than moral in its essence."[1] So while Simondon only briefly and somewhat obliquely addresses Bergson's work, we should be wary of underplaying its significance for IPC.

After Simondon foregrounds the relationship of individual and society on the basis of their temporal reciprocity, it would not seem improper for us to find a point of engagement between Simondon's IPC and Bergson's *The Two Sources of Morality and Religion*. Not surprisingly, perhaps, Simondon rejects Bergson's approach out of hand. Still, this does not mean that their ways of articulating the problem are incompatible, nor should we merely dismiss the notion that Simondon's own approach reflects a negotiation with Bergson's. For rather than fully rejecting Bergson *tout court*, it would be more accurate to say that Simondon rethinks the central distinction at the heart of Bergson's work.

> The individual and society are implied in each: individuals make up society by their grouping together; society shapes an entire side of individuals by being prefigured in each one of them. The individual and society thus condition each other, circle-wise.[2]

Our natural social instinct, "a force of unvarying direction, which is to the soul what force of gravity is to the body," attains two forms: the closed society and the open society. The closed society is solely concerned with its own survival, its own justification for existence, with each member composing it indifferent to the larger humanity. The open society embraces the very idea and reality of humanity. Where a closed society stands in "perpetual readiness for battle" against anyone or anything, including Nature, considered a threat to the society's subsistence, an open society invites a new relationship to Nature. In either instance, the cohesion of the group results from bending individual wills toward an end. Or we should say, "moral obligation" is the external institution of the internal and individualized force of the psychosocial instinct, exerting a pressure that drives us, despite ourselves, collectively together. In a closed society, religion is its apotheosis.

"Between the society in which we live and humanity in general there is, we repeat, the same contrast as between the closed and the open."[3] Between any particular nation-state and "humanity," Bergson argues, is the distance between the finite and the indefinite, the closed and the open. For this reason, an open society, such as he defines it, while acknowledging the instinctual conditions of its genesis, nonetheless seeks to transcend individualism; and to do that it must maintain within itself a degree of vital indefiniteness carried by the impetus it bears within itself. It must also ensure that an individual society remains dynamic, creative, open. "What we need are new reserves of potential energy – moral energy."[4] In this way, an open society lays the groundwork for a "dynamic" religion to counter a closed society's "static" religion.

Thus, "What is specifically religious in religion?" Bergson asks. In the end, it is how the social demand is grasped, infra-rationally or supra-rationally: in short, sociability. Or rather, we grasp the difference between a static morality ingrained in customs and a dynamic morality, which expresses the impetus related to life more generally, experienced supra-rationally in social demand. Hence, a society requires a new, higher individuality, expressive of dynamic morality, to encompass both the vital and the social: a new spiritualism of humanity. For Bergson, this idea of humanity achieves its purest and most absolute form in the ideal of democracy.[5] It genetically reflects, without denial, the vital and natural imperatives compelling individuals, while at the same time ensuring a search for obligations on the basis of an expansive notion of humanity, necessary if a society is to harmonize often-competing desires.

THE GROUP AND THE INDIVIDUAL

Any overtures made toward bringing together individuated beings is made on the basis of their respective temporalities, their respective pasts and futures, more so than by any pre-constituted identities or unities. The individual being seeks a relationship of *belongingness*, each individual being searching for "the ensemble of other beings not subjects but a reticular structure through which it must pass" (177). Hence, for Simondon, the social operates at a temporal "limit" between the individual and the group – extending the limits of the "I" to the frontier between "in-group" of shared temporalities and the "out-group" by constituting the reticulated structure of time.[6] A social scheme has a temporal structure that extends the limits of the self to the frontier distinguishing the in-group and the out-group. The development of "personality" marks the extension of this limit. So, for example, religious communities organizing themselves around belief, as a mode of membership in a group, represents the expansion of personality, that is, a scheme of incorporation, setting the boundaries for the in-group. The form of belief provides the non-structured tendency for an individual's membership in the "group of interiority," providing the individual with a *futural* presence. "[Belief] conflates with the individual future, but it also assumes the past of the individual, for the individual gives itself an origin in this group of interiority, real or mythic: he or she is of this group and for this group; future and past are simplified, brought to a state of elementary purity" (179).

> The integration of the individual to the social is done by the creation of a functional analogy between the operation defining the individual presence and the operation defining the social presence; the individual must find a social individuation that recovers its personal individuation – its relation to the in-group and its relation to the out-group are one and other, like the future and the past; the in-group is the source of virtualities of tensions, like the individual future; the "in-group" is a reservoir of presence by which it precedes the individual in the encounter with the group of exteriority; it represses the exterior group. (178)

We must be careful here. Simondon is not suggesting that all groups merely reflect the so-called "cult of personality," whereby a group revolves around a single individual. Instead, each individualized personality is itself "the individuation of an individuated being." For this reason any one individuated being, in belonging to a group, embodies a particular schema of temporality and, thus, a psychic structure which maintains, as a result, "the coherence of the individuation and permanent process of individualization" (IL 277).

Any one individual being's participation in a group is "affected with a certain precariousness" (179). But from where does this precariousness stem? It stems from its being constituted only ever in relation to some other potential being; its being is purely relational. And, subsequently, it maintains within itself, as the condition for any new individuation, a share of pre-individual reality. The precariousness of the human individual being describes its potentiality as only ever socialized, which directly corresponds to the relationality that engenders it and, at the same time, to its metastable being. This is why Simondon argues that it is difficult to put the social and the individual into direct opposition, except in the most extreme theoretical cases, such as certain lived pathological situations. Simondon stresses, "the true social is not substantial, for the social is not a term of relation: *it is a system of relations, a system which comports a relation and nurtures it*" (179, my italics). The social is a "network of relations." As such, the "interiority of the group" is a certain dimension of the individual personality, fundamentally metastable, rather than some other distinct term. The interiority of the group serves as a zone of participation for the individual. And it is through it that the individuated individual remains inextricably attached to the pre-individual (obviously, pre-societal) reality.

From a more expansive perspective, we see that Simondon conceives the relation between group and individual at the psychosocial level, in terms of transindividuality, as a response to the difference between "genesis" and "structure," which phenomenology and structuralism, on differing grounds, use to justify their respective practices. Simondon distances himself from both by first reformulating "genesis" as "operation," transduction. Genesis is said to structure itself through the ontological complementarity presenting time's operation, a time internal to the genesis of individuation, in relation to the ordinal genesis of structure. Simondon further distances himself from phenomenology and structuralism by proposing that it is *relation* which constitutes the group and the individual, both respectively and reciprocally; and for this reason, relation realizes the "value of being" in the ontology of relation.

PSYCHOLOGISM AND SOCIOLOGISM

Psychologism fails because it supposes that inter-group relations are mere extensions of the relation between the individual and the interiority of the group. Simondon argues that we are left with the illusion of identification between these relations, insofar as this illusion misrecognizes the proper nature of the social relation, since "it misrecognizes the frontier of relational activity between the group of interiority and the group of exteriority" (179). So interiority is reified, let us say, in terms of the cogito or ego, which becomes the starting point for philosophical interrogation, re-duplicated at the social level because it supposedly reflects at the level of subjective identity the unity of all faculties related to a external form of being. By contrast, Simondon seems to suggest that a vital non-resemblance maintains the relationship of the interiority of the group to the conditioned exteriority of inter-group relations. Indeed, it is in this non-resemblance that one discovers the *genitality* of the social object: its problematic being.

Simondon rejects sociologism, on the other hand, because it wants to substantialize social life rather than recognize the relational character of social activity (180). Both psychology and sociology share this mistake of fabricating the social on the basis of presupposing an absolute starting point in either pure interiority (in the form of an inter-psychological schema) or pure exteriority (by the sociological presumption of a social substantialist being). The individual being, as a result, is turned into no more than a figment of these domains, each exceeding the individual existence (180). In other words, each surreptitiously imports transcendence, denying the operational immanence at once conditioned by and conditioning the psychosocial reality of transindividuality: "the continuous individualizing individuation of the individual."[7]

The limitations of psychologism and sociologism can only be

appreciated if we look to how each approaches the analysis of "work." Combes presents some useful pages on Simondon's focus on work. Work, in fact, for Simondon, precisely marks the "frontier between the group's interiority and its exteriority" (180). The sociological attitude "encloses the pre-individual within the social," making it difficult to fully retrieve a sense of the individual reality by reconstituting it (180). From the psychological perspective, work is reduced to the effect of a series of individual needs, which can only be addressed starting from a presumed fully self-contained individual being, as if it were possible that a pure and complete individual could exist prior to its being integrated socially (180). In reducing work to individual need, a human essence is presupposed which conditions this need, clearing the way for the retrieval of discredited notions like the soul, while cynically encouraging intellectual work over manual labor.

The Marxist interpretation, which defines work in terms of the economic-political relation, Simondon contends, exemplifies sociologism perfectly: "Work substantializes as value-exchange in a social system where the individual disappears" (181). Class is the new Form that subsumes the individual for Marxism. It is work that achieves substantiality by means of a system that sacrifices the individual being to exchange-value. More positively, we can take this to be Simondon's description of capitalism's operationality. The notion of class, properly speaking, follows from the substantial being given to work, the exchange-value exteriority allocates to it. Similarly, the interiority of class, properly speaking, is no longer that of a social body coextensive with the limits of personality; instead, it too emerges out of class struggle. Thus, Marxism's overriding concern is to raise awareness of the fact that a proper understanding of class is achievable only once awareness is cultivated of the (ideological) structuring by society of a conflict "with a front line" (181).

This is yet another moment when I must pause to clarify Simondon's treatment of Marxism. So much of Simondon's work seems to draw on Marx and Marxism that one can only be perplexed that he appears to be intent on distancing himself from this kind of analysis. As we try to untangle Simondon's relationship to Marx and Marxist analysis, it appears misleading either to call him Marxist or, for that matter, to suggest that he is profoundly anti-Marxist. Really, the issue, from Muriel Combes' perspective, is that the conflict Simondon has with Marxism is to some extent manufactured from an act of willful misinterpretation on Simondon's part: the reduction of Marxism to a kind of radical economism. While clearly not truthful to Marxism, this reduction reflects a strategic maneuver, on Simondon's part, to manufacture a justification for distancing his analysis from Marxist analysis, in spite of their shared points of commonality.

Combes suggests, "at the very moment he critiques Marx, Simondon is far closer to him than he thinks."[8]

Etienne Balibar not only corrects for us the image of Marx that Simondon presents but, more importantly, he demonstrates how close Simondon's work is to a Marxist analysis and what is innovative in this approach, without distorting Marx's thought. Balibar asserts in *The Philosophy of Marx* that a true picture of "Marxism" begins with its rejecting the primacy of the individual, most particularly "the fiction of an individuality which could be defined *in itself*," from whatever perspective – biological, psychological, or economistic. As has been incessantly emphasized, this is a foundational postulate of Simondon's entire project. Similarly, Balibar argues that Marx rejects the "organicist" perspective, which defines society as one whole indivisible unity made up of distinct individuals. Both the whole and the parts are individuals, distinguished only functionally. These rejections on Marx's part require a shifting of theoretical emphasis to the "constitutive relations, which displaces the question of the human essence while, at the same time, providing a formal answer to it (and one which thus contains in embryo another problematic than that of theoretical humanism)."[9] In fact, Balibar suggests that Marx's most powerful accomplishment is the theoretical shift to relations, which he endorses. This leads to the interrogating of being from the ontogenetic perspective of an ontology of relations, displacing the ontology of substances and essences. And so, too, Marx offers us the philosophical invitation to rethink humanity "as a transindividual reality." Balibar writes, "Not what is ideally 'in' each individual (as a form or a substance), or what would serve, from outside, to classify that individual, but what exists *between individuals* by dint of their multiple interactions."[10]

And yet, interestingly, this is where we might discern Simondon's divergence from Marxism, even when they share the exact same terminological innovations. For Marxism, it is "practices" which determine being, becoming. Balibar himself says that relations are "in fact nothing other than differentiated practices, singular actions of individuals."[11] Simondon begins not from practices but from operations, or more specifically a theory of operational transformation. Simondon's Allagmatic theory has a prime goal of providing a perspective on being as operationality, that is, the grasping of being through the operation of structures converting into other structures. Operations and structures are ontological complements. Therefore, structures in themselves are not real, only their conversions are real; if what is real in beings is relation, the genesis of relationality is the operation. Operations are what constitute relations and relation is what constitutes the individual. But what is the impetus for the being of the individual as the process of its becoming individuated? Missing from

Balibar's description of relational ontology is the source or operation (relation of relation) engendering the relation itself; in other words, missing is Simondon's notion of pre-individuality, which he credits with generating relationality. Thus, while not denying human practices, they are only a mode of the operation of individuation, and, as such, modes that stabilize metastable pre-individual being. It is not individuals that create relations; individuals are themselves only relations that constitute relations.

The point of my turning to Balibar's work is not to rescue or defend Marx against Simondon's somewhat cavalier treatment. Nor is it my intention to characterize Simondon as secretly Marxist or to suggest that his thought can be read as one more tributary branching from the main river of Marx's thought. In fact, it is evident that Balibar's own reading of Marx takes certain liberties and is clearly read through the screen not only of Simondon's work (admittedly only belatedly encountered) but also post-Marxist and postmodernist concerns, not to mention his adapting the more all-embracing perspective of Spinoza (with which I have an obvious sympathy).[12] The point of turning to Balibar's work is to support my contention that Simondon does himself a great disservice by not fully exploiting a dialogue with Marx. This path will be left to others to develop, not just Balibar and Stiegler but also important Italian Marxist philosophers like Vittorio Morfino and Paolo Virno.

THE INSUFFICIENCY OF THE NOTION OF THE ESSENCE OF MAN AND ANTHROPOLOGY

Simondon composed IPC at a time when the debate concerning the human sciences and their relation to anthropology was enlivening post-war French philosophical discussions. The ground had been set by the contentious debate Husserl carried on with Heidegger. Husserl's concern is that Heidegger's privileging of human being will lead to philosophy receding back into anthropologism and psychologism. Instead of grounding itself on an unimpeachable and solid rationalist foundation, Husserl argues that Heidegger opens the way for the most "naive" objectification of human experience, relegating philosophical inquiry to nothing more than subjective reflection. Husserl advocates phenomenological methodology on the basis of its better achieving the true meaning of an interior psychology ("transcendental Ego").[13] For Husserl, Heidegger's so-called fundamental ontology, introduced via the analytic of Dasein, is nothing more than a disguised anthropology. Husserl never seemed to grasp that, for Heidegger, Dasein was precisely conceived to provide a way to avoid the concept of subjectivity, with all its accompanying metaphysical and epistemological baggage. Yet more important than the particularities of Husserl's disagreement with Heidegger is the influence this debate had on establishing the definite anti-humanist strain present throughout the French after the Second World War. Driving French anti-humanism was the belief that it provided a bulwark against the threat of anthropologism and, so, freed the human sciences to rethink human relationality in all its diverse aspects: language, economy, sexuality, culture.

It is not surprising that Simondon feels obliged to address the threat of anthropologism, especially considering the intellectual climate he was working within and his proposing an axiomatic of the human sciences. Simondon argues that philosophy must struggle against the anthropologistic tendency to substantialize either the individual or the social in support of the essence of man. Simondon does not call for an outright rejection of anthropology but rather for its reformation, the creation of a "new anthropology" that might more accurately reflect "human relational activities." In short, he seeks a study of human being which takes its cues from his relational ontology, that is, a general theory of operations (IL 559) or a "general theory of transformations" (284). In brief, if relation is the principle for anthropology, then any other type of ontology that has the starting point of an unprovable human "essence" is unrecognizable. Simondon's ontology is ontogenetic to correspond with his larger goal of proposing a different kind of humanism, one that is opposed to the substantialist and essentialist metaphysics of the previous humanism. "Being as relation is primary and must be taken *as principle*; the human is social, psychosocial, psychic, somatic, without any one of these of aspects to be taken as fundamental, while others would be judged accessories" (182).

GROUP INDIVIDUATION AND VITAL INDIVIDUATION

According to Simondon, a group's "interiority" is no more a complex structure than that of a single person. As was previously discussed, Simondon distinguishes himself both from traditional sociological and psychological theories (in addition to those inspired by Husserlian phenomenology) by arguing that any "interiority" of a group must be composed of the "superposition of individual personalities"; hence, he refuses any tendency to reduce the group formation to a simple matter of an "ensemble of individuals." Nor, for that matter, is the basis for a group's formation to be a "contract," as is the case for contract theorists (from Hobbes and Rousseau to Carol Pateman and Charles Mills), which likewise implies at least two totally pre-individuated individuals (a specifically individuated individual or specific individuated group) who are necessary for ratifying it.

Thus, we are not speaking of structures of personalities anteriorly defined, constituted, and entirely individualized prior to the moment the group of interiority constitutes itself, to encounter itself and recover itself. Each individual personality is coextensive with the "personality of the group" – that is, instead of individual personalities in joining together being constitutive of the group. The envisioning of the group in this manner avoids psychologism in two ways. First, personality is neither purely psychic nor purely psychological; it is wholly psychosomatic, including tendencies, instincts, beliefs, somatic attitudes, significations, expression. Second, and most importantly, this conception, Simondon asserts, *recovers* the individual personalities, which play a role in structuring a group's interiority, in conditioning its auto-constitution. "This recovering [of the psychosomatic level] is an individuation, the resolution of a conflict, the assumption of conflictual tensions in organic stability, structural and functional" (183).

Nonetheless, the parameters that prescribe the group's interiority emerge from a fundamental conflict, a disparity resonating throughout the group; this interiority is, in short, only ever problematic. Or, to use Simondon's term, it is "syncrystalline."[14] In other words, the group's cohesiveness and structural integrity remains only ever partially undetermined, in a state of tension like the state of the oversaturated liquid conditioning the genesis of a crystal; it is pre-individual prior to its being individuated by a process of individuation. And so this tension extends to the individual being conditioned, which, like the group, maintains within itself the precondition for its coming into being – a share of pre-individuality. Without emotion, without potential, Simondon insists, without this dynamism pledged by this preliminary tension, the individuation of the group is impossible.

It likewise follows that "an absolutely complete and perfect individual" could not enter into a group. Every individual *as* individual is a carrier of tensions, tendencies, potential structurable reality – not yet structured – "so that the group of interiority is possible; the group of interiority is born when the forces of the future received by several living individuals lead to a collective structuration . . . in this instant [there is the] individuation of the group and the individuation of individual groups" (183–4). The individuation that gives birth to the group is one and the same with the individuation of those individuals grouped. As Simondon stresses, not unaware of the fact that it might be construed as a critique of Husserl's fifth *Cartesian Meditation*: "a society of monads does not exist" (184).[15]

Every individual only ever exists as already a "*grouped* individual; *a group individual*" (185). And it is not because the group exercises some influence over individuals. As the group no longer presents itself an inter-individual (inter-subjective) reality, at once separate and dependent upon the individual, it exists more so as "the complement of a vast plane of individuation reuniting a plurality of individuals." Consequently, one is able to think this reality, but only if a "mutual convertibility of structures in operations and operations in structures" is accepted and if one accepts "relational operation as having a value of being" (185). We are obliged to think the group as anterior to the individual, instead of the individual as anterior to the group, unlike sociologism and psychologism. And because the group is nothing more than pure relationality, contrary to any desire on the part of sociologism and psychologism to ascribe to it some level of substantialism, we are left to grasp the individual's fragility within the psycho-sociological domain. It is this domain that is the transcendental, and not the inter-monadic, inter-individual, inter-subjective domain. The relation of the individual to the group is always fundamentally the same: it depends upon the simultaneous individuation of individual beings and the group. In other words, as we saw above: "It is presence" (186), that is, "living time."

The implications of Simondon's physio-biological theory of genesis fully outlined in the first part of his doctoral thesis, *L'individu et sa genèse physico-biologique*, reach fulfillment in this chapter in IPC. Finding evidence in physiology to support the rejection out of hand of any notion that societal human being exists in opposition to Nature, Simondon, instead, describes two pathways for individuation: the first, the individuation of the individual, the second, the individuation of the group.

> Everything happens as if above a specific first individuation, man sought from it another, and had need of the second individuation. Received as living in the world, it can associate itself with exploiting the world; but it still lacks something, it remains hollow, an incompletion. To exploit Nature does not satisfy to that end; what faces the world is not the group's interiority; another relation is necessary in addition that makes each man exist as a social person, and for that, this second genesis is necessary, which is the group's individuation. (189)

Once the individual being attains its individuated being, she, he or it immediately enters a "new" process of individuation, where "forces and tensions" are at play which go much further than those a person supposedly faces in nature. It is this second individuation and not the former, Simondon argues, where we might find justification for why "man thinks of himself as spiritual being." But Simondon also warns against turning the spirit into a substance, even if we feel ourselves justified, with the best of intentions, as in Descartes' somato-psychic dualism (body and mind split) (189).

Animals possess a certain "coefficient" corresponding to what Simondon describes as "spirituality," except "in a more fugitive, less stable, and less permanent manner" (190). And, hence, one might argue that the human social group is different from animal groups only to the extent that their specific adaptive responses to Nature are different.

Human social reality never divorces itself completely from the vital level. Simondon offers the example of laborers, who would only be a group if realized at its most stable level, where *living* labor maintains itself. Taking up where he left off in the previous discussion of work, Simondon argues that "living labor" makes useless the Marxist schema of superstructure conditioned by the economico-political infrastructure. Work opens the group to the nature of its own vital conditioning in the structuring operation transforming a life: "Work, is a structure or better a tension, a potential, a certain fashion of being linked to the world through activity that calls for a structuration without being a structure itself" (191). Marx reduces work to inter-individual relationships, and so gives work or labor a form that inhibits a second individuation – "it does not produce the second properly human individuation." The inter-individual relation goes from individual to individual without penetrating individuals. Marxist theory posits what it requires: an individual biologically determined "already given" (191). Simondon, by contrast, argues that "beyond these biological relations, biologico-social and inter-individual, exists another level that one could name the transindividual level: it is this level which corresponds to the groups of interiority, a veritable individuation of the group" (191).

The "second" individuation is the transindividual event, for this second individuation is reducible to neither the specific group nor the exploitation of Nature by the association of human beings. The group arising out of this second individuation as the group of action must be distinguished from the group of interiority:

> Transindividual action is what causes individuals to exist together like elements of a system comprising potentials and metastability, expectation and tension, then discovery of a structure and functional organization that integrates and resolves this problematic of incorporated immanence. The transindividual passes into the individual as from individual to individual: individual personalities congregate together by recovering and not by accumulation or specialist organization as in the biological grouping of solidarity and division of labor. In the instance of the division of labor, individuals are closed up into their biological unities, as a result of practical functions. The transindividual does not localize individuals: it makes them coincide; it is necessary to communicate individuals by significations: these are the relations of information, which are primordial, not the relations of solidarity, of functional differentiation. (192)

Transindividuality is the achievement of immanence, though of a kind that is purely operational and functional, for it brings about the attaining of signification, distinguishing itself from any conception that would attempt to define it as absolute or substantially complete. "The transindividual is with the individual but it is not the individuated individual. It is with the individual according to a more primitive relation than membership, inherence, or the relation of exteriority . . . beyond the limits of the individual" (193).

Indeed, identical to the operation that brings it into appearance, *transduction* is a structure and a structuring action, at once the form achieved, however transitory a phase, and what is necessary to engender it. As such, immanence is the means of engendering the different domains of reality and the form (now reformed) which this operation gives itself. Immanence in this sense is altogether the effect of the converting of operation into structure and structure into operation, investing into each succeeding structure from the antecedent structure that is going to be transformed the charge of pre-individuality internally resonating at the "very center of being," within each subsequent structure. This internal resonance is what spurs being toward invention. A true and absolute immanence is not one that designates the immanence "of" or "to" an individual being; rather, it is the being of the individual being, grasped entirely and only ever in the event of convertibility, of transformation. If Simondon's critique of transcendence is total, his critique of immanence is provisional. For, in short, "true" immanence dramatizes more purely the *operationality* of becoming, that is, "information" *in becoming signification* or meaningfulness. As Simondon writes (in a text delivered at a conference in 1962 but not published until 2010): "Information is not a thing but the operation of a thing arriving into a system and producing there a transformation."[16]

"The psychosocial is transindividual: it is this reality that the individuated being transports with him, this charge of being for future individuations" (193). And it is precisely the always-present charge of pre-individuality which initiates and ensures that the individuated is prepared for the second individuation, its transindividuation, when it becomes *grouped* and structured concurrently as subject. With transindividuation the individual being is individualized, subjectivized, if not necessarily subjectified. For once the group acts as milieu for the next event of individuation, a "personality" is likewise formed which comprises, after structuration, an individual aspect and a complementary aspect of this individual. This other aspect ultimately derives from the pre-individual reality, existing prior to splitting into individual beings.

In work, for example, we find a way to grasp the pure operationality of immanence: impersonal and personal, pre-individual and metastable, it expresses at once the movement of individuation and the momentary phasing of singularization at the psychosocial level, ratified as a result. Pre-individuality provides the necessary impetus of disassociation cultivated by the tension and forces it maintains, the antecedent to the division of labor, while, at the same time, the pre-individual instills in the divided laboring individual the necessity for participating in association with others. The coincidence of personalities resulting from this is not reductive because it is not based on the elimination of individual differences, nor their reduction to usefulness or the ends of functional differentiation (which would close the individual in its particularities). Instead, there is "a second structuration" whose starting point is left "unresolved" in living individuals (192).

"Life is a first individuation" (192). But this first individuation has not been able to exhaust and absorb all force.

> This is not a *vital* force; *it is pre-vital*; life is a specialization, a first solution, complete in itself but leaving a residue outside of its system. It is not as living being that man brings him what spiritually individuates, but as being, who contains in it the pre-individual and the pre-vital. This reality can be called transindividual. It has neither a social origin nor some other individual origin. It is disposed in the individual, carried by the individual, but it does not belong to it and cannot be apart of its system of being as individual. (193)

The pre-vital, pre-individual tensions and singularities expressive of purely impersonal potentialities pass into the individual, or rather, they become individual and milieu, as condition for engendering a new individuation; the "unresolved" charge of reality, still non-individuated, is the initiator for the human individual to seek out other human beings to form a group in which she or he will discover "the presence" by way of the second individuation. The second individuation "gives" or manifests "presence." This means that the individual is to be grasped as a "reserve of being" held in suspense, however momentarily (193).

THE THIRD INDIVIDUATION: THE COLLECTIVE

"The individual *is* not only itself but it *exists* as superior to itself, for it carries with it a more complete reality, which individuation has not exhausted, which is yet new and potential, animated by potentials" (194). One must not speak of the tendencies of the individual that lead toward joining the group, for these tendencies, properly speaking, do not belong to the individual *qua* individual. Rather, they are the "non-resolution of potentials that precede the genesis of the individual" (193). The individual in becoming individuated is not totally resolved in the individual and the milieu. The individual conserves the pre-individual within itself. And every individual carries with it, as a result, a kind of non-structured ground (*fond*), which provides the individual with a "point" of departure for a new individuation to originate.[17]

No longer can spirit be said to institute the communication between individual consciousnesses, or between one and another higher form of consciousness, in the way a belief system might define it. According to Simondon, we must think of it as the dimension where the "synergy and common structuration of beings" occurs (193). "It is at the level of the transindividual that spiritual significations are discovered, not at the level of the inter-individual or social" (196). Wholly ontological, spirituality directs us to the overflowing of individual limits, to grasp true immanence in the operation of the spiritual, in the transindividual and not in the individuated individual, be they priest or shaman, soul or God.[18] The individuated being bears within a possible future of relational significations to discover: "it is the pre-individual which grounds the spiritual in the collective" (196). Individuals bring with them something that can become the "collective," but which is not yet individuated into the individual. Individuals are at once animated and fixed by the group. One cannot, therefore, speak either of immanence or transcendence of spirituality in relation to the individual being. The true relation is that of the individual to the transindividual.

Simondon resolves the Cartesian psychic and somatic split by arguing that there is no such thing as a purely spiritual group, without body, without limits or attachments. The collective as individual is "psycho-somatic." Still, the collective body and collective soul separate more and more, despite the production of myths and opinions that would seek to keep them coupled to one another. Simondon claims that the aging and decadence of the group derives from this detachment of soul and body from one another (195–6).

PRE-SOCRATICS AND NATURE

As I asserted previously, Simondon's turn to the pre-Socratics is precipitated by the search for a principle of complementarity that would, on the one hand, make possible the integrating of different realities, while, on the other hand, repudiating any appeal to a universal will, most obviously in terms of God, without ignoring the successes of religion in forming relationships of complementarity – the notion of the "elected people" is the very existence of the Christian community, which I mentioned previously. Still, Simondon asserts that we must be aware of the so-called law of unintended consequences: a universalizing divine finality, or universalizing principle of sufficient reason that compensates for our interjecting inequality in the form of the relationship between the creator and created. Simondon's unwavering insistence on the relevance of the pre-Socratics for resolving the problem of individuation goes hand and hand with how

141

he conceives and responds to this problem in terms of his characterizing his own work as fundamentally a philosophy of Nature.

And what is Nature for Simondon? It is "this pre-individual reality that the individual carries." And so, in the final pages of this first chapter of the second part of IPC, we see the definite linkage of his descriptive analysis of the psychosocial imperatives, which, he argues, direct the individualization of the individual human being toward the collective, with the metaphysics of Nature directing the formulation of this relationship. For Simondon, to disclose the ontogenetic role pre-individuality plays is to recover the meaning Nature had for the pre-Socratics.

The spirituality emerging in the collective, while grasped at the level of the transindividual, ultimately, as I have already suggested, is founded on the pre-individual Nature. Thus, Nature is not the contrary of humanity but rather "being's first phase." Its "second being" is the opposition set up between the individual and the milieu. Simondon's pre-Socratic inspiration lies in those Ionian physiologists, most particularly Anaximander, who discover the origin of every being anterior to individuation: Nature is the "*reality of the possible*, under the species of this απειρον [apeiron or the "indefinite"], the cause of every individuated form" (196). This απειρον, the indeterminate, couples together individuated being and Nature. It is precisely in the engendering role that Anaximander gives to the "indefinite," identifying it, therefore, with potentiality, that Simondon finds a perfect analogue with pre-individuality. And it is through this persistent Nature that the individuated being communicates with the world and other individuated beings, discovering significations *a priori* and *a posteriori*.

Simondon then extends this analogy to a hypothesis: απειρον persists in the individual as a crystal reserves within itself the "mother-water" so that the charge of the απειρον will compel a second individuation (196). As a result, Simondon writes, "The individual carriers of απειρον discover in the collective a signification," a meaning, naming a being's "destiny." From the indeterminate comes individual destiny, once being has become individuated.

Further, extending the analogy, Simondon describes the charge of απειρον as offering a "principle of *disparation*," setting up a relation to other charges of the same Nature contained in other beings (197). The collective is an individuation that reunites natures of several individuals without being contained in any one, particular individuality. "It is why the discovery of signification of the collective is at once transcendent and immanent in relationship to the anterior individual; it is contemporary with the new group personality, in which the individual participates via its nature" (197). But *we must not confuse Nature with the nature of the individual's individuality*.

Following the first individuation, promised by the vital, to the second individuation, enacted by transindividuality, the collective serves as a third phase: the individuation of joint natures of individuated being. "It is the persistence (*remanence*) of the primitive and original phase of being [pre-individuality] in the second phase [individuation of the individuated: individualization] . . . this persistence [of pre-individual being] implicates a tendency toward a third phase, the collective" (197). Only in this restricted sense might it be said that the "individuated being is the bearer of *absolute origin*" (197). It is an origin only ever deferred by moving toward it, receding further as we move closer toward it. For this reason, the individuated being is as much reinvented as it is recollected.

Although it will be discussed in the next chapter, let us at least broach the question: might we consider the collective, as the third individuation of being, to be the point at which we finally grasp values transvalued? It is here that we discover Simondon setting the stage for developing an ethics, the focus of my final chapter.

THE ROLE OF BELIEF IN THE GROUP INDIVIDUAL: THE EMERGENCE OF THE COLLECTIVE

The most compelling example of the co-individuation of the individual and the group is the role "belief" plays in not only religion but, more broadly, in our taking this world as real. Simondon's definition of belief shifts the terrain from previous theories and their account of belief by finding in it a confirmation of the precariousness of the individual's participation in the group. For Simondon, belief is "the latent collection of references in relation to which significations can be discovered." It is not, as such, reducible to doctrine, dogma or, for that matter, ideological commitment; it is as much operational as structure, and as much ontological as emotional – existing as much at the collective level as the individual. Indeed, "belief is this collective individuation in the midst of its existing; it is the presence of other individuals of the group, the recovering of personalities" (186).

Collective belief is equivalent – in the personality – to belief of the individual. But this belief does not exist *qua* belief. Belief exists when some force or obstacle obliges the individual to define and structure its membership in the group, in an intelligible and expressible form, to those who are not group members. Its necessity is found in the question: "Why do you belong to the group?" The instant the group's identity is put into question, belief is there to provide the individual associates with a way to cement their inter-individual relationships (186). So Simondon takes those theories that begin with belief to be insufficiently appreciative of the process by which one becomes a group member.

EXCURSUS

الربيع العربي [*al-rabī* *al-ʿarabī*]: Arab Spring

Why do societies transform themselves, why do groups modify themselves? How are individual beings transformed in becoming a part of a collective? These questions are answerable for Simondon as a function of the conditions of metastability. More important than stability in the life of social groups are those particular moments when groups become *"incapable of conserving their structure: they become incompatible in relation to themselves, they de-differentiate and oversaturate themselves"* (63). Suddenly it is no longer possible to put on a false face in order to hide incompatibilities and inequalities – for example, "The West versus the Rest" – beneath a forced harmony. New structures are called for to account for those potentials "emerging from invention, a sudden appearance of form," so that this state of invention might "crystallize itself" (64). Hamid Dabashi describes this "pre-revolutionary state" quite well when he writes, "The mystical consciousness our world has inherited hangs around the binary of the 'The West and the Rest,' the most damning delusion that the European colonial map of the world manufactured and left behind, with 'Islam and the West' as its most potent borderlines. It is precisely this grand illusion that is dissolving right before our eyes. But that is not all: the challenge posed by these revolutions to divisions within Islam and among Muslims – racial (Arabs, Turks, Iranians, etc.), ethnic (Kurds, Baluchs, etc.), or sectarian (Sunni and Shi'i in particular) – has at once agitated and (*ipso facto*) discredited them. These revolutions are collective acts of *overcoming*. They are crafting new identities, forging new solidarities, both within and without the 'Islam and the West' binary, overcoming once and for all the thin (material and moral) colonial divide. The dynamics now unfolding between the national and the transnational will, as they do, override all others."[19]

We are able to witness the theater of individuation in which the transindividual nurtures itself with the fires of metastability in what Simondon also calls the "pre-revolutionary state." For Simondon, the pre-revolutionary state not only introduces a new idea of social organization, it introduces a different kind of temporality which in a collective being is structured. There is no "before" and "after" in a pre-revolutionary state. A pre-revolutionary state of being is not dissipated once a revolution is attained. There is only ever a becoming-revolutionary because every revolution maintains within itself necessarily the same vital metastability that makes it possible, powerfully sustaining structures with its energy. And it is this same vital metastability that continues to threaten a revolution's hopeful dreams, always threatening it with the collapse into utter powerlessness. We fool ourselves into thinking that somehow we can predict or have a reasonable guess at a revolution's outcome. How many governments continue to miscalculate based on impossible predictions?

Indeed, there is no "state" before or after a revolution because every state of being or state of a group is only ever a "phase" in different degrees of relative instability or vital metastability at distinct levels, and different speeds of becoming, on the way to revolution. To de-differentiate is to encourage incompatibility and tensions within a system "whose state becomes metastable" (59). A field or system will more efficiently receive a form when potential energies accumulate, constituting a vital metastability favorable to transformations. Consequently, Simondon describes the pre-revolutionary state of a governing system as "a state of oversaturation," dynamic and capricious, strained to the point of collapse by a surfeit of potentialities. It is where new structures are ready to burst forth. All that is needed is some seed, some act – accidental or not – to be the crystalline germ, if you will, for an operation that takes on a life of its own, transductively feeding on the pre-individual forces latent within the system itself, that is, those who make it up. A revolution is itself the solution to whatever accident, person, or idea sparks it. But more than that, it is a departure from the pre-individual, a "dimension of systematic discovery," time itself really, and so it follows the path that individuation journeys in carrying itself out (28). A revolution begins before *and* after the act that names it.

The revolutionary wave that has traversed the Arab nations for nearly four years, overthrowing monarchies and dictators in Tunisia, Egypt, Yemen, Libya, continues for some, even at this moment as I write (and, perhaps, you read), with a young woman's voice in the background reporting on the struggle raging within Syria. This specific phase of struggle, like phases that preceded it and will follow, can be grasped in the event of December 17, 2010, in the rural town of Sidi Bouzid, Tunisia, where Muhammad Bouazizi doused himself with petrol and set himself on fire in front of the local government building. This act unites a date and place. But more than that, the apostrophe of Bouazizi's life signals what had been up to that point anonymous misfortune, *hogra* – that is, humiliations in the daily struggle of trying to feed himself and his family.

A revolution found significance in the obscure life of an obscure man not because his act gave us yet another lesson to ponder and to forget. In itself Bouazizi's act was not unique – self-immolation has a long history as a form of protest. Bouazizi's act achieves signification because of what it initiates, what it comes to symbolize, for the process of de-differentiation it begins. More important is the becoming catalyzed in those beyond his own action, for his act transductively amplifies beyond him, to other systems, other individuals. In this way, Bouazizi's action is not like the false ones that invade our memories in the form of the horrors to follow, or glorious deeds that become bedtime stories.

Muhammad Bouazizi should not be remembered as a Martyr (nor as a Sage, nor a Hero). He is a *singularity*, "in contrast to becoming individual." As Hardt and Negri write, it is singular subjectivity that "discovers there is no event without a recomposition with other singularities, that there is no being together of singular subjectivities without rebellion. A process of singularitization is thus incarnated: a self-affirmation, a self-valorization, and a subjective decision that all open toward a state of being together."[20] Bouazizi, or rather his action, brings those extreme and crushing social realities into communication. As such, his self-immolation is a "pure event at the dimension of the emerging individual (*en train d'apparaître*)" (IL 51). He appears before us only in the process that exceeds him, a phase in an event that he incarnates. Together this act and this milieu constitute a systematic event, which survives in the living individuals, in the form of an associated milieu, in which individuation continues to operate: "a perpetuated individuation, a continuous individuation through time, prolonging a singularity," that of the "event" of individuation not only of the individual psyche but of the collective (IL 27).

Bouazizi's self-immolation is the crystalline germ for the Arab revolution precisely because it can be defined and dismissed as abnormal, even "pathological." His "brusque and definitive" action introduces a degree of indefiniteness that creates a new domain of reality, a compulsion for new structures. His act modifies a problem (injustice, inequality, oppression, or the emotion of humiliation) and rewrites history in the fervor of becoming-revolutionary. Simultaneously, a subject or subjectivities are born through a transindividual act of individuation that upsets binaries and their logics predicated upon predestined individuated identities.

Behind the refusal to privilege belief, denying it full credit for providing a way to grasp the relationship of an individual to a group, is the fundamental and innovative idea motivating the ontogenetic leap, as Simondon conceptualizes it: individuation as such (of an exterior being to the knowing subject) cannot be grasped using the same mode of knowledge as that which designates the reality of something to be objectively real. Merely applying objective knowledge proves inadequate for "grasping" individuation, the being of becoming. We require instead a kind of "comprehension without knowledge," an ontologizing and ontologized form of gnoseology; it "intuitively grasps" instead of "knows," simultaneously, as Chateau describes it, "reflexively reprising ontogenesis."[21] It can only be "analogically attributed to the known being by a thought that grasps in itself, by *reflection*, the individuation of its own knowledge." Belief, on the other hand, counters reflexivity with unreflective homogeneity; and yet it is also "a phenomenon of disassociation or alteration of groups, not a basis for their existence; it has a compensation value of consolidation, of provisional reparation rather than a relatively fundamental meaning for the genesis of the group and the mode of existence of individuals in the group" (187).

NOTES

1. Bergson, *The Two Sources of Morality and Religion*, 234.
2. Bergson, *The Two Sources of Morality and Religion*, 199.
3. Bergson, *The Two Sources of Morality and Religion*, 32.
4. Bergson, *The Two Sources of Morality and Religion*, 310.
5. Bergson, *The Two Sources of Morality and Religion*, 281.
6. It should be noted that Simondon's use of the terms "in-group" and "out-group" is borrowed from social theory. An in-group is a social group in which a person finds psychological meaning in identifying with it as a member. An out-group is a social group with which an individual does not identify. However, it should be noted that Simondon's terms "group of interiority" and "group of exteriority" seem to be conflated with in-group and out-group.
7. Chateau, *Le Vocabulaire de Gilbert Simondon*, 60.
8. Muriel Combes, *Gilbert Simondon and the Philosophy of the Transindividual*, Technologies of Lived Abstraction (Cambridge, MA: MIT Press, 2013), 73.
9. Etienne Balibar, *The Philosophy of Marx*, trans. Chris Turner (New York: Verso, 1995), 30.
10. Balibar, *The Philosophy of Marx*, 32.
11. Balibar, *The Philosophy of Marx*, 32.
12. "My surprise was even greater when I realized the extent to which Simondon's

arguments in fact are truly spinozistic, literally converging with some basic propositions of the *Ethics*, although Simondon himself (as many theoreticians in history) denies that he owes anything to Spinoza and even rejects his doctrine which, in a rather conventional way, he sees as 'pantheistic,' or a negation of individual reality." Etienne Balibar, *Spinoza from Individuality to Transindividuality*, Mededelingen Vanwege Het Spinozahuis (Delft: Eburon, 1997).

13. Husserl, *Psychological and Transcendental Phenomenology and the Confrontation with Heidegger*, 494.

14. "It is necessary to begin with the individuation of the group, in which individual beings are at once milieu and agents of a syn-crystallization; the group is a syn-crystallization of several individual beings. The group personality is the result of this syn-crystallization" (183).

15. "There naturally corresponds, in transcendental concreteness, a similarly open *community of monads*, which we designate as *transcendental intersubjectivity*. We need hardly say that, as existing for me, it is constituted purely within me, the meditating ego, purely by virtue of sources belonging to my intentionality; nevertheless, it is constituted thus *as* a community constituted also in every other monad (who, in turn is constituted with the modification: 'other') as the same community – only with a different subjective mode of appearance – and as necessarily bearing within itself the same Objective world. Manifestly, it is essentially necessary to the world constituted transcendentally in me (and similarly necessary to the world constituted in any community of monads that is imaginable by me) that it be a *world of men* and that, *in each particular man*, it be more or less perfectly constituted *intrapsychically* – in intentional processes and potential systems of intentionality, which as 'psychic life,' are themselves already constituted as existing in the world." Husserl, *Cartesian Meditations*, 130. This specific passage, I would argue, provides as definite a reason as possible for why Simondon diverges from Husserlian phenomenological orthodoxy. On almost every count, almost point by point, concept by concept, beginning most obviously with a primary refusal to reduce group being to a kind of monadology, Simondon answers or reconceives Husserl's position. I hope to save this comparative analysis for a future exploration. Unfortunately, for now I can only speak in generalities.

16. Gilbert Simondon, *Communication et information: cours et conférences* (Chatou: Transparence, 2010), 159. This fascinating text, entitled "L'amplification dans les processus d'information," is imensely important, for it throws a clarifying light on Simondon's work and its logics, transductive amplification, modulative amplification, and organizational amplification. Hopefully, the executors of Simondon's estate will some day permit its translation into English.

17. Simondon stresses that we must not confuse the transindividual movement with Bergsonian *élan vital*, "for it is not exactly in continuity with vital individuation, though [transindividual individuation] prolongs life – the first individuation" (193). "Bearer of pre-individual reality, a person encounters in other people another charge of this reality; the sudden appearance of struc-

tures and functions that can happen at this moment is not inter-individual, for it brings a new individuation that superposes and exceeds the old, connecting several individuals in a group being born" (193).

18. "The divergence of transcendence and immanence of spirituality is not a divergence in the transindividual itself but only in relation to the individuated individual" (194).

19. Hamid Dabashi, *The Arab Spring: The End of Postcolonialism* (London and New York: Zed Books, 2012), xix.

20. Michael Hardt and Antonio Negri, *Declaration* ([New York?]: Distributed by Argo-Navis Author Services, 2012), no page.

21. Chateau, *Le Vocabulaire de Gilbert Simondon*, 98–9.

6

The Collective as Condition of Signification

THE PRESENCE OF SIGNIFICATION

In order for the collective to exist, it must come-into-*presence*, which is to say, come-into-signification. The collective attains presence, a being-in-the-world, through signification. "But this apparition of signification supposes also a real *a priori*, the liaison to the subject of this charge of Nature, remnant of being in its original, pre-individual phase" (197). The linking of the creation of signification or meaning to the subject reflects more generally the individuation of being. In this sixth and final chapter (Chapter 2, Part II) of IPC, having already discussed the role of signification as criterion of individuation (Chapter 3, Part I), Simondon returns once again to signification, except this time he more explicitly considers it to be the element most essential for structuring the genesis of the collective. For this reason, Simondon takes it to be the key to unlocking the double-becoming of thought and being.

Information acquires a *significative* status once the collective comes into existence. It is both the operation of signification as it comes into being and the means by which that presence is accomplished. Once we recall that every individual being, particularly if already individuated, carries the original charge of Nature, we also realize the degree to which indeterminacy is carried by individual beings. The subject, therefore, receives information by carrying out an individuation within itself that discloses the "collective relationship with being."

Simondon's concept of the subject is complex. Its overt role is to mediate between the pure indeterminacy, which it incarnates, and the collective, through which it expressively signals its participation. As we spoke of previously, the psychic being is incapable of resolving within

150

itself its own metastable indeterminacy. "At the same time as its charge of pre-individual reality individuates as psychic being, it exceeds the individuated living being's limits and incorporates the living into a system of the world and the subject" (19). The subject is the ensemble formed by the individuated individual and the απειρον, *apeiron* of indeterminacy, which the individuated carries. Hence, "the subject is more than individual" – it is metastable, *larval*. And it is precisely the subject's being "more-than-unity" and "more-than-identity" which permits its participation in the individuation of the collective: "individuation in the form of the collective makes the individual a 'group-individual,' associated with the *group* by the pre-individual reality that it carries within and that reunited to those other individuals, *it individuates into a collective unity*" (19).

The signification of the two individuations of the psychic and the collective resolve themselves through the movement, the forces, that constitute the transindividual. Simondon is not speaking here of a hierarchical structure, nor of dialectic, or even successive levels of individuation. The psychic and the collective, interior individuation and exterior individuation, are instead reciprocal, simultaneous, and codeterminant, so that each individuated individual psychically becomes individualized as a subject in concert with the individuation of the collective.

Nor is there any difference between the discovery of signification and collectively existing because "signification is not being but *between* beings, or rather *through* beings: it is *trans*individual" (199, my italics). Signification is, in short, the being of relation, while the transindividual is action through the "relation of two relations" (IGPB 81); the signifying subject and the signified object are unified and given their distinct presences through a relation of signification. Transindividuality is the genesis and purest expression of the achievement of signification or meaning. Yet what sets apart Simondon's discussion of signification is that signification is said by him to be achieved not by synthesis or a realized unity; rather, it is "*disparation*," which exists in constituting the two phases or relations of being, contained in the subject but "enveloped by the constitution of the transindividual" (199–200).

THE PROBLEM OF LANGUAGE

Now that we have been reminded of how Simondon defines signification and how he establishes the relationship between signification and individuation, a question presents itself to us: given that Simondon defines signification as expressly non-linguistic, what role might language play in the process of individualization?[1]

We are have been guided to this question after surveying the landscape of late twentieth-century and early twenty-first-century philosophy. While the details are less important for now, we should appreciate how philosophy turned toward language and made an appeal to it, not just as an object of study. Language seemed to offer itself to thought as a model, a structuring principle for all the facets of human action and, beyond this, as an invitation for us to poetically dwell within its novelties. It seems unimaginable that IPC would show so little evidence of the "problem of language," since this problem was ubiquitous throughout European intellectual life at the time Simondon was writing, when language was looked upon as providing the key for unlocking the secrets of the human psyche and social life. One cannot help but be puzzled by Simondon's seeming indifference toward language. Information, he argues, not language is the central issue. This becomes one of the pillars of his thought. Language is a secondary effect of the operation of information, of information's operational transformation through the process of communication to signification. Information, not language, structures the world, conscious and unconscious.

In a 1970–71 course "On Communication," Simondon describes communication as requiring at least two nearly closed systems, the "in-put" and the "out-put," "effector" and "emitter." Communication couples the incidents of weak energy through amplifying their effects either within the same or between several different systems, each system existing at various states of metastable equilibrium. This process of amplification changes the initial energy input, transforming it by different orders of magnitude. For Simondon, communication is not linguistic, it is more basically energetic and, thus, ontological. Now, if we return again to the above description and consider "information" to be synonymous with the input of weak energy, then information becomes the tension that accrues between at least two real *disparates*, incompatibilities. Originating from a process that resolves these tensions in a system, information is communicated by producing a transformation in both the "resolved" incompatibilities and the resolving system. Simondon points to the incidence of the transmission of changes through the nerves influx or the emission of hormones, the appearance of catalyzer in a mixture, or the dropping of a crystal germ into an oversaturated solution: all are incidences, he argues, where we find the emission and reception of information and, therefore, the establishment of communication (CI 60). We communicate before we have language; we have language only because of the psychosocial imperative to belong to a group. "Communication exists *prior* to life" (CI 61).

We recall Simondon's basic Allagamatic principle that says that all operations and structures are ontological complements: "operation is what causes a structure to appear, or modifies a structure" (IL 559). Each is the condition for the bringing into presence of the other. Consequently, Simondon wants us to see that the operation of information and language structures are ontological complements. Certainly, a discussion of language, while not *totally* absent, is so thoroughly demoted within Simondon's work that it seems superfluous to how the individuated individual becomes collective. This would not be the case for Simondon. Human language sustains action, the practices Balibar speaks about which synchronize a group's organized behavior, while, at the same time, providing criteria for recognizing, excluding, and maintaining distance from the "stranger," whatever or whoever threatens from outside the group. As one form of signification, language marks the psychosocial partitioning of an interior from an exterior.

Simondon argues that if there were not signification to begin with, there would not be language: signification *precedes* language, not vice versa.

> It is not language that creates signification; [language] is only what carries (*véhicule*) between subjects information which, in order to become significative, requires encounters with this απειρον [*apeiron*: the indefinite or boundlessness] associated with individuality but defined in the subject; language is the instrument of expression, the vehicle of information, but not the creator of signification. (200)

Simondon displaces language by reducing it almost solely to a mode of communication and expression – and, as such, language is made a secondary effect of information and, thus, of individuation. Communication aids individuation in completing itself, maintaining, regenerating, and transforming itself. Language, verbal or written, is one mode of communicability, only secondarily a phase of the more primary state of attained signification. Signification has causal priority over language.

But we feel compelled to ask, does the structure of Simondon's metaphysical descriptions of individuation of the collective warrant this reduction of the role of language? Or, might the addressing of the problem of signification, signification *as problem*, bring the collective presence into being, just affectively, to counter the ontological privilege given to the individual over individuation? What if there were a language that took itself as communicating its own problematic being as well as the meaning it pretends, by calling its own expressiveness into question *as language*? What if there were a real language operational only ever in conflict with its originating structure and, thus, fully expressive of those pre-individual tensions giving rise to it? How is it possible for such a language, seemingly at odds with itself, to be the effect of a community and unify a group?

"PARTISANS OF NEGRITUDE"

If we say that communication allows one to identify a stranger, a "deviant" who must be excluded or quarantined, then, according to Simondon, language serves the dual function of identification and exclusion: that is, it synchronizes and organizes behavior and action, while at the same providing criteria for judging who is excluded. It is a question not only of the spoken accent, Simondon suggests, but also the vocabulary, the grammar, and the syntax spoken and written; the general expressive manner operational in a language is what filters within the group's interior (determining who is the stranger, the deviant, the leader) and which relationships must be maintained between groups (cultural stereotype relative to communication) (CI 65–6).

It might be argued that Simondon's dismissal of language is really an extreme reaction to the tendency in the opposite direction, against what he perceives is happening with those philosophers' appropriations of linguistics who emphasize the supposed innateness of language, disconnecting it from its proper function as "an instrument of mediation between living beings in a relation of communication" (CI 113). Simondon returns language to a functionalist role by shifting emphasis more thoroughly on to the communicative. Ironically perhaps, here is where we might find the expressive power of language. Simondon's reduction of language to mediation does not evade the operational; quite the contrary, it means that language *qua* language forces whatever discourse it structures to confront those pre-individual forces that have led to its genesis. We are forced to see that whatever use a group makes of language reflects the "operative" nature of language. A language often unbeknownst to itself is able to bring to expressive visibility the mute metastability nurturing within its apparent stable expression. And even if a language tries to structure itself by ignoring the pre-individual "voices of silence" which make its articulations possible, we remain exposed to them by the invention of new collective perspectives. With this disclosing of the operational nature of language – "as action, as offense and as seduction" – we note how integral it is to language's functionalist responsibility, that is, to its mediating the relationship of the subject to its milieu. Equally communicated with every word is what murmurs within it and is borne by it – those tensions it subsumes, rehearses, and forms through the transformation of information into signification: "all the deep-rooted relations of the lived experience wherein [language] takes form, and which is the language of life and of action but also that of literature and poetry."[2]

In the introduction that Simondon wrote for a series of lectures he gave during the 1970s, he makes mention, off-handedly, of those he calls the "partisans of 'Negritude'" who reject the "Banania laughter." "Banania laughter" is an oblique reference to the image of a laughing black man used in France to advertise a particular brand of chocolate breakfast drink.[3] This striking statement is made in the context of a discussion of the doubledness of language, to exclude and to provoke encounters. It is a surprising moment for a number of reasons. One reason in particular is that, although in other places Simondon writes admirably about the plastic arts, architecture, and indeed, music, he seems utterly indifferent to literature, for the most part. More surprising perhaps is that this reference to Negritude foregrounds for us the problem of race by linking it to the problem of language.

But who are these "partisans of Negritude?" Here it would be fair to say that Simondon refers to the African and Caribbean poets and principal theoreticians of the Negritude movement, most of whom came from current or former French colonies. Foremost among these "partisans" were Aimé Césaire and Léopold Senghor. The reason for these poets' rejection of the advertising image, writes Simondon, is that it "represents the myth of the Good Black, inferior, sympathetic but not threatening, a comfort to European ignorance about African culture and the black soldiers" dying in the name of republicanism.[4] In other words, the reason for its rejection by the partisans of Negritude is psychosocial. As Simondon allows, the image of the smiling Good Black is an effect of the doubledness of language: it provokes action and synchronizes behavior, while excluding and identifying in order to distance oneself from the "stranger," the deviant, the other. Senghor exploits this doubledness by extracting a poetic use of language, whose very operation puts into question the communicable being of language and, so too, the one who speaks and the one who speaks back.

> I shall not let the words of government ministers nor generals,
> No! I shall not let words of scornful praise secretly bury you.
> You are not empty-pocket poor men without honor
> But I will tear off the *banania* grins from all the walls of France.[5]

This smiling *Banania* is a transindividual image. Overtly symbolic of the joyful Good Black, it is also the bearer of a pre-individual reality both psychic and social. "Man encounters in the other another the charge of this reality" (193). It is this pre-individual reality that provokes, in this instance, the individuation of two mutually opposed groups, who, nevertheless, are born and bring into a new reality a share of the same "primitive" pre-individual reality: the partisans of Negritude, who shudder anxiously in front of this image, and the partisans of the Good Black, who are comforted by its certainty and shudder anxiously when they notice those joyless partisans of Negritude. How do the partisans and non-partisans look at the same image but draw different conclusions, especially when we consider that both share the same linguistic community and, in some instances, the same group affiliation? All the while both participate in the same group as a result of the catalyst to their individuation (individualization) and, thus, leave themselves exposed to the same pre-individual reality: the smiling *Banania*.

Simondon writes, "Signification is a relationship of beings, not a pure expression; signification is relational, collective, transindividual, and cannot be provided by the encounter of expression and subject" (200). As the effect of signification, language must *disindividuate itself*, if it wants to move beyond subjective expressiveness and grasp the signification of collective individuation. Combes describes this disindividuating event as provoking "a putting into question of the subject that necessarily takes the form of a momentary loosening of the hold of constituted individuality, which is engulfed by the preindividual."[6]

For the Martiniquean poet and philosopher Edouard Glissant, the dynamics of the Creole language *live* the emergence of Caribbean culture and the individual. Characterized by puns, assonance, ambiguities of origin and borrowings from multiple languages, Glissant asks: "Is it a language?" "Is it a deformation of French speech?" The one who speaks Creole places these questions in suspension by shifting the focus from Creole as a linguistic entity, fully individuated with its own proper syntax, vocabulary, and grammar, to Creole as a "continuing process of undermining its innate capacity for transcending its French origins." Creole reflects on who and how it is spoken in the *hic et nunc* of its being spoken; and so, it reminds the Martiniquean that to speak French is to speak a language that at once constitutes itself *and* dispossesses the other – "you know, the one who must learn to speak French *properly*." But the Martiniquean answers: "You wish to reduce me to a childish babble, I will make this babble systematic, we shall see if you can make sense of it."[7]

Créolisation is a perfect test case for the idea of the psychosocial transindividuality of language; it enacts, performs, and reflects the doubledness of language, bringing together the reciprocal individuations of the psychic individual and the collective, psychosocial anxiety and nonhistorical fear, mixing to provoke the "strange *totality* impossible to close,"[8] the Caribbean. For Creole is the very personification of a disindividuating act, throwing into question the French language, the colonizer's language, opening this language to its role in the individualization of the colonized. "The climax of the Creole speech," Glissant writes, "does not release any appreciative smile but the laughter of participation."[9] It operates as a purely transindividual language in action, putting the individual into question in order to expressively account for the systematic unity of interior (psychic) and exterior (collective) individuation. Glissant emphasizes that when he speaks of "*Créolisation*" he is not at all referring to the Creole language but "to the *phenomena* that has structured the Creole language, which isn't the same thing."[10] In this regard, I would posit that Glissant credits Creole with carrying out a *kind of transindividual disindividuation* of the French language. *Créolisation* is the Martiniquean's response to the collective alienation of the Antilleans from their own language, the colonizer's language.

> Today the French Caribbean individual does not deny the African part of himself; he does not have, in reaction, to go to the extreme of celebrating it exclusively. He must *recognize* it. He understands that from all this history (even if we lived it like a nonhistory) *another reality* has come about. He is no longer forced to reject strategically the European elements in his composition, although they continue to be a source of alienation, since he knows that he can choose between them. He can see that alienation first and foremost resides in the impossibility of choice, in the arbitrary impositions of values, and, perhaps, in the concept of value itself. He can conceive that synthesis is not a process of bastardization as he used to be told, but a productive activity through which each element is enriched. He has *become* Caribbean.[11]

Frantz Fanon writes, "A man who has language consequently possesses the world *expressed* and implied by that language . . . Mastery of language affords remarkable power."[12] Power derives not from the linguistic structural elements alone but from their synchronous activation of transindividuality, emerging from the pure operation of expression through and beyond language itself. Expression *through* language and the operation of language are one and the same, the result of the process of individuation, which invites the ontological complementary between operation and structure (the conversion of the structure of language into another structure); in doing so, language is brought to signification, at once *outside* the verbal structures of its presentation and *inside* the operation of its actualization, the collective.

Hence, it must be said more accurately Simondon does not make language inconsequential, so much as he gives it a different operational status relative to its becoming, an effect that directs language beyond itself, to history, to anxiety, even if it is not the cause itself of engendering and structuring signification. Have we brought language to a place more distant than any form of exteriority and, for this reason, infinitely closer: like the smiling Senegalese joyfully interrogating our faces while he stands guard over our breakfast cereal?

SEXUALITY AND SIGNIFICATION: FREUD

Having already discussed sexuality in the previous chapter, what has changed that would require Simondon to return to it again in this chapter?

Like language, sexuality is "a mixture of nature and individuation." Simondon argues that because the individuated being is the "psychosomatic immanence of pre-individual nature," it can only be grasped as a kind of "individuation in suspension, arrested in the asymmetric determination of the elementary collective" (201). For this reason, sexuality provides the inspiration and incitation *toward* the collective, *toward* spirituality.

In the previous chapter Simondon clearly preferred Janet's formulation of split personality over Freud's. Now Simondon holds open the possibility of a fruitful dialogue with Freud. The basis for this dialogue is Freud's theory of drives. Once an organism encounters the outside world, the psyche provides the quantities of energy with a form. The problem from Simondon's perspective is that Freud's economistic model cannot answer how one is able to equate the *quantitative* distribution of energies with the *qualitative* human being in the world.

In order to ensure the constancy of individual unity, according to Freud the most simplified form of the living organism, which he describes as "an undifferentiated vesicle of substance," turns its surface toward the external world so that it is permanently altered, differentiated, "dying" so that its outer layer becomes to some extent nonliving, in order to receive stimuli. The membrane preserves the existence of the living being by regulating the quantity of energy filtering into the interior. Embryology reveals a similar origination for the nervous system, in particular the cortical layer, of higher-level animals' brains. In the absence of this "shield against stimuli," the organism would be destabilized, its interiority compromised, and, thus, it would be killed by the "destructive influence of the monumental energies operating outside."[13]

Out of this systematic regulation of energies, distinguishable into quantities or levels of tension reflecting either pleasure or un-pleasure, Freud's formulation of the "pleasure principle" is intended to describe the mechanism necessary for equalizing the difference between external stimuli and internal excitation. According to Freud, the pleasure principle defines the process by which the psyche seeks to minimize and keep constant the quantity of excitation. As stimuli raise internal excitation, the pleasure principle carries out a "release" of tension. The system's dynamism of tension and release is self-perpetuating, a kind of closed loop. For in competition with the pleasure principle, indeed as a way to moderate its excesses, Freud posits a "reality principle," which will frustrate the immediacy of pleasure's satisfaction, ensuring that the organism has a way to recognize and then negotiate with the difficulties in the world for its self-preservation.

If we extend the economic logic of the pleasure principle, we find that thermodynamically it reflects a taking part "in the universal striving of all living things to return to the peace of the inorganic world."[14] Freud's speculative turn, therefore, corresponds with his appeal to the universality of inertia present in all organic life. It provides a way for him to designate from where the internal drives get their impulse to return to the earlier inorganic state. In this way, Freud argues ultimately, the pleasure principle is at the service of the "death drive" (*Thanatos*). Life drives are but the accomplishing of the death drive. And so, in this constancy of movement, we seek to die in our own way.

The forces behind the tensions deriving from the somatic demands or the psychic affects of physical needs are instincts that direct human activity. There are the "life instincts," which drive us to seek food and water, while compelling us toward sex, toward perpetuating the species, at least initially. Freud makes a clear connection between "sex drives" or the "libido" and the life instincts. According to Freud, it is "the libidinal character of the self-preservation drives . . . the sex drive as all preserving Eros," which increasingly becomes most dominant in the human psyche.[15] The Id is the "great reservoir of the libido," that is, of sexualizing forces or instincts. Eros is the operational form from which the sex drives derive. It grants unity to the living being as a result of its directing instinctual impulses toward objects with which the individual identifies. Still, given that various drive impulses are in constant play within the organism, most are incompatible with their joining into a comprehensive unity of the ego. And Eros is itself the form Freud gives to the "life drive." Its incessant and insistent struggle with the "death drive" constitutes the identity of the psychic individual.[16] Therefore, Eros gives form to the ego. Indeed, only the agency of Eros stands against the destructive impulses; it therefore acts as a countervailing force of agency to redirect potentially damaging impulses from the self toward the external world.[17]

It would be a lie to claim that Simondon is rigorous or, for that matter, totally accurate in how he draws distinctions between Freud's four attempts to conceive the psyche; indeed, he tends to conflate the structural (ego/id/superego) and the dynamic (tension and release of competing forces), with the economic model (the distribution of quantities of energy as outlined in the *Beyond the Pleasure Principle* above). It is the latter that draws most of Simondon's attention.

Still, Freud's attempt to address the problem of "how to procure for the group precisely those features which were characteristic of the individual but extinguished in him by the formation of the group" begins from the "fundamental fact" that an individual in a group is subjected to the "intensification of affects" that as a result reduces intellectual ability, while inviting the approximating or imitating of other individuals in the group. This becomes possible upon the removal of those inhibitions upon instincts peculiar to each individual, as control over those inclinations belonging to him or her is relinquished to the "higher organization" of the group. Freud is interested in providing a psychological explanation for this mental change, which becomes necessary with the individual's participation in a group.

In a group the individual is brought under conditions that permit the individual's being liberated from repressions of the unconscious instinctual impulses. Hence, the individual's seeking the group manifests this unconsciousness. In this characterization Freud appropriates and extends Le Bon's analogy of the mental life of the individual in the group with primitive people, children, and neurotics: "A group is impulsive, changeable and irritable. It is led almost exclusively by the unconscious."[18] A group's "critical faculty" is suspended: "It thinks in images, which call one another up by association (just as they arise with individuals in states of free imagination), and whose agreement with reality is never checked by a reasonable agency . . . a group knows neither doubt nor uncertainty."[19] Thus, a group can only be excited by an excessive stimulus (not logic but exaggeration, intensity).

Here Freud identifies the role of libido, the energy regarded as a quantitative magnitude (though not actually measurable) of those instincts which relate to sexual love, as well self-love, love for parents and children, friendship, love for humanity, for abstract ideas and concrete objects, etc. All are traceable to the same instinctual impulse. "Love relationships . . . constitute the essence of the group mind."[20] First, identification is an original form of emotional tie with an object; second, in a regressive way it becomes a substitute for a libidinal object-tie via introjection of the object into an ego; third, it may arise with a new perception of a common quality shared with some other person who is not an object of the sexual instinct.

With the formation of a group, intolerance vanishes *within* the group, but only so far as the group persists. "Such a limitation of narcissism can, according to our theoretical views, only be produced by one factor, a libidinal tie with other people. Love for oneself knows only one barrier – love for others, love for objects."[21] Further, the libido attaches itself to the satisfaction of vital needs and, thereby, decides in favor of people who will benefit it. Thus, in mankind as a whole as in the individual, love alone acts as the civilizing factor to transform egoism to altruism. Yet if we absent the sexual object-cathexis aim, which is not so easy for the individual, what is the nature of the tie existing in the group? Here love instincts are diverted from the original sexual aims, though without the diminution of energy. It is precisely the inhibiting of sexual impulsions that achieves the lasting ties between people. Still, this is to maintain an energy of sexual impulsions; for it is the fate of sensual love to be extinguished when it is satisfied.

Therefore, if mixed from the beginning with purely affectionate elements, inhibited in their aims, love undergoes a transformation that preserves the intensity of its energy without extinguishing it via direct satisfaction.

The same "libidinal tie" holds in ensuring the power of a group's leader: one who loves every individual in the group, Christ and Commander-in-Chief equally. Each individual is bound by libidinal ties to the leader and to other members of the group. An individual is provoked into fear either by the scale of a danger or by the cessation of emotional ties (libidinal cathexes).

Freudian psychoanalysis wants to prove that nearly every intimate emotional relation between people contains the sediment of aversion and hostility, which escapes perception insofar as it is the result of repression.[22] In the undisguised antipathies and aversions toward strangers, Freud recognizes the expression of self-love, of narcissism and, likewise, the striving toward equalization at the level of both impulses and other persons. Thus, the herd instinct is a psychosocial feeling that reverses what was hostile into a positive connection between individuals via identification. This reversal seems to be motivated by an affectionate tie established to a person outside the group. All members want to be equal to one another but ruled by one person. Man is not a "herd animal," Freud writes, but rather a "horde animal, an individual creature in a horde led by a chief."[23]

SUBJECT AND INDIVIDUAL: BEYOND FREUD AND FREUDIANISM

Simondon's initial critique of Freud and Freudianism takes place on two fronts. First, Freud acts as if the subject and the individual are the same, ontologically, which confuses the processes of individualization, as a secondary individuation, with the more anterior individuation engendering the still impersonal individual being. Individualization is the "individuation of an individuated being" (IL 267). Once achieved via the transindividual systematic unity of the interior individuation (psychic) and the exterior (collective), an equalizing phase is reached, at which point the individuated being is *subjectivized, personalized, individualized.* An identifiable subjectivity is inaugurated and formed where previously there had been an anonymous living individual being (no less metastable because of the share of pre-individual indetermination (Nature) constitutively present within it). Second, Freud conceives sexuality as if it were something that could be contained and enclosed within the individual. To do so, of course, means that Freud must equate sexuality with a kind of "substance" or matter in relation to the granted "form" of the individual being. Thus, carrying forward his critique of Aristotelian and Platonist metaphysics, the implicit hylemorphism that structures Freudian theory and the substantialist metaphysic it presupposes afford Simondon the justification for rejecting Freudian psychologism.

Simondon's rejection of Freud's psychosocial theory is driven by his refusal of its underlying theory of instincts. Really, at the most basic level, Simondon refuses Freud's attempt to identify sexuality as the sole principle for all tendencies at play in the individuated being. As a result, "one can no longer separate into the two principles of pleasure and the death instinct" (202). Simondon proposes, instead, a reformulation of those modalities constituting individuation, most particularly sexuality, in contradistinction to its Freudian structuring as solely responsible for the individual's psyche. Once again, Simondon reveals himself to be closer to Jung than to Freud, insofar as he shares the former's criticism of the latter. Simondon is troubled by the Freudian conception because it presupposes the subject to be only ever a formed individual, so that "sexuality is placed in the individual like something the individual contains and encloses" (202). For Simondon, on the contrary, sexuality is "first and foremost" a modality of psychic individualization. It is neither individuation *in total* nor for that matter the "content" of some given actual individual. It follows that the relationship between the life instinct and the death instinct is distributive rather than oppositional, with its criteria always only emerging out of the process of individuation. Sexuality organizes itself in its ontogenetic development "with what we have called 'Nature' in the subject; as a result, it individualizes itself or, on the contrary, it is connected with the world and the group" (202).

Simondon alters the Freudian basis for characterizing psychic pathologies and pathogenesis. He redefines them as conflicts between sexuality, a modality of individuation, and the charge of pre-individuality or Nature, which is to some degree within the subject, though without being thoroughly contained within the individual. Certainly it is the case that a sexualized being is fulfilling every desire, satisfying every tendency, and the relaxation of all tensions cannot bring the individual to agreement with himself; it cannot end the conflict between the modality of individuation (sexuality) and Nature internal to the subject. Hence, neither the study of the individual nor the study of social integration accounts for pathogenesis. The only resolution is the subject's discovery of significations or meanings, which will bring the individual and the collective into accord to develop, in a synergetic manner, at the transindividual level (202–3).

> The pathological relation to the other is that which lacks significations, which dissolves into the neutrality of things and leaves life without polarity; as a result, the individual feels itself to have become an insular reality; abusively

crushed or falsely triumphant and dominating, the subject searches to recon-
nect the individual being to a world that has lost its meaning; the transindividual relation of signification is replaced by the subject's powerless relation to
neutral objects, of which certain of them are alike. (203)

For Simondon, Freudian psychologism restricts our ability to think
through the psychosocial and, thus, to properly diagnose pathologies not as
mental or cognitive instability but, instead, as signaling a failure in achieving signification at the level where it materializes: at the level of the transindividual. Perhaps more self-consciously than it might appear, Simondon
undercuts any attempt to extend Freud's psychoanalytic hypotheses
by later Freudo-Marxist attempts (like Herbert Marcuse's *Eros and
Civilization*) to explain society and its relation to the individual on the basis
of ontologically privileging the notion of the individual via the "sociological" mechanism of identification.

Simondon argues that a primary effect of the Freudian approach, at
least at this point, is that it does not clearly distinguish between instincts
and tendencies (*tendances*).[24] Why is Freud's error significant? Instincts,
Simondon argues, are purely individual, insofar as they transmit via the
vital activity of time and space. On the other hand, tendencies, everyday
and continuous, do not possess the aspect of irreversibility of creative
nature like instincts, which, at some level, displace the constituted individual, often to the point of the individual's non-integration in the vital
community; perhaps, in this final way more than any other, instincts are in
contradiction to tendencies. According to Simondon, this is Freud's fatal
mistake. "If tendencies and instincts are of the same nature, it becomes
impossible to distinguish the transductive character of those belonging to
the membership of a society" (IL 170).

For example, sexuality is said to testify to a sexual instinct – a sexualizing tendency is conflated with sexual need. But they operate in dynamic
opposition to one another. It is precisely because of their continuousness
and stability that tendencies are integral to the life of a community, for they
provide the means by which the individual is integrated; hence his nutri-
tive and defensive needs are met. The sexual instinct is itself a function of
a change of a regime of behavior. Rather than being the cause of society and
its sublimations (as Freud claims in *Civilization and its Discontents*), strictly
speaking the sexual instinct is an effect or phenomenon of "transductive
amplification," the operation by which a society forms itself.[25] Simondon,
in other words, turns Freud on his head.

So how does instinct become an element of transductive amplification?
And what exactly is amplified? First, let us recall that any constituted
"relation" of the individual to the world or to the collective or to "society"

is a dimension of individuation, and, so, what the instinctive drive discloses for us is our being compelled by the share of pre-individual being, which the individual already contains in being individuated, to participate in a dimension of being that is "more-than-unity, more-than-identity." In other words, instinct compels us to belong to a group or some collective by disclosing that the individual is not an absolute but rather a relative reality: "a certain phase of being which supposes before it a pre-individual reality," whose metastable is rich in potentials (IL 24). Instinct points us in the direction of our essential insubstantiality and, so, dependency.

In Freud's positing a principle of genesis that is anterior to the operation of individuation itself, which can explain and produce individuation, Simondon finds the same error that he discerns more generally in scientific and metaphysical attempts to conceptualize individuation. The individual is engendered by the encounter between form and matter – in this instance, the "ego" and the "id" via the cathetic processes of "identification" and its presupposing of an absolute individual being.

Freud's hylemorphism ontologically privileges the individuated individual – foregrounding the result as an analytical starting point, as opposed to the operation of individuation itself. As a result, it structures itself in presupposing a "substantialist" ontology, whereby being is given to itself and founded on itself, as a unity. What is lost is precisely the dynamism that Freud's model pretends. The "matter" of individuation is already prefigured in the "form" of the constituted individual and, so, we are left without a true idea of individuation, which, from Simondon's perspective, must maintain within its operation some degree of indetermination. Freud's notion of the "super-ego," as "ideal," functions as if one might discover a condition of absolute unity in the passage into action of its virtual content. In other words, it functions as Freud's Good Form. For Simondon, Freud's hylemorphism is only able to take into account the essential duality of instinct and tendency by appealing to an inhibiting alienation constituting the individual. So, if Freud importantly improves upon Aristotelian entelechy by theorizing the instinctive drives, even so, from Simondon's perspective, he makes a mistake by neglecting the fact that the individual is a "transduction" and *not*, as Freud claims, a repressed inhibition destined to be actualized, a "virtuality."

According to Simondon, the conflict Freud sets up between the ego and sexuality transforms the psyche into nothing more than an automaton. As we saw previously, Freud conceives the ego as an agent of the totality of the individual; it is topologically and genetically differentiated at the surface as a function through adaptation; it is a prolongation of the individual, a kind of living "safety valve" between the organic individual and the external world, whose role is to dispose of the surfeit of energy produced by neurotic or psychotic conflict. Are we speaking of the ego as an actual effect of differentiating the biological organism, or rather is the ego, either in part or whole, what makes up some kind of virtual "psychical individual"? And what does the latter mean? Jean Laplanche among others has forcefully discerned this as an unresolvable difficulty within Freud's economic formulation.[26] At issue for Simondon is, first, Freud's theorizing the ego differentiation by adaptation and, secondly, Freud's presumption that the individual, like some kind of physical envelope containing the psyche, exists anterior to the psychical process. One might go so far as to argue that the entirety of Simondon's notion of the psyche is formulated in opposition to these two errors, as he characterizes them.

And yet, in truth, both errors ultimately have their common origin in Freud's unacknowledged mechanistic conception of the ego as the effect of adaptation. What distinguishes the automaton from the living individual is the capacity for self-creation, invention. An individual is able to integrate large quantities of information, potentially dangerous to its existence, by changing its structure to adapt. Thus, a structure reflects those informational thresholds, which establish the limits of its adaptability. An automaton, however, is incapable of changing its structure, for there is never an incompatibility between the structures it possesses and the information it acquires. Its structure determines in advance the type of information it is able to incorporate; thus, there is no need for it to adapt to information that is not homogeneous with its predetermined scheme. Freud's structure of the ego, founded on the pleasure principle, seems to reflect a kind of automatic ideal, structurally static, always seeking homeostasis, that is, tending toward zero equilibrium or the "death drive."

On the contrary, the individual, as Simondon describes it, possesses an open faculty for acquiring information, not necessarily homogeneous to its actual structure. Always subsisting within the individual is "a certain margin between the actual structure and acquired information which, being heterogeneous in relation to the structure, necessitates the successive recasting of the being, and the power to put itself in question" (273). As a result of this margin a degree of indeterminism is present, which ensures the structure is always to some degree open and, so, capable of resolving a difficulty or problem, no matter if the information introduced is heterogeneous. For that is what an individual is: the resolution of an incompatibility, a problem. "The problem is resolved thanks to a change of structure of the individual subject, according to an action which creates a veritable relation between the anteriorly structured individual and its new charge of information" (274).

On Freud's own terms, the ego fails to bridge the psychic and the vital, insofar as it fails to be adaptable enough and, thus, is incapable of moving beyond the autonomic. Thus, for Simondon, the individual is "dynamically unlimited." It is not a matter of adapting to external circumstances, mediating internal excitation with external excitations via the reality principle, for, on the contrary, the individual problematic "requires in effect solutions from overstepping, and not by the reduction of the gap (*écart*) between the being and its milieu" (274).

In short, Simondon requires us to formulate a new vitalism where we see that, finally, Freud's error lay in his assuming a particular kind of "vitalism . . . which valorizes forms closest to the human species, in constituting an anthropocentrism" (IL 171). Simondon argues that a vitalism that ignores the difference between two functions – tendencies and instincts – is unable to establish the difference between those two functions and the structural dynamism which permits the exercise of these functions in maintaining vital stability. Thus, the "death instinct," as proposed by Freud, is inaccurately theorized if it is assumed to be symmetrical with the "life instinct" or "sex drives." Instead, the death instinct is, in effect, "the dynamic limit for the [life instinct], and *not* another instinct" (IL 171). What does this mean? For Simondon the death drive marks a "temporal frontier" beyond which the positive vital instinct can no longer be exercised.

It can no longer be a surprise for the majority of readers that, when an important thinker like Freud, whose theory of instinct is ultimately rejected, is found wanting and dismissed, almost immediately Simondon returns to Spinoza: "In the Spinozist sense of *conatus*, the tendency of the being to preserve in its being belongs to an instinctive ensemble that leads to the 'death instinct'" (IL 171). Spinoza's *conatus* describes a relation of forces. Chantel Jaquet suggests that this Spinozist concept does not describe the effort to strive toward existence so much as to preserve an already individuated existence. *Conatus* is the effort exhibited by a living being to preserve its *being*, to strive to remain existing. However, the effort of striving to exist implies something more than the conservation of the same state, for it is equivalent neither to simple resistance nor the reproduction of existing effects. *Conatus* expresses all the power of the individual being, affirming as much as possible all the properties contained in its essence. The essence of a thing is, thus, dynamic, the power to act and to be acted upon, to individuate and to be individuated. Thus, a thing or individual is nothing more than its *conatus*, or the degree of power that essentially defines its existence. And, so, every individual is to some degree a pure *potentia* or collection of tendencies. "It is in this Spinozistic sense," Simondon writes, "that we are able to discover a relation of the reproductive (*génésique*) instinct and the death instinct, for they are functionally homogeneous. The reproductive instinct and death instinct are, on the contrary, heterogeneous in relation to different tendencies, which are a continuous and *socially* integral reality" (IL 171, my italics).

A CHOICE

Sartre famously declared, "We are our choices." Simondon rethinks the notion of "choice" and its constitutive role in creating subjectivity on ontogenetic grounds. And in this manner, Simondon begins to point us toward not only a metaphysic and a philosophy of psychosocial being but a new ethics as well. Again, the starting point is pre-individual reality, which Simondon suggests guides the subject in whatever positive choice is available to it. A choice reflects what is individuated in the subject, but it is the discovery of a relation of being through which the subject constitutes itself in joining a collective unity. The choice is a mode of individuation. As such, though it would seem that choices belong solely to the subject, who must take responsibility for them, in fact every choice creates an opportunity that discovers and institutes the collective: "The choice is not solely the act of the subject; it is structuration in the subject with other subjects; the subject is the milieu of choice and at the same time agent of this choice" (204). Reassembled with others, the subject can be correlatively theater and agent of a second individuation, which causes the transindividual collective to be born and reattaches the subject to other subjects. Truly, it is not as individuals that beings are reconnected to one another in the collective but as "subjects,"that is, as beings who incarnate the pre-individual.

"Choice is thus the advent of being" (204). What seems to be individual or individualizing is in fact the complete opposite; it is a demonstration of collective individuation in operation. For "Ontologically, every true choice is reciprocal and supposes an operation of individuation more profound than a communication of consciousness or an inter-subjective relation. The choice is collective operation, foundation of the group, transindividual activity" (204). Hence, Simondon argues that the subject, more so than the individual, is "implicated in choice," for a "choice makes itself at the level of subjects, and entails individuals constituted in the collective" (204). Every subject is implicated in a choice, as a result of his or her contribution of a pre-individual nature, providing a milieu necessary for the choice to be realized. The collective is not a milieu for the individual but an ensemble of participations that it enters by this second individuation, which is choice.

> The collective is the signification obtained by superposition in a unique system of being, which, one by one, diverges (*disparates*): it is an encounter with a system's edified dynamic forms, a realized signification, consummated, which requires passage to a superior level, advent of the collective as unified system of reciprocal beings. (206)

The individual achieves its "collective personality" with the individuation of the collective *in concert* with the emergence of transindividual signification given to the collective more generally and the individual, more specifically, individualized as a participant in the collective. The advent of the collective, therefore, resulting from a second individuation initiated by this reciprocal causality, is, simultaneously, the birth of transindividual significations that live beyond the individual subjects incarnating them.[27] As Simondon writes, "What there is in the subject-being of pre-individual nature survives in the form of signification passed along to the living individual" (207). As Simondon describes it, participation in collective individuation allows the subject "to infuse something of itself (which is not individuality)" into a more stable reality than itself: information attains signification.

> It is no longer individual, its hardly the subject who outlives itself; it is the charge of nature associated with the subject who becomes signification integrated in the collective, survives in the *hic et nunc* of the individual contained in the subject-being. The sole chance for the individual or, rather, for the subject, to survive in some fashion is to become signification, to cause something to become signification. (207)

EXCURSUS
Once again we have an example of the not always advantageous structure that Simondon crafts for IPC. As Simondon has discussed the transcendental/empirical split, which I covered in Chapter 4, and the problem of anthropology, covered in Chapter 5, we must wonder why he chose to return to these questions once again in this chapter. An element has been added: the *disparation*. In this section, for the first time, in labeling his own thought "pre-Critical," he situates himself tangentially to Kant. *Disparation* is Simondon's evidence to support this self-characterization.

BEYOND THE EMPIRICAL AND THE TRANSCENDENTAL: PRE-CRITICAL ONTOLOGY AND ONTOGENESIS

Simondon repeatedly asserts that once the ontogenetic perspective has been adopted, no longer is it possible for our starting point to be being; it must instead be genesis, for no longer can the individuated be ushered into the phenomenal as a result of its finitude. There is only the insistent and interminable individuation. "Therefore, it is a question of assisting the genesis of individuated beings starting from a pre-individual reality, containing potentials that resolve themselves and fix themselves in the system of individuation" (206). And so it follows that it only becomes more difficult, if not outright impossible, to propose, as the absolute departure point for devising the knowledge of man, anthropology, as this human science structured itself at the time Simondon wrote IPC, which mandates as a condition for employment the positing of its object's supposed essence. "Man" is anthropology's "Good Form." As was already argued in the prior chapter, for Simondon, anthropology is a dead-end axiomatically speaking – in particular, for characterizing the ontology of relation necessary for the analysis of the social. "It is not by starting from an essence that one is able to indicate what a Man is, for every anthropology would be obliged to substantialize either the individual or the social in order to give Man as essence" (181). As was previously described, life rescues us from the abstraction of essence, in that it cannot be reduced to a substance or a matter but is only ever exceeding the thought said to capture it. A living being amplifies rather than exhausts the initial problem, whose resolution defines his existence. Thus, nothing is gained by separating Man[28] from the vital, as anthropology does, except to reduce the complexity of the problematic structuring the individuation of the social. In the end, *philosophical* anthropology's failure is apparent from its inability to fully grasp the fundamental constitutive role pre-individuality plays in individuation, given that it has the need to posit an essence of Man for explanation. Simondon joins the distinguished company of late 1950s and early 1960s thinkers who contest philosophical anthropology specifically, and the human sciences more generally, and who are taken to ground its practice and promote its goal by justifying the primacy of the notion of "Man" as providing the Good Form. Its purpose is to provide the forces of finitude with a form of representation, that is, knowledge.[29]

The individual, in terms of being, can neither be totally contained nor reduced to being a figment of the Man-Form, because it is the result of a prior individuation – as such the individual bears within it some degree of pre-individuality – the potential now actualized in the individual. As a result, Simondon finds the justification for what he calls a "pre-individual knowledge" (206). If we think of all knowledge in terms of a synthetic activity that answers, as Kant describes it, to conceptions whose objective reality is provable, verifiable by experience, and, consequently, apodeitic, that is, universally and objectively necessary if judgments are to be sufficient, then, certainly, Simondon's call for a "pre-individual knowledge" correlate with the functional role given to pre-individuality in the coming-to-be of the individual would seem to be an odd formulation, or at worst a return to the kind "pre-critical" dogmatism that Kant worried about.

And yet, where Kant saw failure in reason's resignation before a "state of nature,"[30] Simondon sees the opportunity for creating a new kind of knowledge – one that invites and, indeed, serves as a propaedeutic for the leap into ontogenesis. For presupposed by the prior theories of knowledge, in particular the Kantian variety, is the ontological privilege granted to the individual or individuated being, and supported by a purely logical synthesis. Being is not a predicate; it does not contribute to the subject of a judgment but designates "merely what is possible, by my thinking its object."[31] Only once the conditions of synthetic knowledge are acknowledged, permitting the unity of experience, is it possible for us to think being as such. This is the core of Kant's critical philosophy.

However, for Simondon, being is not reducible to a logical category. It is real. Or, more rigorously perhaps, let us say that although it is not necessarily actual *all at once*, it remains no less real because it is potential, pre-individual. *Not in spite of* but *because* being is never absolutely given in terms either of an individuated object or subject, Simondon enacts a fundamental upending of Kantian critical philosophy, refashioning the domain of philosophical examination in the light of the ontogenetic perspective that is made available once individuated being is deprived of its absolute primacy in conditioning epistemology. As a result, those ontological postulates presumed by critique are finally overcome and given a secondary status as effects relative to the more primary event of individuation. What is refused as a result is any classification of beings into kinds without their corresponding to the genetic operation that brought them into being. We require a "knowledge engaged *after* genesis," conditioned by individuation and not the already individuated object and subject, which, as Simondon stresses, returns us to "the foundation of Scholasticism," not Kantianism (206).

"In order to try to lead to the institution of ontogenesis, which is this *pre-critical ontology*, we wanted to create the notion of phases of being" (206, my italics). Simondon describes his ontology as "pre-critical," not to mean what Kant says must be lost, but for what it permits: a return to ontology, or more specifically, to an *ontologizing* of thought that permits our grasping coming-to-be as the pure event of becoming, the being as no more and no less than a dephasing movement, neither an instant or a now but the phasing of action.

Obviously aware of Bergson's well-known (if not always properly characterized) criticism of the tendency for epistemology and science to reduce time to the divisible quantity of the "instant," Simondon develops this notion – "phases of being" – on the basis of his connecting it to the wholly qualitative and intensive exchange of information destined, as he characterizes it, to replace the notion of form.

170

EXCURSUS
The return to a theory of emotion in this final section of Chapter 2, Part II seems somewhat redundant. Why would a discussion of emotion be necessary given that Simondon has already defined it and then assigned to it an important role in Chapter 2, Part I, "Individuation and Affectivity"? Perhaps, looking forward more positively, we should ask a different question: What was left unsaid, *necessarily*, in the earlier chapter?

THE CENTRAL OPERATIONAL ZONE OF THE TRANSINDIVIDUAL: A THEORY OF EMOTION

In the previous chapter concerning affectivity, the primary goal had been to establish clear distinctions among affectivity, perception, and emotion, related to the way each reciprocally prepares the way for the other. Emotion is born from failing to integrate a being's actual state with an affective dimension; thus, an emotion is an affective contradiction, the non-coincidence of affections that, nevertheless, discovers a new psychic unity. For this reason, Simondon describes emotion as a kind of psychic of individuation, not merely a mode of affectivity. Emotion is "of the order of the metastable" (121) and, as such, it is through the experiencing of emotional ruptures – as we saw in Simondon's analysis of "anxiety" – that being encounters its limit, the threshold where being is put into question. Simondon's return to his discussion of emotion in this final chapter further amplifies the criticism of the hylemorphic scheme which initiates his study and continues to fuel the rejection of any scientific theory and philosophy that would seek to avoid the fundamental problem of individuation at its basis.

If one is to truly grasp form in the act of its coming into presence, one must think through the operation of individuation exceeding the realized form. It cannot be reduced to the form itself. For the notion of individuation to be entirely disengaged from the hylemorphic scheme requires, as Simondon defines it, "a process of thought that refuses an appeal to classification, and that does without definitions of essence by inclusion or exclusion of character" (209). Accordingly, one must be "able to think the realization of form starting from individuation but not individuation starting from the paradigm of the realization of form" (208). So, though it initially appeared that Simondon simply rejected outright the hylemorphic scheme, he is, in fact, more interested in using the ontogenetic perspective in order to reflect back upon the genesis of the hylemorphic scheme itself, to find within it the resources restricted but inseparable from its operation, to find the zone where its specific individuation is nurtured, the "obscure zone, which is precisely the central operational zone" (208).

171

As Simondon describes the obscure zone, it provides a model for every logical process by which a fundamental role might be attributed to the limit-cases, that is, to the threshold marking the boundary between extreme terms organizing a reality. We can find evidence of the appropriation of Simondon's notion of this "boundary" concept, the "obscure zone," not only in Deleuze's *Difference and Repetition* and *Logic of Sense* ("obscure zone," "zone of indetermination") but also Giorgio Agamben's *Homo Sacer* and *Remnants of Auschwitz*.

If we focus briefly for now on Agamben's works we witness the richness of Simondon's concept. The "zone of indistinction" – homologous with Simondon's "obscure zone" logically and metaphysically – Agamben argues, marks the threshold of the constituting power, the potentiality of bare life, in relation to constituted power – that is, the relation between *potentia* and *potestas* (in the Spinozist distinction). "At the limit, pure potentiality and pure actuality are indistinguishable, and the sovereign is precisely the zone of indistinction."[32] As such, this zone helps us to look beyond how power has been constituted by sovereignty, the already individuated given a form (via the imposing of the hylemorphic schema) toward an ontology of potentiality, disclosed by the concept of "bare life," which for Agamben is the "always present and always operative presupposition of sovereignty."[33] Bare life is compared with the eruption of nature in Hobbes; it is the most "sacred life" and, therefore, the most authentic, operational, political being. Its emergence forces a reflection on sovereignty. For this reason, Agamben argues that bare life is "the new political subject."[34]

And the pervasive alienation felt vaguely and indirectly throughout *Remnants of Auschwitz* is given powerful expression through the analysis of "shame," the emotion that Agamben identifies which opens us to the indiscernibility between the human and the inhuman. For this reason, "shame is truly something like the hidden structure of all subjectivity and consciousness."[35] Shame, as an emotion, opens before us the collective experience; in this regard, we can say that it acts as a mode of transindividual being. Explicitly carrying it forward into the political, Agamben (while certainly filtered through the work of Deleuze) is one of the most important of Simondon's speculative heirs.

Social morphology is able to describe a group's "body," its organizational form, while inter-psychology and sociology are able to describe those representations by which social coherency is instilled, a common identity; only ontogenesis, that is, the study of the individuation of groups, can disclose the existence of this "obscure relational zone" out of which emerges "the real collective" (209). Group reality is not a sociological fact that comes after the individuation that founds the collective. Nor does the group precede the individuation, predetermined by inter-psychological postulates, which in turn confirms for us that the individual's psychic dynamism, social tendencies, and needs originate from the group. The true collective is contemporary with the operation of individuation. "The social and the psychic are only case-limits; they are not the foundations of reality, the true terms of the relation" (209). Thus, Simondon's challenge is "grasping being in its center of activity" without restricting its action either to the purely psychic or the purely social, the purely interior and the purely exterior, form and matter (209).

> The relation can never be conceived as relation between pre-existing terms but as a reciprocal regime of exchange of information and causality in a system, which individuates itself. The relation exists physically, biologically, psychologically, collectively as internal resonance of individuated being; the relation expresses individuation, and is at the center of being. (210)

To properly grasp the relationality at the center of being, Simondon feels obliged to remind us once again that constitutively a "certain charge of the undetermined, i.e. of pre-individual reality, which passes through the operation of individuation without being effectively individuated," belongs to individuated being ... Without individuation there is no being and without being there is no relation" (210). For Simondon, we might call this the charge of undetermined "nature" – and it is what maintains and preserves, to whatever degree, a level of metastability as always present, even once being is overtly fully individuated. A metastable system is not the difference of reality or being; rather, it is difference at the level of action and organization.

The collective is born out of the charge of pre-individuality within every individuated being and cannot, therefore, be attributed to the encounter between an already existing form and matter. And it is this charge of nature that provides the condition for the birth of an inter-subjective relation, as a result of returning pre-individuality back to individuated beings (211). "The collective possesses its own ontogenesis, its own operation of individuation utilizing potentials brought by pre-individual reality contained in already individuated beings. The collective manifests itself via the internal resonance at the collective's interior; it is real insofar as it is a stable relational operation; it exists φυσχως [physically] and not λογιχως [rationally]" (211).

Simondon finds that his raising again the central if ambiguous role that pre-individuality plays in collective individuation is necessary to redress the problem of emotion. But how, and what additional element is gained in the process? Initially we are able conclusively to identify the reason as the failure of psychology to fully appreciate emotion's psychosocial dimension;

the purely psychological explanation restricts emotion to the function of a totally individuated being. Simondon rejects the purely psychological explanation on the grounds that emotion manifests the remnants of the pre-individual as constitutively a part of the individuated being; moreover, it is the real, if undetermined, potentiality that provokes the subject to become the collective. Emotion is the "exchange, within the subject, between the nature's charge and the stable structures of individuated being; the exchange between the pre-individual and the individuated; it prefigures the discovery of the collective" (211–12).

Emotion is not, however, the disorganization of the subject; it is "the beginning of a new structuration" stabilizing itself in the moment of the collective's emergence. "The essential instant of emotion is the collective's individuation" (213). The essential and resonant incompatibility between the charge of nature and individuated reality coalesces into "emotional latency," which indicates to the subject that it is "*more than* individuated being, that it receives from it the energy for an ulterior individuation." For this reason, Simondon argues, this ulterior individuation cannot be carried out in the being of a single subject alone; it can only be accomplished through a transindividual collective, carried out by multiple subjects (213). Emotion is neither implicitly social nor a deregulating operation of individuality; it is, instead, more essentially a structure of being, the "obscure zone of the psycho-somatic relation," through which an individuated being expresses its possible participation in other hidden individuations, incorporating whatever remains of pre-individuality in the subject. The social and the individual are only antithetically extremes, to the extent that they mark the mobilizing limits, never absolute, of the transindividual. "The transindividual has only been forgotten in philosophical reflection because it corresponds to the obscure zone of the hylemorphic schema" (214).

NOTES

1. Again, we remind ourselves: individualization is "the individuation of an individuated being" (133), that is to say, the individuation of a being already individualized but not yet individualized, not yet personalized.
2. Merleau-Ponty, *The Visible and the Invisible*, 126.
3. Like the similar uproar over the Aunt Jemima image used in American advertising, the Banania figure has been criticized for perpetuating an aggressively colonialist racial stereotype, the happy, benign and stupid Negro.
4. Simondon, *Communication et Information*, 66.
5. Léopold Sédar Senghor, *The Collected Poetry*, trans. Melvin Dixon (Charlottesville: University Press of Virginia, 1991), 39.
6. Combes, *Gilbert Simondon and the Philosophy of the Transindividual*, 38.

7. Edouard Glissant, *Caribbean Discourse: Selected Essays*, trans. J. Michael Dash (Charlottesville: University Press of Virginia, 1989), 20.
8. Patrick Chamoiseau, *Ecrire en pays dominé* (Paris: Gallimard, 1997), 226.
9. Glissant, *Caribbean Discourse*, 20.
10. Edouard Glissant, *Introduction à une poétique du divers* (Paris: Gallimard, 1996), 29.
11. Glissant, *Caribbean Discourse*, 20, Glissant's italics.
12. Frantz Fanon, *Black Skin, White Masks*, trans. Charles Lam Markmann (New York,: Grove Press, 1967), 18. My italics.
13. Sigmund Freud, *Beyond the Pleasure Principle*, trans. Gregory C. Richter (Peterborough, Ont.: Broadview, 2011), 68.
14. Freud, *Beyond the Pleasure Principle*, 98.
15. Freud, *Beyond the Pleasure Principle*, 89.
16. "Through its work of identification and sublimation it gives the death instincts in the id assistance in gaining control over the libido, but in so doing it runs the risk of becoming the object of the death instinct and of itself perishing. In order to be able to help in this way it has had itself to become filled with libido; it thus itself becomes the representative of Eros and thenceforward desires to live and to be loved." Sigmund Freud, *The Ego and the Id*, trans. Joan Riviere (New York: Norton, 1989), 59.
17. "And from the struggle against Eros! It can hardly be doubted that the pleasure principle serves the id as a compass in its struggle against the libido – the force that introduces disturbances into the process of life. If it is true that Fechner's principle of constancy governs life, which thus consists of a continuous descent towards death, it is the claims of Eros, of the sexual instincts, which, in the form of instinctual needs, hold up the falling level and introduce fresh tensions. The id, guided by the pleasure principle – that is, by the perception of unpleasure – fends off these tensions in various ways" (Freud, *The Ego and the Id*, 46).
18. Freud, *Group Psychology and the Analysis of the Ego*, 13.
19. Freud, *Group Psychology and the Analysis of the Ego*, 13–14.
20. Freud, *Group Psychology and the Analysis of the Ego*, 31.
21. Freud, *Group Psychology and the Analysis of the Ego*, 43.
22. Freud, *Group Psychology and the Analysis of the Ego*, 41–2.
23. Freud, *Group Psychology and the Analysis of the Ego*, 68.
24. The specific technical meaning in psychology for "tendance."
25. Simondon's 1964 course "On Instinct" is central for getting a definitive idea concerning the difference between instinct and tendency. Cf. Simondon, *Communication et Information*, 247–373.
26. Jean Laplanche, *Life and Death in Psychoanalysis*, trans. Jeffrey Mehlman (Baltimore: Johns Hopkins University Press, 1976).
27. "The collective is what results from a secondary individuation in relation to vital individuation, taking back what the previous individuation had left of brute nature unemployed in the living. This second individuation cannot totally recover the first; in spite of the collective, the individual perishes as

individual, and the participation in the collective cannot save him from this death, consequence of the first individuation. The second individuation, that of the collective and the spiritual, gives birth to transindividual significations which cannot die with the individuals through which they are constituted; what there is in the subject-being of pre-individual nature can survive in the form of signification to the individual that had been living" (206–7).

28. At this point one can no longer avoid a critique of the gender-exclusive language that is pervasive throughout Simondon's work. While one would like to render his language and the problems it raises wholly gender neutral (which I have tried to do at specific points in this work), the problem is that Simondon's critique of anthropology is precisely the critique of the absolutist ideal of the Man-Form. Foucault, Deleuze, and others of course offer innovative interrogations of this Form. But that takes me too far beyond this work.

29. We recall here Foucault's more or less contemporary critique of anthropology (in *The Order of Things*), which in a similar manner, though of course utilizing different methods, sought to contest the epistemological significance of the "Man-Form." We find this to be more explicitly the case in the various critiques carried out by feminist philosophers, like Luce Irigaray.

30. Kant, *Critique of Pure Reason*, A 751/ B 779.

31. Kant, *Critique of Pure Reason*, A 599/ B 627.

32. Giorgio Agamben, *Homo Sacer. Sovereign Power and Bare Life*, trans. Daniel Heller-Roazen (Stanford: Stanford University Press, 1998), 47.

33. Agamben, *Homo Sacer*, 106.

34. Agamben, *Homo Sacer*, 123.

35. Giorgio Agamben, *Remnants of Auschwitz: The Witness and the Archive*, trans. Daniel Heller-Roazen (New York: Zone Books, 2000), 128.

7

An Ethics of Ontogenesis and a Non-human Humanism

TO HAVE DONE WITH JUDGMENT

Deleuze's appropriation of Antonin Artaud's phrase "Have done with judgment" is meant to act as a wedge to separate philosophy from what Deleuze calls the "entire doctrine of judgment." This is why he uses Artaud's phrase as the title of one his most important essays. And it is this doctrine of judgment, Deleuze believes, since its outcomes are pre-determined, that has transformed philosophical critique into judgment's enabler. "The condition of judgment lies in a supposed relation between existence and the infinite in the *order* of time."[1] The eternal is the order of time claimed for the infinite. He who judges and is judged gains the power of the eternal, Deleuze argues, by transforming himself into a plea for this relation. Judgment is an action that, to whatever degree, makes a petition, an invocation, a prayer to the eternal. Whosoever embraces the infinite and takes it to be inseparable from human existence is worthy to judge and to be judged. But one must first prove this worth.

Judgment, for Simondon, is incarnated by the figures of transcendence – the Sage, the Hero, and the Martyr-Saint. These are but figments of an illusory eternity, a false intemporality. But they do so by coordinating the relation of existence and the infinite. They are in short figures of judgment. As such, for Simondon, we must not only take the Sage, the Hero, and the Saint to be figures that demarcate the threshold where transcendence falters in grasping individuation, but we must also appreciate how they bring about the dissolution of figuration itself: where the Figure (Good Form) gives way to transformation, metamorphoses, transfiguration. For judgment and figuration or representation reciprocally determine one another. This is why Simondon says that the best thing these figures can

177

offer us is a kind of "negative revelation," a cautionary tale, if you will, of what is at stake and what might be lost when a society, a group, is built on the pledge of communication between a superior reality promised by the infinite transcending the living current of existence. We must learn from them if we want to create new values.

It is not judgment itself, however, which is really at issue; it is what conditions the act of judging, making it possible by directing its capacities. Every judgment reflects a definitive arbitration before the "tribunal of the pure form of reason," according to Kant; and so, ultimately, judgment's role is to represent being as subject and legislator – the subjective form of principles *and* the objective form of law that acts as the determining ground. To have done with judgment is to have done with the values presumed by the ontological and epistemological privilege granted to the (subjective) individual on the basis of the highest good, the Good Form. This is why, for Artaud, Deleuze, and certainly for Simondon, to "have done with judgment" is to finally surpass the transcendental value given to God, to subjectivity, to Man. We liberate vital forces and invite the emergence of new modes of existence to discover those potentials not in the predetermined possibilities of the *a priori* but, rather, in the existence of a pre-individuality, only ever metastable, inexhaustible and threatening whatever representations that would direct thought toward those ends representing the maxims directing a subject's actions. "Herein, perhaps, lies the secret: to bring into existence and not to judge."[2]

In the Conclusion to IPC (which is really the conclusion to IL), Simondon does something completely unexpected: he broadly sketches the outlines for an ethics. Simondon occupies a position unique in relation to thinkers like Foucault and Deleuze who have been most credited with establishing the basis for developing an explicitly post-Nietzschean ethics. Those who have chosen to pursue this path are expected to share their fundamental skepticism with regards to any hint of ethical normativity. A post-Nietzschean ethics has come to be characterized as equating the formulation of norms with the desire for moral absolutism or autocracy. By contrast, Simondon argues for a fuller appreciation of normative criteria – and, indeed, the need for creating new norms – as the precondition for carrying out any ethical action. However, what Simondon means by normativity is not the same as prescribing a moral absolute. Indeed, his search for an axiomatic of the human sciences on the basis of an ontogenetic speculative shift is inseparable from his calling for a genetic analysis of those values said to give birth to the moral norms of right and wrong, good and evil. Here is where we uncover the payoff for Simondon's committed Nietzscheanism. For it is exactly the return to the "innocence of becoming" (as Nietzsche describes it) that is the incentive for a "transvaluation" of a system of values, transforming the catalyst for the development of a normative ethics; ethics becomes indistinguishable from the operation of ontogenesis more generally.

There are at best very oblique suggestions that the problem of individuation might lead to a fundamental revaluation of values as preparation for an ethics coming to light with the perspective furnished by ontogenesis. Really, only Simondon's recurrent engagement with the notion of spirituality might suggest an ethical component. But he does not exploit even this possibility. Why wait until the conclusion to introduce his ethics? Unfortunately, Simondon leaves us with the sense that this aspect of his work was to remain largely uncompleted, particularly as it gestures toward a new conception of political subjectivity. The only instance that we can find in which Simondon directly engages in the formulation of an ethics of ontogenesis is in a fragment that the editor helpfully appends to IPC.

THE ETERNAL RETURN OF BECOMING

Contrary to the perspective offered by Christianity (and by religion more generally), which requires a principle of complementarity drawing from the value of transcendence, Simondon turns to the pre-Socratic concept of the *apeiron*. For the pre-Socratic philosopher Anaximander, the *apeiron* [ἄπειρον] or the "unlimited" or the "Indefinite" was theorized as the engendering principle of being – the becoming of being – "the source of coming-to-be for existing things is that into which destruction, too, happens, 'according to necessity'."[3] It constitutes the flux of time, while it exists itself in timelessness. "According to the hypothesis presented here," Simondon writes, "something of the *apeiron* remains in the individual as a crystal retains its aqueous solution" (197). Once again, in this passage we find Simondon using the crystal image as a paradigm for an operational process. The *apeiron* is a share of indeterminate nature, which acts as the catalyst, as I detailed previously, to invite the second individuation individuating the amorphous milieu, lacking structure; and so it is metastable and structurable. By adding this charge of energy, of information, the aqueous system is "shocked" and becomes polarized, organizing itself along these energetic thresholds into structures of being and, with the release of energy from this reaction, into a milieu for a potentially new individual being. Hence, every individual being exists only to the degree that it maintains within itself the potential for transformation; and this potentiality becomes available to being via the element of asymmetry, which in turn discloses within each individual being, to whatever degree, the state of its own vital amorphous metastability. If we think of reality as only ever the interminable movement of the "phasing" of being in and out of phase,

179

each transformation, each becoming, birth and death is an "ensemble" of these phasings or becomings. Each phase of being is the affective becoming that is the operation of individuation. What this means, according to Simondon, is that any one individual being having an existence in the world is only a "dephased" singularity when the movement of becoming slows or suddenly deviates, if only ever momentarily. Not yet phased, this catalyst of nature remains unexhausted, and hence the constituent within each subsequent phase, in persisting, ensures the interminable and yet, to whatever variable degree, indeterminable movement of individuation toward a third phase.

This is why it must be stressed that, for Simondon, more profoundly significant than the claim that the individual is the product of the propagation of order out of chaos is the idea that whatever an individual being becomes, it is only ever incomplete – it is *in-between* metastabilities, a not-yet individuated "phase" within the transductive continuum of becoming. Simondon's Allagmatic theory, which works by associating levels of reality through a series of real analogues, advances a perspective from which to explain how a relation of complementarity is engendered between the "natures born by many individuals but not yet contained in the individualities already constituted from these individuals" (197). It is the shares of nature that incite individuals together to form a collective in order to resolve incompatibilities within and without.

Importantly, while Simondon describes a "persistence of the primitive and original phase of being" incarnating the tendency toward the "third phase of the collective" (197), there is never really any "original" event, a point of absolute singularity, in that this first indeterminate primitive event is only ever constituted as such "after" individuation has begun. Every individual is, therefore, pre-individual. An individual being's existence is determined by the potential it has for another individuation; there is no real origin, it is only ever repeated, a pure dynamism only ever displacing its beginning with every new subsequent individuation at multiple levels, often simultaneously.

At the same time that the third phase of individuation most apparently brings forth the collective, Simondon's individuation acts as the "eternal return" of the common becoming of all metamorphoses, bringing into the actual present – here and now – *again*, all the phases of becoming. For this operation brings all the preceding contraries, extremes, in all the individuated degrees of power into communication with one another. In this regard, the collective provides an excuse for the disindividuating return of the pre-individuality from which every individual "originates." Before the individual can become collective, it must first plunge back into the pre-individual; the individual must lose itself before it, she, he can find itself in the collective being. For the individual it is obviously exhilarating and potentially dangerous.

Simondon linking of the pre-Socratics with Nietzsche's eternal return is made more explicit when he suggests that the Heraclitus' discovery of the condition of the birth of life in death is "the complementarity of the sum of becoming" expressed by Nietzsche's notion of the eternal return. Further, this association between Nietzsche and the pre-Socratics is strengthened, ironically, by Simondon's oblique reference to Spinoza: that this myth of the eternal return is essential for the pre-Socratics as well and, so, points to their common pantheism (250). Here again we have an example of Simondon's eccentric Spinozism – a Spinozism that does not to want to admit its Spinozism. As we saw in Chapter 4, Simondon justifies the disqualifying of Spinozist ontology precisely because it is pantheistic. How, then, is he able to turn around and associate the pre-Socratics, in whose thought he finds analogues for his own ontogenetic project, with Nietzsche's eternal return on the basis of their shared pantheism, when it is precisely for this reason that he rejects adopting Spinoza to metaphysically describe ontogenesis? We need not forget that Nietzsche saw Spinoza as his precursor. Perhaps the best that might be said (to paraphrase Combes' position relative to Simondon's attitude toward Marx) is that, more than Simondon himself wants to admit, his thought is closer to not further from Spinoza's. We have to leave an examination of the reasons for this for another time.[4]

NORMS AND VALUES

At the heart of Simondon's formulation of an ontogenetic ethics is the opposition between norms and values. It would appear that this relationship is oppositional. It is not. In truth, the distinction maintained between norms and values is, for Simondon, wholly non-oppositional and, as such, reciprocal and a relationship of codetermination. What defines a norm and a value is not the fact that they stand fully defined opposed to one another in an asymmetrical relationship, or that one negates the other, yielding an ethics as their synthesis. On the contrary, they are the extremes of the relationality constituting them. In themselves they are nothing but the relation, the effect signaling a relational being. The distinction drawn between norms and values only makes sense, according to Jean-Hugues Barthélémy, as an "articulation" of the resistance to their being reduced to a relationship of simple opposition. Barthélémy instead argues that the difference constituting norms and values provides the *"common soil* of an ethics of being ["pure" ethics] and ethics of becoming ["applied" or "practical" ethics]."[5] And in this regard, they remain never fully resolvable, and so are only ever *problematic* and *problematizing* of their own particular status. Therefore, as I survey how Simondon defines norms and values, it is important to remember that the particular definition given to them is only ever reflective of one in relation to the other, to the way each problematize and make use of the other.

To summarize: Simondon's ontogenetic ethics must be distinguished from any and all forms of Kantian moral philosophy (his primary target)[6] on the basis of what I am calling the ontologizing leap, and what Simondon calls the leap into the "pre-critical." Ethics is transformed once the perspective for choosing "right" or "wrong" action is made on the basis of an appeal to becoming and the presumption that all being is only ever incomplete and indeterminate (to whatever degree). In doing so, we replace the Kantian presumption on which moral choices are made: the total and complete individual being, with its corollary, conscious and coherent subjectivity. What this means is that the normative is only an effect of affective practice and, therefore, expressive of the particular problem of incompatibility – of existence and necessity, between the individual and the world and between other individuals – that elicits the decision to act, to be, or not to be. An ontogenetic ethics is one that raises the question of how an individual lives its problematic being (255). But to raise this as a question one must always have presupposed the problematic being of the individual.

Value, alternatively, acquires its "sense" or meaning as a result of its expressing the compatibility within and between a culture's civic and religious domains. Still, whatever sense value obtains is possible only because the individual cannot be characterized as a substance or "an aspirant toward substantiality." The individual is instead "grasped as *the singular point of an open infinity of relations*" (254). For Simondon, the actual flowering of a relational ontology is achieved by the formulation of an ethics; further, this ethics affirms for us the necessity of loosening the determination of finitude and individual being, so that the presumption of individuality might relinquish its ontological and epistemological privilege to the eternity of the process of becoming engendering it. It is the ontological leap from *hic et nunc* to *sub specie aeternitatis* that correlates with the descriptive shift of metaphysical perspective from individuality to individuation. This is what lies behind the discussion of eternity which I carried out in Chapter 3 of this study.

Being is never fully exhausted once it is realized in the form of the individuated individual being. The reason for this is that the potentiality of becoming remains always available to the individuated individual in the form of pre-individuality; its potential for becoming other than it is constitutively preserves itself within the individual being. It is the pre-individual that determines for the individual being its "force of existing." And, for this reason, we find in value the particular conjunction of existence and necessity, compelling and exceeding its normative realization. The relation has the value of being because it exceeds its being reduced to the opposition between the desire for eternity and the necessity of the collective (254–5). Value, or rather its sense, is inherent to the relation; it spurs the creation of relations. A value's affectivity can be felt; it takes the form of the passion prompting us to action, to search for a solution not already given by the world or personal identity, without guarantee of success. Indeed, values are what invite our investigating into what determines our choices, what conditions the choices made: "the subject's self-constitution through its actions" (256).

Simondon reallocates the moral problem to the level of action. It is not some abstract issue of good or evil. The moral is dependent on the value of an action, the "permanent constructive mediation thanks to which the subject becomes progressively conscious" of the reality that its existence is synonymous with resolving problems in action (256). The subject does not provide norms, nor does it adopt them for directing action. "It is itself the norm of its action." A norm's invention springs from the auto-creation of a regime of compatibility. An individual being seeks resolution to the conflict of existence and necessity through instituting regimes of compatibilities between the normative aspects of her or his existence. The ethical individual, in carrying out a moral action, does so by resolving an ontological problem arising out of its existence, but affectively experienced, into normative categories ("good"/"evil," "right"/"wrong"). If we return to Simondon's language, we might say that the invention of norms is produced during the process of an individual being's *individualization*: during becoming a *subject*. A moral consciousness is born from the need of the individualized being to regulate its own subjective existence. "Moral consciousness is a regulative consciousness submitted to an internal auto-regulation; this double regulative consciousness can be called a normative consciousness" (257).

Simondon contends that ethics diverges into two paths, "never to rejoin." The one path is what he calls a "pure" ethics and the other, "applied" ethics. Simondon tends to use "ethics" and "morality" interchangeably. However, I would like to restrict "morality" to what Simondon calls pure (sometimes "theoretical") ethics, but I retain his term "applied" or "practical ethics."

I hope to show that, although Simondon initially seems to oppose them, ultimately both morality and practical ethics originate from the non-opposition of norms and values. Norms are the form values take once they are categorized. Rather than call "theoretical ethics" "normative ethics" (which might seem a more likely option), "morality" seems more definitively to follow from the adopting of transcendent values to direct personality, whereas ethics more thoroughly captures the sense of value emerging out of the immanent modes of existence in relation to one another. A practical ethics is an emergent value, while morality is a projective normativity: it projects a norm to explain value. But we must be careful here, for while pure and applied ethics never come to a point of synthesis, nevertheless, just prior to their becoming actualized, values and norms must continuously interact. I will describe the nature of this interaction below.

Simondon institutes this dichotomy between a pure or "theoretical" morality and an applied ethics to parallel the ontological difference he discerns between the two ways to grasp being: as the essence of a fully individuated substance and as only ever an indeterminate and incomplete event of becoming. A pure ethics or morality takes place at the level of essences, which for Simondon has the purpose of preserving the "theoretical substantiality of the individuated being; in fact, [a morality] surrounds it with an illusion of substantiality" (236). And so, for this reason, Simondon asserts that morality demonstrates "a contra-existence, an anti-becoming, which gives the impression of substantiality." It would be more accurate to call this morality a "substantialist ethics," which co-opts the perceptive and affective (237).

Practical ethics, strictly speaking, opposes morality on the basis of its using values defined by the latter in order to constitute itself in a stable manner. "The ethics of becoming and action in the present needs the ethics [morality] of wisdom according to eternity in order to be conscious of itself as ethics of action; it agrees with itself in what it refuses more than what it constructs, like the ethics of wisdom" (237). In this regard, both morality and ethics are required to achieve signification. Morality seeks out the immutability of being, whereas a practical ethics acts to compose a normative correlate with the being of becoming. Only in tandem is the signification possible that completes individuality. This is why Simondon once again returns to the notion of information as a way to locate the point of correlation between a practical ethics and becoming.

> The notion of information as identical to the internal resonance of a system on the way to the completion of individuation . . . endeavors to grasp (*saisir*) being in its becoming without privileging an immobile essence of being or becoming *qua* becoming; there is only a complete ethics to the extent that the becoming of being is grasped (*saisi*) as being itself, in other words, to the extent becoming is known as becoming of being. (237–8)

Information as identical to the internal resonance of a system is, for Simondon, the means for testing the sufficiency of morality and practical ethics. What he finds is that when both are placed in opposition to one another, separately they are insufficient. As Simondon suggests, each respectively favors either interiority, in the case of morality, or exteriority, in the case of practical ethics, on the basis of their continuing to ontologically fixate on the individuated being. The evidence for this is that they situate individuation anterior to an individual being's realization. A practical ethics retains a "perpetual nostalgia" for the purity of individuated being, something it shares with morality ("theoretical ethics"). Neither is able to truly grasp and accompany being in the act of its individuation. It is only when we consider individuation to be conditioned by the internal resonance of a system, that is, as information, that we might truly grasp the successive constitutions of metastable equilibria, without needing to resort to either the morality "of the eternity of being," devoted to a definitive, absolute, and eternal structure, or to the practical ethics and its unexamined presumption that whatever action is chosen is from the perspective of the "perpetual evolution of being." Morality and practical ethics structure themselves by instituting a formal principle that continuously modifies norms to match the incessant evolution of their milieu. Contrary to the "absolute stability of the unconditional," Simondon offers, "it is necessary to substitute the notion of a successive series of metastable equilibria" (238). And it is with this shift that the notions of values and norms must be rethought.

NORMS	VALUES
Stability	Metastability
Individuated	Pre-individual
Individual	Relational
Being	Becoming
Structure	Operation

Values are operational. Norms are structural. Values are operations. Norms are structures. Which is to say, values exist so that the norms of a system can become new norms for another system through the operational conversion of structures into other structures. Values express the moment in which the "structures of a system translate themselves into structures that replace it" (238). In this regard, values are the "becoming of norms" (238). Values incite and establish the norm's transductivity. Norms, on the other hand, constitute "lines of internal coherence" and, thus, reflect their attained states of equilibria (however brief). In other words, as pure relationality, values are the expression of the convertibility of structures, of normative structures; in being expressive they give what they grasp in acting out the event of this transformation. This is why we can say that

Simondon's Allagmatic "general theory of transformation" (284) is really only most immediately and concretely experienced via how he sets up the relationship between values and norms. In either case, metastability is foregrounded rather than coherency and stability.

Instead of their being transformed into more permanent or "noble" norms, values leave behind "a sense of the axiomatic of becoming," for each value conserves a metastable state (239). As Simondon writes, "values are information contained in norms," or more accurately, in their being de-differentiated, norms are brought to the state of information: they are what conserves one state to another. Once de-differentiated, now disindividuated, norms are prepared for their potential conversion into other norms. Hence, norms and values together determine the ethical system to be only ever relative. "Everything is relative, except the very formula of this relativity, according to which a system of norms is able to be converted into another system of norms" (239).

An ethical system's desired "completeness" is only an illusory distortion that all the same positively discloses the destructive element internal to the system of normativity. And it is this internal element that ensures the possibility of the ethical system's transductive translation into another system. It is the determination of its relativity. Consequently, it is necessary that the system gain knowledge of the "relativity" constitutive to itself – that its attained equilibrium incorporates a fundamental metastability. For not only does this metastability provide the condition for morality (purely theoretical) and practical ethics to coincide, it also specifies the tendency for our conceiving eternity in terms of "consciousness of the relative." No longer must ethics coincide with the will to arrest becoming or to render an origin absolute, while normatively privileging a structure; instead, an ontogenetic ethics, from Simondon's perspective the only true ethics, correlates with the "knowledge (*le savoir*) of the metastability of norms" (239). The will-to-absolute norms "mimes eternity and intemporality at the interior of a life" – a Sage's life, or a Saint's life, or a Hero's life. These figures encase and memorialize a false eternity. Such an absolutist morality is dependent upon the pretense of controlling becoming, directing it toward some end, some purpose predetermined, so that once it has been achieved salvation is guaranteed. But Simondon reminds us that the Sage, the Saint, the Hero, or other "styles of individual life are only extremes that illustrate poles of the moral life; they are not themselves the elements of the moral life" (240).

There is no real hierarchy of values to norms. Values are not superior to norms, nor vice versa. Rather, values traverse and transect norms. Values open norms to their own variability, to that tendency which they carry within that invites transformation. And, as such, values act as a kind of *apeiron* of indetermination. In this way, Nature is present within norms by way of the internal resonance forming them, fostered by this share of inde-termination. Neither things, categories, or forms, values are the *tendencies* or forces that compel a "putting into question the subject that necessarily provokes a momentary losing of the hold of constituted individuality, which is engulfed by the pre-individual" (240–1). As such, values are the direct expression of transindividual individuation, stipulating the condi-tions of possibility for new individuations.[7]

Still, norms are only secondarily conceivable as expressing a defined individuation and have, as a consequence, a structural and functional sense at the level of individuated beings, while "values can be conceived as tied to the very birth of norms, expressing the fact that norms arise with an individuation and only last as long as this individuation exists as a present state" (240–1).

A contradiction between the different norms of systems is possible only if one transforms the individual into the absolute rather than taking it to be nothing more than "the expression of an individuation creating solely a metastable state" (241). The "moral" status assigned to norms only ever reflects the ontological status of the system overall. But what really invites the shift of morality to the ontological and, thus, to ethics (and back) is the constitutive role Simondon gives to metastable pre-individuality. "Being becomes moral subject insofar as it is individuated reality and non-individuated associated reality" (241). Thus, to privilege the primacy of being, as individuated or not individuated, is to oppose norms (relative to individuated being in a system) to values (relative to the non-individuated reality associated with individuated being). "Morality is neither in norms nor values but in the continuum that spreads values to norms, grasped (*saisi*) in its real center. Norms and values are the extreme terms of a dynamic of being, terms which neither consist in themselves alone nor support them-selves alone" (241). Ethics distances itself from moral pronouncements or judgments or, for that matter, the franchising of an immutable eternity to justify them (falsely, according to Simondon). More significant is grasping the ontogenetic grounds that become necessary if one hopes to provoke and maintain the dynamism of convertibility of values into norms, and norms into values, to parallel the individuation of being.

INNOCENCE OF BECOMING: ETHICS AS SENSE OF INDIVIDUATION

Ethics is exigency according to which there is a significant correlation of norms and values. To grasp (*saisir*) ethics in its unity requires that we *accompany* ontogenesis: *ethics is the sense of individuation*, the sense of the synergy of successive individuations. It is *the sense of the transductivity of becoming*, the sense according to which in each act resides at once the movement of going further and the scheme that will integrate other schemes; it is the sense according to which the interiority of an act has meaning in exteriority. (242, my italics)

So we see that Simondon takes ethics to be the most direct and pure way to grasp ontogenesis in the "here and now," *hic et nunc*, that is to say, *in the act* of carrying out the transductivity of becoming. Ethics must be distinguished from morality by the fact that the former looks for the impetus to invent new norms in those values expressive of its engendering imperatives, grasped from the perspective of ontogenesis. In this way ethics accompanies ontogenesis. An ontogenetic ethics furnishes individuation with meaning that, otherwise, remains an anonymous, stubborn, if equanimous trek of becoming, indifferent to all but the motive it provides for itself.

Certainly, Simondon's characterization of a new ethics that not only grasps but also ontogenetically expresses the conditions of its possibility is interesting. But now what? How is the ethical act changed? What becomes the ethical act, the ethical choice or decision relative to this ontological ground, now fully clarified by our taking the ontogenetic perspective?

There is ethics insofar as there is information, in other words, signification surmounting a *disparation* of elements of beings, and making what is interior also exterior. The value of an act does not lie in its universalizable character according to the norms that it implicates but the effective reality of its integration in a network of acts, which is becoming. It is very much a question of a network and not a chain of acts. (242)

No ethical action is itself the result of its own single motivation, nor is its effect limited to itself. An ethical action only acquires its affective intensity when integrated with and operative within a larger network or informational web of actions. This is what gives an ethical action its sense or signification. Moral action, on the other hand, draws its motive ultimately from an ontology that privileges the status of the individual; for even if a moral action is related to the relations between individuals, it remains the effect of an *inter-individual* assemblage, however contingent or supposedly influenced or anteriorly determined by historical determinations.[8] What most distinguishes moral action from ethical action is that the latter finds itself to be determined by something internal to the act as it is carried out. It is from this ethical perspective that moral questions take on a different caste. For example: Was Muhammad Bouazizi's act of self-immolation an ethical act? There are moments in the life of a social group when it is no longer able to conserve its structure, when it becomes incompatible with itself, according to Simondon. In those moments a society expresses the tendency, only always internally constitutive of its structure, to de-differentiate and over-saturate itself. Might Bouazizi's act become ethically significant (and explicitly not a moral act) in provoking what Simondon calls a "pre-revolutionary state" of oversaturation, the crystalline event that initiates a whole series of transductive ethical and political acts of collective individuation – from Tunis to Libya to Egypt – transforming societies, raising to the level of signification the group's modifying of itself in responding to conditions of metastability? Unlike moral reality, an ontogenetic ethics offers a perspective on a reality structured in terms of a network of relations. An ethical act elevates to its highest intensity of value the relationality of its own genesis, that is, the resonance of acts in relation to one another, but directly within the system that it foments. "Each act is centered but infinite; the value of an act is its breadth, its transductive expansion" (243). One cannot divorce the act from the infinity of its transductive expansion, its relations with other relations, ensuring that it completes itself – who knows when? If norms are, for Simondon, analogous to variants of the Good Form, then an ethical act spreads, dephasing into lateral acts, and joins with other acts in spreading from its own active and unique origin, as if from yellow-green to green and yellow, via the augmentation of a larger band of frequency. As neither form nor matter, an ethical action is only ever "becoming *in the midst of becoming*; it is being insofar as it is in the process of becoming" (242). Ethics is this reality that is more "than unity and itself," whose existence is inseparable from the other realities with which it connects.

And freedom? Freedom "is that which has enough reality in order to go beyond itself and re-encounter other acts." While all decisions or acts have an organizing motive or source, there is no *external* limit to freedom. This does not mean that freedom is somehow absolute. A goal, end or purpose fixed by some outside or anterior absolute principle or force to supposedly explain the end toward which all things are directed is not what determines an ethical act's necessity. This presumption of an end is a form of prejudice that denies becoming. From the ontogenetic ethical perspective all things proceed from a certain eternal necessity of Nature, which Nature provides to itself.

Thus, the necessity for an action is internally generated in relationship to other realities, other acts. An action's freedom is one carried out on the basis of its grasping (though without necessarily fully comprehending) that it emerges from the necessity of the imperative internally engendered within itself, within the operation of individuation making it possible, this operation conditioned by those potentialities available to it as a result of the share of nature every individual being bears within her or himself. Freedom is not in the free judgment but in the free necessity – to accompany becoming – to persevere along and within the interior of whatever courses psychic and collective individuation lay before the individual being.

AESTHETICISM AND THE ACT OF MADNESS

"An act that is only itself is not a moral act." A "moral" act is one that emerges from a decision, which inserts itself into becoming without arresting its movement, bringing to completion "this dephasing of being that *is* becoming" (243). Simondon describes the non-moral act as "lost in itself"; it "buries itself" and in so doing, it likewise "buries a part of the becoming of the subject." A loss of signification, of meaning, is brought about by the immoral act, for it destroys the signification of acts that either exist or would be summoned to exist by its preventing other acts from structuring themselves in the network. In this sense, there is not, properly speaking, an act but the inverse of an act, an illusory "becoming" that absorbs and destroys the relational significations of other acts, which might seem to suggest a transductivity while, in fact, it misleads the subject in relation to itself. Simondon calls it a "parasitic act, a false act that draws its appearance of signification from a counter-signification" (244).

For Simondon, this false act takes the form of what he calls "aestheticism." "Aestheticism is a parasite of moral becoming" (244). Morality as aestheticism transforms ethical acts into pure exterior ritual, the creation of monuments, the worshiping of icons, the emptiness of contemplation without action. If, for Nietzsche, the only true values are aesthetic values, it is the reduction of ethics to the aesthetic that is Simondon's concern. More specifically, for Simondon, aestheticism demands the adopting of an extrinsic norm, an ideal or a form, which becomes the "given" for invention: for example, God, the Good Man, the Worker, etc. Aestheticism is contra-moral because it institutes a unification of acts accorded by imposing a certain "common style" that, consequently, restricts (if not totally eliminates) the power of transductivity. The imperfection of the non-moral or immoral act, for Simondon, is most evident in its refusal of a "constitutive relative inadequacy." The Ancient Greeks sought the reduplication of the perfection of the Athenian city in the idealized symmetry of the human form and vice versa. The exterior form shared by the human body and the city supposedly unifies the relativity of values. It is on the basis of the devotion to the form of beauty, determined as embodying the pure perfection of the common social and religious ideal, that a moral action must be judged. The principles that emerge for the invention of values and action originate from exterior comparison, with the extrinsic form of one the model for the other. Aestheticism restricts the moral perfection sought and achieved to an exterior affair: a matter of the representation of a wholly exterior aesthetic model.

In actuality, an act's perfection emerges from within the interior of its own limits. Every moral act includes information in the form of values that situate and limit it as an act: it develops according to a certain partially inhibiting regulation, which translates its existence as act into a network or web of acts. "In a certain sense, the act of madness (*l'acte fou*) is identical to the perfect act" (245). Only a "crazy act," an act of madness, is somehow isolated from the totality of all other possible acts. As a result, it is left without a way to measure its "perfection" against those acts of others; without a way to activate and inhibit it, to explain its being (*aseity*); the act of madness is left to imagine that it possesses some property or "substance." The act of madness confirms for itself its own realness by finding itself reduplicated everywhere, in every individuated object. Indeed, it takes itself to be the source for the individuation of everything.

> The act of madness (*l'acte fou*) is that which tends to be a total individuation, and only admits as real that which is totally individuated. Acts exist in a network insofar as they are realized on a ground of nature, a source of becoming by continuous individuation. This act is no longer an internal normativity; it consists in itself and enters into the vertigo of its iterative existence. (245)

Simondon argues that becoming is *denatured* by morality. In its need to reject a positive role for inadequacy in the creation of norms, particularly from Simondon's perspective in the form of an internal disparity constitutive of the act itself, morality justifies *for itself* the belief in the reality of an achievable complete perfection. The act of madness, therefore, must be defined by what it presumes: it presumes becoming as identical with the process of degradation and adaptation. Change is externally measured on the basis of degrees of dissimilarity relative to the presumed perfection of the aesthetic form that judgment gives to itself.

Here too we find further evidence supporting the notion that the guarantee of the immorality of a moral act is found in the purely egoistic act in relation to other acts. The immoral act seeks only the domination of other acts. As Nietzsche argues, the supremacy of the moral judgment's accomplishment requires the presumption of the perfectibility of the entire human "subject" to justify for itself the righteousness of its action.

> This type of man needs to believe in an unbiased "subject" with freedom of choice, because he has an instinct of self-preservation and self-affirmation in which every lie is sanctified. The reason the subject (or, as we more colloquially say, the *soul*) has been, until now, the best doctrine on earth, is perhaps because it facilitated that sublime self-deception whereby the majority of the dying, the weak and the oppressed of every kind could construe weakness itself as freedom, and their particular mode of existence as an *accomplishment*.[9]

What distinguishes the moral "subject" from the ethical subject? It is the degree to which the ethical subject reflects and affirms by its action its own share of pre-individuality, the "insufficiency" of imperfection at the heart of its being and the impetus for the creation of values, instead of denying or suppressing its assumed imperfectibility. The ethical subject exists only ever in the act of the self-overcoming of the moral subject. In the end, the act of "madness" that Simondon describes, as it strains to become moral, rests on denying the very same pre-individual reality that is associated with propagating the genesis of individuated being. To deny the pre-individual – Life, Nature – is to deny the generating and inhibiting source of normativity. This is what lies behind Simondon's evoking of Nietzsche's description of the "ascetic priest" as the most dangerous of moralists, the great co-opter of values who, nonetheless, offers us a method of valuation that, on the promise of salvation, turns life *against* life.[10] In this regard, Simondon's post-Nietzschean ethical formulation is particularly unusual and nuanced.

What is immoral is the morality of a devaluation of life; thus, it is morality that becomes immoral, unaware of its own ethical practice. It is the moral act that is the greatest act of madness. And it is ethics that brings us back to the *innocence* of becoming.

> Ethics is that by which the subject remains subject, refusing to become an absolute individual, closed domain of reality, detached singularity; it is that by which the subject remains in an internal problematic and externally always tensed, i.e. in a real present, living in the central zone of being, not wanting to become either form or matter. Ethics expresses the sense of perpetuated individuation, the stability of becoming, which is that of being as pre-individuated and self-individuating. (246)

The ethical act is both *anterior and internal*, Simondon argues, to morality and to its forming judgments of "good" and "evil," "right" and "wrong." Ethics puts into practice in the form of moral action the ontogenetic principle. This principle is what affirms that every moral act is "more than the unity" specified by the judgment uttered. Although it concentrates all emotion and action in the form of the subject, judgment confirms that the moral act alone is meaningless, but realized in and through the infinity of other acts. Morality becomes actual owing to the transvaluation of values, of the movement of information to signification, carried out at the transindividual level of our most profound relationships. In other words, judgment is but a response to the problem of life posed by becoming a collective. Perhaps it must be said that, in the end, the principle that Simondon's *Psychic and Collective Individuation* dramatizes is that grasping the problem of individuation is fundamentally ethical, insofar as it is one with grasping life.

CULTURE OF VALUES

Values symbolize the most "perfect integration possible," the point at which the relationship between individual beings achieves "unlimited complementarity." While the functional complementarity of values assumes diverse symbolic forms at different levels, still the most well-known forms assumed by values are, respectively, universal will, divine finality, and the principle of sufficient reason. What all three forms share in traversing the ontological, moral, and epistemological dimensions is their being taken as representing the stages in which whatever incompatibility present in reality and between realities is ideally resolved. They are all realizations of the state of being in total compatibility.

Simondon finds an ideal example in value given to "God" by Christianity, originating in the dissymmetrical relationship of the creator and the created. "God" is the attainment of the value of complementarity. It incarnates the function of the synthesis of three distinct levels of reality: at the first level, is the birth of an "elected people," resulting from the appeal to "God" as the means for creating a "direct liaison" between a community and the decreed divine plan; at the second level, "God" is given the power to found the constitution of a "virtual" Christian community of the elected, the heaven presumed to exist beyond this terrestrial world; and at the third level, "God" is invoked by the Saint or Priest's ascetic practice as the promise of "indefinite progress," a retreat that leads to salvation. Through the group, the community, the personal, "God" acquires value. More broadly speaking, Christianity subsumes the pagan and initiatory cults preceding it, replacing the plurality of their respective external rituals of sacrifice and resurrection with a single culture making their internal compatibility possible (253). In all these realities, value operates through the moral, social, and psychological levels, often simultaneously, to create relationships of complementarity between the individual and the collective.

In a fascinating fragment entitled "Values and Research of Objectivity," appended to IPC, Simondon fills in a crucial element of values largely absent elsewhere in this volume. This fragment confirms that values bridge the psychological and the social realms; that the ontogenetic perspective is a useful one, if we hope to grasp fully not just values but those conditions directing their formation, which are likewise the conditions guiding the individualizing process leading to the individualized being. The individuation of values is an *analogue* for the individualization of the individual. Though the former operationally shadows the latter – sharing the movement and the way it structures itself through a process of conversion – they remain, nonetheless, two distinct processes. Yet, more than it confirms what is said in IPC, this fragment introduces something which IPC largely neglects: it speaks to the central role culture must play. This struggle over values taking place in culture is, quite honestly, Simondon at his most Nietzschean. For Simondon, culture is not a totally self-subsisting reality; its existence is relative to the individuals who comprehend it and bear significations. As was discussed in the previous chapter, the process of individuation is identical to the process of coming-to-signification. The only question left to answer is: does the moral solution aid or inhibit the activity of living, preserve or exhaust life?

In either case, for Christianity and the pre-Socratics, values provide the means for establishing complementarity between actions. Culture is what emerges as a result. It integrates values. It is where the technical life and the organic life are brought into their most direct relationship with one another. It is where symbols are created. And so, too, it is where values are invited to enter into affiliations with one another. Culture is, according to Simondon, the place and means for resolving "human problems." But just because cultural aspects are brought into a complementary relationship with one other does not mean that the antagonisms existing among them disappear altogether. On the contrary, beneath any complementarity "virtual" tensions remain. These virtual incompatibilities (as suggested previously) are not simply eradicated but survive in a new form: in the case I am speaking to here, the relative opposition between culture and religious culture.

And it is in response to this internal split that Simondon asserts, "culture is reflexive" (251). Culture dramatizes the valuation of value, for it is a canvas for expressing the transindividual. The transvaluation of values results from reflexivity, which discloses for us transindividual being, the putting into question of the human. In this way, culture serves as the zone for disclosing "the necessity of a mode of compatibility between both lives [organic and technical]," integrating them within a single life of human existence (252).

Only reflexive thought, according to Simondon, that is to say, thought that risks its own coherency, its "completeness," in disclosing the nature of its action, is able discover a unifying sense of values in this antagonism (254). Reflexivity in thought grasps what compels the transformation of ethical values into normative categories of morality. At once it delineates and surmounts the threshold holding the civic and the religious in their productive tension.

Finally, for Simondon, what is most at stake is the revaluation of the value of technology. And it is culture that regulates human beings' relation to the world and our relation to ourselves. Yet technology after all sometimes acts literally as a prosthetic, and sometimes figuratively by organizing our relationship with the natural world and with one another.

It is a relationship constantly recalibrating itself. But, Simondon argues, if culture had not incorporated technology, it would not consist of an obscure zone and, as a result, it would not be able to provide a regulative normativity in coupling man and world (MEOT 227).

> Philosophical thought must, therefore, take up again the genesis of technicity, integrated into the ensemble of genetic processes which precede it, follow it and surround it, not only to be able to know (*connaître*) technicity in itself, but finally to grasp (*saisir*) the very basis for the problems that dominate the philosophical problematic: theory of knowledge (*savoir*) and theory of action, in relationship with the theory of being or ontology. (MEOT 158)

THE TEST OF THE TECHNICAL OBJECT TO FREEDOM'S INVENTION

In "Individuation and Invention," which the editor places as the second chapter of the "note complémentaire," Simondon asserts that technical activity offers an introduction to "social reason," and is the initiator for the individual's achieving freedom. This stems from the role given for the technician to play in a community. It is the technician who acts as a "mediator between the community and some hidden or inaccessible object" by creating a technical object which "crystallizes" a creator's human gestures, thereby perpetuating the technical object into being (262–3). The technical object is "more than a tool, and less than a slave" (271).

Acting to mediate human effort and conferring upon it autonomy, otherwise possibly not granted by a community, the technical object's nature does not reside solely in actuality but "in the information that it fixes and constitutes" (263). It is, therefore, potentially inexhaustibly rich "insofar as information," for it maintains itself in its openness to every human gesture that would make use of it, "inserting itself into an *élan* of universal communication" (264).

Hence, Simondon finds that the technical operation realizes what other functions of a community cannot: a norm for determining what it means to act. It provides an image for what it means to act, which permits us to gain an awareness of our relationship to the world, to ourselves and to others, as a kind of "permanent mediation," the individual's striving to exist by the continuous operation of reactivating action, existing as its own norm. So, if objects are often hidden or inaccessible, technical norms are "entirely accessible to the individual without it being forced to have recourse to a social normativity." We live these norms; technical norms structure how we live, how we invent our lives, even if oftentimes we are unaware of them. Our grasping the specificity of a technical object's being discloses the intrinsic normativity which it provides for its own genesis.

> The technical object is valid or not valid according to its internal characteristics that translate the effort's inherent schematism by which it is constituted. An intrinsic normativity of the subject's acts, which requires their internal coherence, originates from the inventive technical operation. These norms are never sufficient to produce invention, but their immanence to the subject conditions the validity of their effort. (264)

The technician's freedom is dependent on the normativity intrinsic to the action that constitutes it. And it is precisely the unique nature of technical inventiveness which demonstrates the specificity of this norm; for it is, as was said previously, the crystallization of human gesture, providing it with value. "Technical normativity," Simondon writes, "modifies the code of values of a closed society because there exists a systematic of values, and every closed society which, admitting a new technics, introduces inherent values to this technics carries out by this action a new structuring of the code of values" (265). The invention of a new technics is the invention of new values, which operationally (that is, ontologically) creates a structuring and, thus, a transvaluation of all values. And so a community, as incarnating the code of obligation in relation to individuals, is obviously transformed.

In building the characterization of the technical object as crystallizing the human gesture, it logically follows that Simondon should call for a rethinking of humanism on the basis of integrating "a study of technics" (266). Simondon does not completely reject humanism but rethinks it on different grounds, without the ontological and epistemological privileging of the human being. And so he theorizes a humanism beyond good and evil. According to Simondon, good and evil are affections of the imagination that has conferred on them the status of judgments.

A technical object introduces a different basis for norms: not the human as model but the act of invention itself. As Simondon writes, "Technical being exists, therefore, as the germ of thought, harboring a normativity that extends the good beyond itself" (267). In a way not unlike the way an organism organizes itself during growth, invention is the discovery of mediation between the problem and the regime of reality in which the problem is posed. The conditions for invention, the new, point to the conditions for the invention of the technical object. The subject belongs to the particular reality posing the problem; the technical object's invention resolves the problem. It exemplifies the most immediate way to transmit from individual to individual a "certain capacity of creation" or invention, of posing a problem to be communicated as the common source linking together society and community, the psychological and the social, the human and nature.[11]

The value of the dialogue the individual has with the technical object is, therefore, to conserve the human effort, and to create a transindividual domain, distinct from the community, in which the notion of freedom takes its sense, and which transforms the notion of destined individual, but does not annihilate it. The fundamental character of technical being is of the integrating of time to concrete and consistent existence; in this is the correlate of the individual's self-creation. (268)

The technical object puts the human individual into question. In other words, the human individual becomes a problem. For subsisting within the individual is a "certain margin between the actual structure and acquired information." The latter is heterogeneous with the former, according to Simondon, and for this reason requires the successive reorganizing of being, prepared for by "the power to put itself into question" (273). This indeterminate and obscure margin is a wellspring for inventiveness insofar as it is the fount of information. With the potentiality it maintains, it is where the problem resolves itself "thanks to a changing of an individual subject's structure, according to an action that creates a veritable relation between an anteriorly structured individual and its new charge of information" (274).

The technical object is, in short, the most powerful initiator of the psychosocial transindividual operation. It provides the means by which individuals are made to coincide and communicate via their significations. But it can do so only because it makes the disindividuation of individuals possible, transforming their relationship with the world and among themselves into encounters between pre-individual configurations of information. It is this reality which the technical object makes available to us if we allow ourselves to adopt this perspectival shift, disclosing, as a result, that every individuated being transports this charge of pre-individual being for future individuations, potential inventiveness.

So, while the individual's exploiting of its capacity for calling itself into question endangers the community, it also provides an affective stability which becomes "the fundamental criteria," the norm, permitting "the permanent integration of the individual to the group" (275). The technical object's being makes it necessary to rethink the relation of the human to the machine, the human to Nature, in taking us beyond the community.[12] As a result, we are presented with a test: whether or not to risk a revaluing of the very value accorded to a human being opening itself to the world. Simondon's response to this risk is a call for a corresponding humanism, which in accounting for the productive challenge presented by technology and the being of the technical object, aims "to liberate this world of technical objects, which are called to become mediators of the relation of man to the world" (289).

BEYOND THE HUMANISM OF THE HUMAN

Let us recall my prior discussion of Simondon's critique of anthropology. As was suggested, Simondon shares Heidegger's rejection of philosophical anthropology on the basis of its presupposing an abstracted essence enclosed within human being, which it exploits for the purpose of the study of "man." Man as determined by this "essence" is closed within himself, a wholly ontologically and epistemologically *complete individual being*, precluding, as a result, the proper study of the social relation. While Simondon's critique in manner lines up with Foucault's own critique of anthropologism in *The Order of Things*, one great difference ensures that these two thinkers are irreconcilable: Foucault remained unwaveringly anti-humanist, whereas Simondon sought a new kind of humanism, without the presumption of a human essence, which would be fatal. In fact, this is what sets Simondon apart from nearly every philosopher of his generation: where most philosophers, like Foucault and Deleuze, were (in some cases) radically anti-humanist, Simondon asserts that one might rescue the humanist project if one rethinks those metaphysical conditions presumed by it. This would likewise require a recalibrating of the epistemological, ethical, and political goals of this humanism, though, now, in relation to a new concept of "humanity." In other words, it is the problem of "humanism" or the signification that names what is "human."

An 1872 text written by Nietzsche anticipates the impetus for the anti-humanist strain in post-war thought, while isolating the element necessary for it to be reformed.

> If we speak of *humanity*, it is on the basic assumption that it should be that which *separates* man from nature and is his mark of distinction. But in reality there is no separation: "natural" characteristics and those called specifically "human" have grown together inextricably. Man, in his noblest, finest powers, is all nature and carries nature's uncanny dual character within himself. Those capacities of his which are terrible and are viewed as inhuman are perhaps, indeed, the fertile soil from which alone all humanity, in feelings, actions and works, can spring forth.[13]

Combes argues that Simondon's brand of humanism is predicated on the description of human "incompleteness." Whereas the rejected version of humanism presumes and constitutes a notion of human being as "complete" – "Man" – given the status of absolute form, that is to say, wholly an individuated individual, Simondon takes "incompleteness" to be what defines the being of the human. I would suggest that this must be at the heart of any interpretation of Simondon's work. Still, this does not mean, as Combes emphasizes, that a human being is "essentially" incomplete. Incompleteness expresses the being of a human individual, as it points only ever beyond itself to its being "more-than-individual," to the charge of pre-individual reality held in reserve within every subject as the "real potential" available and waiting. In other words, it signifies that it is a transindividual being, conditioned by the pre-individual allotment of nature and what it conditions, the mode of existence structured as collective. As a result, the transindividual operation ensures that human being must remain wholly incomplete. Human being is becoming, the self-overcoming of being. Nietzsche calls this the "Übermensch." And so a new humanism is called for, Combes writes, "a humanism without the human," a "humanism substituting the Kantian question 'What is man?' with the question 'How much potential does a human have to go beyond itself?' and also 'What can a human do insofar as she is not alone?'"[14]

The relation between individuals emerges out of the process of collective individuation. Inter-individual relationships are determined not by the individuals themselves but, rather, in the coherence of a systematic individuation, incorporating individuals into a vaster unity. "It is individuation that founds the relation thanks to a relationship between successive states of individuation remaining reattached by the energetic and systematic unity of being" (229). Now freed from a humanism of the human, Simondon looks to a theory of individuation to lead to an ontogenetic theory of ethics (236).

NOTES

1. Gilles Deleuze, *Essays Critical and Clinical*, trans. Daniel W. Smith and Michael A. Greco (Minneapolis: University of Minnesota Press, 1997), 127, Deleuze's italics.
2. Deleuze, *Essays Critical and Clinical*, 135.
3. G.S. Kirk, J.E. Raven, and M. Schofield, *The Presocratic Philosophers: A Critical History with a Selection of Texts*, 2nd edn (Cambridge: Cambridge University Press, 1983), 118. Nietzsche also has an interesting gloss on Anaximander in his early lectures on the pre-Socratics. Friedrich Wilhelm Nietzsche, *The Pre-Platonic Philosophers*, trans. Greg Whitlock (Urbana: University of Illinois Press, 2001).
4. Even in the French secondary literature, the connection between Simondon and Spinoza has not been fully addressed. It should be said that Jean-Hugues Barthélemy makes a convincing case for the importance of Bergson to Simondon's formulation of an ethics. I would not disagree, although I would suggest that it is an overstatement to call Simondon's ethics a "Bergsonian ethics." Jean-Hugues Barthélemy, "Simondon et la question ethique,"*Cahiers Simondon*, ed. Jean-Hugues Barthélemy, vol. 1 (Paris: Harmattan, 2009), 140.

It should be quite evident from my own interpretation that I place a greater emphasis on Spinoza and Nietzsche.

5. Barthélémy, "Simondon et la question ethique," 139, Barthélémy's italics.

6. Barthélémy, "Simondon et la question ethique," 145–8.

7. Combes, *Gilbert Simondon and the Philosophy of the Transindividual*, 38.

8. "The ontological status of an assemblage, inorganic, organic or social, is that of a unique, singular, historically contingent, individual." Manuel De Landa, *A New Philosophy of Society: Assemblage Theory and Social Complexity* (London and New York: Continuum, 2006), 40.

9. Nietzsche, *On the Genealogy of Morality*, 29, Nietzsche's italics.

10. Nietzsche, *On the Genealogy of Morality*, 93.

11. According to Simondon, a primary difference exists between a society, as "interiority" constituted by the relation between individuals, and a community, as a "code of extrinsic obligations" maintained and maintaining the relationships between individuals (267).

12. "Between the community and the isolated individual itself there is the machine, and this machine is opened on to the world. It goes beyond the community reality in order to institute the relation with Nature" (290).

13. "Homer on Competition," Nietzsche, *On the Genealogy of Morality*, 187.

14. Combes, *Gilbert Simondon and the Philosophy of the Transindividual*, 50.

Conclusion

Six motives have directed my writing of this critical introduction and guide to Gilbert Simondon's *Psychic and Collective Individuation*. First, Simondon's IPC is one of the most innovative and prophetic, if neglected, works of European philosophy. It deserves to be placed alongside the defining works of his French generation: Michel Foucault's *History of Madness* and Gilles Deleuze's *Difference and Repetition*. Second, it is necessary to correct the imbalance that has placed a greater critical weight on *Du mode d'existence des objects techniques* and *L'individu et sa gènese physico-biologique*, primarily because these works were published much earlier than IPC. Third, Simondon's principal goal is to provide the human sciences with a foundational axiomatic which avoids the seduction of philosophical anthropology. Simondon for this reason has proven to have lasting implications in laying the groundwork for cultivating the relationship between philosophy and science, in particular cognitive science. Fourth, the fact that Simondon develops a new rationalist ethics – notwithstanding his acknowledging Nietzsche's critique of such a task – places him at the center of any and all contemporary attempts to establish an ethical theory. Fifth, Simondon's work exhibits courageousness in the face of the tide of Continental orthodoxy that embraces Heidegger's call for the "end of metaphysics" and the "death of philosophy." Indeed, nearly an entire generation of French post-war philosophers (Deleuze, perhaps, the most notable exception) has been defined by the Heideggerian injunction. And lastly, evidence for the prescience of IPC is found in the growing notoriety that it has received since its publication in 1989. And if IPC has been up to now less directly commented upon for its own sake, nonetheless one comes across it prolonged through the thinking of other philosophers – sometimes explicitly (Stiegler), sometimes implicitly (Negri).

201

Before completing this study I would like to suggest to the philosopher, the scholar, or the interested reader possible lines of research to pursue. At the same time, I am more than implying Simondon's hidden ubiquity as it is filtered through the work of contemporary philosophers. I will not pretend in this conclusion to fully develop any kind of exhaustive analysis of the thinkers I mention; instead, I would like merely to identify and swiftly sketch the constellation of problems, concepts, and figures traceable to *Psychic and Collective Individuation.*

I would like to distinguish several lines of research possible for extending the theses of IPC. We can discern one line of research in the recent work of post-Marxist thinkers like Étienne Balibar, Antonio Negri, and Paolo Virno. While not unrelated to these post-Marxists, another line of research advances further in the direction of Nietzsche (and Freud and Heidegger, to a lesser extent), who emerges as the more significant figure beneficial for mediating a relationship to Simondon. This is the post-Nietzschean line whose main representatives I would suggest are Bernard Stiegler and Alberto Toscano. Another line of research is prompted by Simondon's analysis of the psychosomatic: the work of biologist Humberto Maturana and the cognitive scientist and philosopher Francisco Varela exhibit definite structural parallels with Simondon's IPC. In particular, Maturana's and Varela's conceiving *autopoietic* organization as operationally structuring the relationship between biology and cognition via "structural coupling" resonates (however fortuitously) with Simondon's description of the movement of transduction in IPC. Their work provides striking evidence for IPC's relevance for cognitive science. Lastly, there is the recent development of the philosophical movement, largely based in Great Britain, called "Speculative Materialism" or "Speculative Realism." From the beginning Simondon's thought has been one of the touchstones used by these philosophers in the search for an axiomatics of (re-ontologized) realism. IPC is not the central text for Speculative Realists; it is rather MEOT. Even so, any connection made between Simondon and the Speculative Realists is strengthened by the fact that François Laruelle, a central figure for this movement, edited the original French publication of IPC. However, I would like to concentrate on the post-Marxist and the post-Nietzschean lines of research. Both of these lines find a point of convergence in addressing the problem of the "biopolitical" or "biopower."

It is not so surprising that Simondon's thought would lend itself to the current interest in the development and use of Foucault's concept of "biopower" and the "biopolitical." According to Simondon, "life" presents the individual being and society with both its motivating problematic and the means for resolving it. The fact that Simondon characterizes the psychosocial as transindividual, and that it is transindividuality that prolongs life in

202

the form of the pre-individual, the first level of individuation, lends itself to this attempt to bring Simondon into dialogue with those philosophers of biopower/biopolitics. At its most basic level, according to Foucault, the "normalizing society is the historical outcome of a technology of power centered on life."[1] It follows that, from the Simondonian perspective, it is through biopower that an individuated being is individualized; the individuated being is transformed ('subjectivated') into a subject. Biopower transforms the individual being into a subject-being as a society individuates (collectivizes) itself by means of biotechnology. Hence, biopower refers "to the possibility of a new ontology that derives from the body and its forces."[2] This is why, for example, post-Marxists like Antonio Negri and Paolo Virno argue that ultimately the concepts of biopower/biopolitics must confront the problem of transformation of "*living* labor" into "immaterial labor." Again, these thinkers invite our returning to the problem of life, to living as the problematic and problematizing event. Life moves to the center of politics for the simple reason that labor power has become immaterial, and, subsequently, more indissolubly structured and structuring of productive potential. "The living body which is a concern of the administrative apparatus of the State, is the tangible sign of a yet unrealized potential, the semblance of labor not yet objectified, or as Marx eloquently says, of 'labor as subjectivity.'"[3] Again, we recall that, for Simondon, psychism and the collective are constituted in the unity attained by the subject-being. Consequently, once the individuated being becomes individualized as subject it resolves the being of the problem presented to us by life. However, "the living is presented as problematic being, superior and inferior at once to unity" (20). But the solution – in the form of the subject – does not exhaust being. As an effect of transindividual reality, the subject constitutively remains – to whatever degree – pre-individual and, thus, potentially more than it is. For this reason it is always "capable of constituting a new problematic having its own metastability" (19–20). And it is here, once again, as we saw in Chapter 7 of this study, that we might find, in the impetus for new biopolitical normativities, new ethical and political categories emerging from the immanence of their own practices.[4]

NOTES

1. Michel Foucault, *The History of Sexuality: An Introduction*, trans. Robert Hurley, vol. 1 (New York: Vintage, 1990), 144.
2. Thomas Lemke, *Biopolitics: An Advanced Introduction*, trans. Eric Frederick Trump (New York: New York University Press, 2010), 72.
3. Paolo Virno, *A Grammar of the Multitude: For an Analysis of Contemporary Forms of Life*, trans. James Cascaito, Isabella Bertoletti, and Andrea Casson

(Cambridge, MA: Semiotext (e), 2003), 83. Cf. also Michael Hardt and Antonio Negri, *Commonwealth* (Cambridge, MA: Harvard University Press, 2009), 56–63.

4. As Roberto Esposito writes, "a conception of a norm that is immanent to bodies, not imposed upon them from outside, a break with the closed and organic idea of a political body in favor of the multiplicity of 'flesh of the world,' and finally a politics of birth understood as the continual production of difference in terms of identity." Roberto Esposito, *Terms of the Political: Community, Immunity, Biopolitics*, trans. Rhiannon Noel Welch (New York: Fordham University Press, 2013), 78.

Bibliography

Agamben, Giorgio. *Homo Sacer. Sovereign Power and Bare Life*. Trans. Daniel Heller-Roazen. Stanford: Stanford University Press, 1998.

—. *Remnants of Auschwitz: The Witness and the Archive*. Trans. Daniel Heller-Roazen. New York: Zone Books, 2000.

Althusser, Louis. *Lenin and Philosophy, and Other Essays*. London: New Left Books, 1971.

—. *Writings on Psychoanalysis: Freud and Lacan*. Trans. Jeffrey Mehlman. New York: Columbia University Press, 1996.

Badiou, Alain. *Deleuze: The Clamor of Being*. Theory out of Bounds. Minneapolis: University of Minnesota Press, 2000.

Balibar, Etienne. *The Philosophy of Marx*. Trans. Chris Turner. New York: Verso, 1995.

—. *Spinoza from Individuality to Transindividuality*. Mededelingen Vanwege Het Spinozahuis. Delft: Eburon, 1997.

Barthélémy, Jean-Hugues. "Simondon et la question ethique." *Cahiers Simondon*. Ed. Jean-Hugues Barthélémy. Vol. 1. Paris: Harmattan, 2009. 135–48.

Bergson, Henri. *Creative Evolution*. Trans. Arthur Mitchell. New York: The Modern Library, 1944.

—. *The Creative Mind*. Trans. Mabelle L. Andison. New York: Citadel Press, 2002.

—. *Ecrits Philosophiques*. Paris: Presses universitaires de France, 2011.

—. *Time and Free Will: An Essay on the Immediate Data of Consciousness*. Trans. F.L. Pogson. Mineola, NY: Dover Publications, 2001.

—. *The Two Sources of Morality and Religion*. Trans. R. Ashley Audra and Cloudesley Brereton, with the assistance of W. Horsfall Carter. Notre Dame, IN: University of Notre Dame Press, 1977.

Butler, Judith. *Excitable Speech: A Politics of the Performative*. New York and London: Routledge, 1997.

205

—. *Gender Trouble: Feminism and the Subversion of Identity*. Thinking Gender. New York: Routledge, 1990.

Canguilhem, Georges. *Études d'histoire et de philosophie des sciences*. 7th edn. Paris: Vrin, 2002.

—. *Knowledge of Life*. Trans. Daniela Ginsburg and Stefanos Geroulanos. New York: Fordham University Press, 2008.

Chabot, Pascal. *The Philosophy of Simondon: Between Technology and Individuation*. London: Bloomsbury, 2013.

Chamoiseau, Patrick. *Ecrire en pays dominé*. Paris: Gallimard, 1997.

Chateau, Jean-Yves. *Le Vocabulaire de Gilbert Simondon*. Paris: Ellipses, 2008.

Châtelet, Gilles. *L'Enchantement du virtuel mathématique, physique, philosophie*. Paris: Rue d'Ulm, 2010.

Combes, Muriel. *Gilbert Simondon and the Philosophy of the Transindividual*. Trans. Thomas LaMarre. Technologies of Lived Abstraction. Cambridge, MA: MIT Press, 2013.

—. "La Vie inespérée: vie et sujet entre biopouvoir et politique." These de doctorat. Universite Paris 8–Vincennes Saint-Denis, 2002.

Dabashi, Hamid. *The Arab Spring: The End of Postcolonialism*. London and New York: Zed Books, 2012.

De Landa, Manuel. *A New Philosophy of Society: Assemblage Theory and Social Complexity*. London and New York: Continuum, 2006.

Deleuze, Gilles. *Desert Islands and Other Texts, 1953–1974*. Trans. Michael Taormina. Ed. David Lapoujade. Cambridge, MA: Semiotext(e), 2004.

—. *Difference and Repetition*. Trans. Paul Patton. New York: Columbia University Press, 1994.

—. "Dualism, Monism, Multiplicities." March 26, 1973.

—. *Empiricism and Subjectivity: An Essay on Hume's Theory of Human Nature*. Trans. Constantin V. Boundas. New York: Columbia University Press, 1991.

—. *Essays Critical and Clinical*. Trans. Michael A. Greco and Daniel W. Smith. Minneapolis: University of Minnesota Press, 1997.

—. *Foucault*. Trans. Seán Hand. Minneapolis: University of Minnesota Press, 1988.

—. "How Do We Recognize Structuralism?" Trans. Michael Taormina. In *Desert Islands and Other Texts*. Ed. David Lapoujade. New York: Semiotext(e), 2004. 170–203.

—. *Negotiations, 1972–1990*. Trans. Martin Joughin. New York: Columbia University Press, 1995.

—. *Spinoza, Practical Philosophy*. Trans. Robert Hurley. San Francisco: City Lights Books, 1988.

—. *Two Regimes of Madness: Texts and Interviews, 1975–1995*. Trans. Michael Taormina and Ames Hodges. Ed. David Lapoujade. New York: Semiotext(e), 2007.

Deleuze, Gilles, and Félix Guattari. *Anti-Oedipus: Capitalism and Schizophrenia*. Trans. Robert Hurley, Mark Seem, and Helen R. Lane. New York: Viking Press, 1977.

—. *Kafka: Toward a Minor Literature*. Trans. Dana Polan. Minneapolis: University of Minnesota Press, 1986.

—. *A Thousand Plateaus: Capitalism and Schizophrenia*. Trans. Brian Massumi. Minneapolis: University of Minnesota Press, 1987.

—. *What Is Philosophy?* Trans. Graham Burchell and Hugh Tomlinson. New York: Columbia University Press, 1994.

Esposito, Roberto. *Terms of the Political: Community, Immunity, Biopolitics*. Trans. Rhiannon Noel Welch. New York: Fordham University Press, 2013.

Fanon, Frantz. *Black Skin, White Masks*. Trans. Charles Lam Markmann. New York: Grove Press, 1967.

Fink, Eugen. "The Phenomenological Philosophy of Edmund Husserl and Contemporary Criticism." Trans. R.O. Elveton. In *The Phenomenology of Husserl: Selected Critical Readings*. Ed. R.O. Elveton. Chicago: Quadrangle Books, 1970. 73–147.

Foucault, Michel. *The History of Sexuality: An Introduction*. Trans. Robert Hurley. Vol. 1. New York: Vintage, 1990.

Freud, Sigmund. *Beyond the Pleasure Principle*. Trans. Gregory C. Richter. Peterborough, Ont.: Broadview, 2011.

—. *The Ego and the Id*. Trans. Joan Riviere. New York: Norton, 1989.

—. *Group Psychology and the Analysis of the Ego*. Trans. James Strachey. New York: Norton, 1989.

—. *The Question of Lay Analysis; Conversations with an Impartial Person*. Trans. James Strachey. New York: Norton, 1978.

Glissant, Edouard. *Caribbean Discourse: Selected Essays*. Trans. J. Michael Dash. Charlottesville: University Press of Virginia, 1989.

—. *Introduction à une poétique du divers*. Paris: Gallimard, 1996.

Guattari, Félix. *Chaosophy: Soft Subversions*. Trans. Chet Wiener and David Sweet. New York: Semiotext(e), 1996.

Hardt, Michael, and Antonio Negri. *Commonwealth*. Cambridge, MA: Harvard University Press, 2009.

—. *Declaration*. [New York?]: Distributed by Argo-Navis Author Services, 2012. Print.

Heidegger, Martin. *Being and Time: A Revised Edition of the Stambaugh Translation*. Trans. Joan Stambaugh. Albany: State University of New York Press, 2010.

Husserl, Edmund. *Cartesian Meditations: An Introduction to Phenomenology*. Trans. Dorion Cairns. Dordrecht and London: Kluwer Academic, 1999.

—. *Psychological and Transcendental Phenomenology and the Confrontation with Heidegger (1927–1931): The Encyclopaedia Britannica Article, the Amsterdam Lectures "Phenomenology and Anthropology," and Husserl's Marginal Notes in Being and Time, and Kant and the Problem of Metaphysics*. Trans. Thomas Sheehan and Richard E. Palmer. Dordrecht and Boston: Kluwer Academic, 1997.

Janicaud, Dominique. *Heidegger en France*. Bibliothèque Albin Michel Idées. Paris: A. Michel, 2001.

Kant, Immanuel. "Critique of Practical Reason." Trans. Mary J. Gregor. In

Practical Philosophy. Ed. Mary J. Gregor. Cambridge: Cambridge University Press, 1996. 134–271.

—. *Critique of Pure Reason*. Trans. Paul Guyer and Allen W. Wood. Cambridge: Cambridge University Press, 1998.

Kirk, G.S., J.E. Raven, and M. Schofield. *The Presocratic Philosophers: A Critical History with a Selection of Texts*. 2nd edn. Cambridge: Cambridge University Press, 1983.

Krtolica, Igor. "The Question of Anxiety in Gilbert Simondon." Trans. Jon Roffe. In *Gilbert Simondon: Being and Technology*. Ed. Arne De Boever, Alex Murray, Jon Roffe, and Ashley Woodward. Edinburgh: Edinburgh University Press, 2012. 73–91.

Lacan, Jacques. *Ecrits: The First Complete Edition in English*. Trans. Bruce Fink. New York: Norton, 2006.

Laplanche, Jean. *Life and Death in Psychoanalysis*. Trans. Jeffrey Mehlman. Baltimore: Johns Hopkins University Press, 1976.

Lemke, Thomas. *Biopolitics: An Advanced Introduction*. Trans. Eric Frederick Trump. New York: New York University Press, 2010.

"Life and Individuation, with Unpublished Texts by Merleau-Ponty and Simondon." *Chiasmi international publication trilingue autour de la pensée de Merleau-Ponty* [dir. Renaud Barbaras, Mauro Carbone, Leonard Lawlor] 7 (2005).

Logan, Shirley W. *With Pen and Voice: A Critical Anthology of Nineteenth-Century African-American Women*. Carbondale: Southern Illinois University Press, 1995.

Loraux, Nicole. *The Invention of Athens: The Funeral Oration in the Classical City*. Cambridge, MA: Harvard University Press, 1986.

Lyotard, Jean-François. *Libidinal Economy*. Trans. Iain Hamilton Grant. Bloomington: Indiana University Press, 1993.

Macherey, Pierre. *Hegel or Spinoza*. Trans. Susan M. Ruddick. Minneapolis: University of Minnesota Press, 2011.

Merleau-Ponty, Maurice. *Notes des cours au Collège de France 1958–1959 et 1960–1961*. Ed. Stéphanie Ménasé. Paris: Gallimard, 1996.

—. *Phenomenology of Perception*. Trans. Donald A. Landes. New York: Routledge, 2012.

—. *The Visible and the Invisible; Followed by Working Notes*. Trans. Alphonso Lingis. Ed. Claude Lefort. Evanston, IL: Northwestern University Press, 1968.

Moreau, Pierre-François. *Spinoza l'expérience et l'éternité*. Epiméthée Essais Philosophiques. Paris: Presses universitaires de France, 1994.

Nietzsche, Friedrich Wilhelm. *Beyond Good and Evil: Prelude to a Philosophy of the Future*. Trans. Marion Faber. New edn. Oxford: Oxford University Press, 2008.

—. *On the Genealogy of Morality*. Trans. Carol Diethe. Cambridge: Cambridge University Press, 1994.

—. *The Pre-Platonic Philosophers*. Trans. Greg Whitlock. Urbana: University of Illinois Press, 2001.

—. *Thus Spoke Zarathustra: A Book for All and None*. Trans. Adrian Del Caro. Cambridge and New York: Cambridge University Press, 2006.

Plato. "Symposium." Trans. Paul Woodruff and Alexander Nehamas. In *Plato on Love: Lysis, Symposium, Phaedrus, Alcibiades, with Selections from Republic, Laws*. Ed. C.D.C. Reeve. Indianapolis: Hackett, 2006.

Sarraute, Nathalie. *Tropisms, and the Age of Suspicion*. Trans. Maria Jolas and A. Calderbook. London: Calder & Boyars, 1963.

Sartre, Jean-Paul. *Critique of Dialectical Reason. Theory of Practical Ensembles*. Trans. Alan Sheridan-Smith. London: NLB, 1976.

—. *The Emotions, Outline of a Theory*. Trans. Bernard Frechtman. New York: Philosophical Library, 1948.

—. *The Transcendence of the Ego: A Sketch for a Phenomenological Description*. Trans. Andrew Brown. London: Routledge, 2004.

Senghor, Léopold Sédar. *The Collected Poetry*. Trans. Melvin Dixon. Charlottesville: University Press of Virginia, 1991.

Simondon, Gilbert. *Communication et information: cours et conférences*. Chatou: Transparence, 2010.

—. *Cours sur la perception: 1964–1965*. Philosophie. Chatou: Transparence, 2006.

—. "Forme, Information, Potentiels." *Société française de philosophie* (1960): 723–65. http://www.sofrphilo.fr/?idPage=34%3E (accessed 10 January 2014).

—. *Imagination et invention, 1965–1966*. Chatou: Transparence, 2008.

—. *L'individu et sa genèse physico-biologique*. 2nd edn. Grenoble: Millon, 1995.

—. *L'individuation à la lumière des notions de forme et d'information* Ed. Jacques Garelli. Grenoble: Millon, 2005.

Spinoza, Benedictus de. *The Collected Works of Spinoza*. Ed. E.M. Curley. Princeton: Princeton University Press, 1985.

—. "Ethics." Trans. Edwin Curley. *The Collected Works of Spinoza*. Ed. E.M. Curley. Vol. 1. Princeton: Princeton University Press, 1985.

—. *Theological-Political Treatise*. Trans. Jonathan Israel and Michael Silverthorne. Cambridge: Cambridge University Press, 2007.

Stiegler, Bernard. *Acting Out*. Trans. David Barison, Daniel Ross, and Patrick Crogan. Stanford: Stanford University Press, 2009.

—. *For a New Critique of Political Economy*. Trans. Daniel Ross. Cambridge and Malden, MA: Polity, 2010.

Virno, Paolo. *A Grammar of the Multitude: For an Analysis of Contemporary Forms of Life*. Trans. Isabella Bertoletti, James Cascaito, and Andrea Casson. Cambridge, MA: Semiotext(e), 2003.

Name Index

Subject Index

aberrant monism, 105–6, 113
adaptation, 54, 107, 164, 165, 191
aestheticism, 190–1
affect; affectivity, 22, 60, 66–71, 72, 77, 78, 81, 82, 83, 86, 88, 89–90, 93n, 96, 98, 99, 104, 105, 107, 115, 116, 130, 153, 159, 161, 171, 180, 182, 183, 184, 188, 196, 197; *see also* affective-emotive; emotion
affective-emotive, 68, 71, 72, 73–4, 75, 76, 77, 82, 86, 88, 89, 91n; *see also* affect; emotion
Allagmatic, 10, 11, 33, 58, 106, 123n, 133, 180
  and epistemology, 37, 38, 44n
  and "general theory exchanges and modifications of state," and "general theory of transformations," 109, 135, 186
  and "general theory of operations," 18
  see also operation; structure
amplification, 32, 41, 111, 148n, 152
  transductive amplification, 163
analogic science, 38, 44n; *see also* science
analogical logic, 20, 39; *see also* Allagmatic; transduction
analogy, 20, 30, 32, 37, 130, 142, 160
anthropology, 15, 91n, 134–5, 168, 169, 176n
  and humanism, 134, 135, 198
  Husserl and Heidegger's debate, 134
  "new anthropology," 135
  see also philosophical anthropology
anxiety, 31, 83–7, 93n, 156, 157, 171
  and affective-emotive, 86

and disindividuation, 87, 104
and Heidegger, 81, 83–4, 87
apeiron, 142, 151, 153, 179, 187
"Arab Spring," 75, 144–6
associationism, 49–51, 53, 62
  and Hume, 50–1
  see also form: formalism
atomism, 5
axiomatic, 19, 21, 26n, 28, 35, 55, 95, 135, 169, 178, 186, 201, 202; *see also* human sciences

becoming, 5, 6, 9, 10, 16, 17, 18, 19, 21, 23, 25n, 31, 32, 33, 35, 36, 37, 38, 39, 43, 45, 46, 47, 58, 67, 71, 78, 80, 84, 88, 90, 92n, 95, 97, 102, 105, 106, 114, 115, 118, 119, 121, 123n, 124n, 126, 133, 139, 146, 147, 150, 157, 170, 175n, 179, 180, 181, 182, 184, 185, 186, 187, 188, 189, 190, 191, 192, 199
axiomatic of becoming, 186
becoming-collective, 88, 192
becoming-individualized, 94, 103, 146
becoming-individuated, 133, 140
becoming-minor, 14, 25n
becoming-revolution, 144–5, 146
ethics of becoming, 181–2, 184, 185, 189
"innocence of becoming," 178, 192
  see also being; collective; desire: eternity; individuation; ontogenetic ethics; phase
being of becoming, 18, 19, 33, 84, 147, 184; *see also* becoming; phase; ontogenesis; transduction
belief, 33, 50, 51, 70, 77, 115, 118, 136, 141
  and the collective, 143, 147